Hegemony and Global Citizenship

Philosophy, Public Policy, and Transnational Law

Series Editor: John Martin Gillroy, Professor of International Relations and Founding Director of the Graduate Programs In Environmental Policy Design at Lehigh University.

http://ir.cas2.lehigh.edu/content/john-martin-gillroy

A Note from the Editor:

This new series for Palgrave-Macmillan seeks, for the first time at a major publisher, to take the philosophical and public policy foundations of legal practice seriously, that is, not in terms of bits and pieces of theory or policy used to illustrate empirical claims, but as a systematic and integral basis for the study of codified law. The series will pursue scholarship that integrates the superstructure of the positive law with its philosophical and public policy substructure producing a more three-dimensional understanding of transnational law and its evolution, meaning, imperatives and future.

For the purposes of this series, transnational law includes the traditional categories of comparative and international law and seeks to understand the role of, not just states, but persons, international organizations, NGOs and governments that create or use law that transcends sovereign states. The series encourages an interdisciplinary approach to transnational law and seeks research reports, original manuscripts or edited collections that explore the essence of legal practice in both the public policy arguments that inform legal discourse and the philosophical precepts that create the logic of concepts inherent in policy debate. The series aims to expand the types and use of philosophical and policy paradigms exploring the nature of transnational law, so that its empirical dimensions are better illuminated for practioners and scholars alike.

An Evolutionary Paradigm for International Law: Philosophical Method, David Hume, and the Essence of Sovereignty
  By John Martin Gillroy

Radicalizing Rawls: Global Justice and the Foundations of International Law
  By Gary Chartier

Hegemony and Global Citizenship: Transitional Governance for the 21st Century
  By Robert C. Paehlke

Hegemony and Global Citizenship

Transitional Governance for the 21st Century

Robert C. Paehlke

HEGEMONY AND GLOBAL CITIZENSHIP
Copyright © Robert C. Paehlke, 2014.

Softcover reprint of the hardcover 1st edition 2014 978-1-137-47601-2

All rights reserved.

First published in 2014 by
PALGRAVE MACMILLAN®
in the United States—a division of St. Martin's Press LLC,
175 Fifth Avenue, New York, NY 10010.

Where this book is distributed in the UK, Europe and the rest of the world, this is by Palgrave Macmillan, a division of Macmillan Publishers Limited, registered in England, company number 785998, of Houndmills, Basingstoke, Hampshire RG21 6XS.

Palgrave Macmillan is the global academic imprint of the above companies and has companies and representatives throughout the world.

Palgrave® and Macmillan® are registered trademarks in the United States, the United Kingdom, Europe and other countries.

ISBN 978-1-349-50191-5   ISBN 978-1-137-47602-9 (eBook)
DOI 10.1057/9781137476029

Library of Congress Cataloging-in-Publication Data

Paehlke, Robert.
  Hegemony and global citizenship : transitional governance for the 21st century / by Robert C. Paehlke.
       pages cm.—(Philosophy, public policy, and transnational law)
  Includes bibliographical references and index.

  1. United States—Foreign relations—21st century. 2. Hegemony.
3. World citizenship. 4. Internationalism. 5. Globalization. I. Title.
JZ1480.P34 2014
327.73—dc23   2014023297

A catalogue record of the book is available from the British Library.

Design by Newgen Knowledge Works (P) Ltd., Chennai, India.

First edition: November 2014

10 9 8 7 6 5 4 3 2 1

Transferred to Digital Printing in 2015

For Freya "Sparrow" Lie-Paehlke Millares

Contents

Series Editor's Preface		ix
1	Hegemony's Comforts, Hegemony's Price	1
2	A Tale of Three Cities: Kyoto, Baghdad, and New Orleans	41
3	The Evolution of Citizenship: From Athens to Earth	87
4	From New American Century to Global Age America?	117
5	Global Citizenship without Global Government	139
6	Conclusion: Building Global Citizenship	169
Notes		203
Index		225

Series Editor's Preface

I am honored to welcome Bob Palehke's book to the *Philosophy, Public Policy and Transnational Law* series at MacMillan. This book represents an interdisciplinary approach to one of the most important transnational policy question facing the twenty-first century: *Global Citizenship In An Increasing Global And Transnational Society*. As well as its political, economic, and moral implications, what we decide in this area of policy will have a profound effect on international law in terms of stateless persons, human rights, humanitarian law, as well as the cosmopolitan future of universal jurisdiction, immunity, and the future of any transnational constitutional law.

Paehlke accurately places the problem as a direct outgrowth of economic globalization and argues for an evolutionary definition of citizenship that transcends the state and ushers in a new era that replaces individual state hegemony with a more egalitarian, democratic, and ecological global society.

This argument is not an end-point, but like all the books in this series, the beginning of a discussion that is critical to the future of humanity and the transnational law that will regulate our interrelationships with one another and the environment in which we live.

JOHN MARTIN GILLROY,
Lehigh University

1
Hegemony's Comforts, Hegemony's Price

Prior to September 11, 2001, most Americans felt secure and blessed. They were grateful for the wealth that nature and hard work had provided and comfortable as citizens of a hegemonic power, a self-identified "greatest nation on earth." This sense of comfort existed even for many who had little by way of a personal share in America's material bounty. Most Americans felt happily isolated from the worst perils of a troubled world.

Most paid only minimal attention to that world even as the US military patrolled it and American corporations profited mightily in it. Americans understood that, but were also content living in a land unto itself—self-protected and free, a nation in some ways much like a cowboy or space explorer. As well, many in "real" (noncoastal, nonurban) America were prone to finding the rest of the world insufficiently American.

Within a year after September 11, however, many Americans and non-Americans (including myself) saw the nation much like Brent Scowcroft, G. H. W. Bush's National Security advisor, viewed Dick Cheney when he said that he "didn't know him anymore." America had seemed to go to a dark place in its national psyche, a place from which it only began to emerge toward the end of the Bush years when Katrina struck New Orleans and Wall Street misbehavior caused the global economy to collapse.

The Bush administration rejected the Kyoto Protocol and occupied Baghdad, and this and the verbal and policy hostility and bluster that came with it provided the world with a disheartening beginning to the new millennium. Unintentionally, those years may also have sparked a nascent global public consciousness in the form of a near-universal rejection of American leadership. Even some Americans began to wonder about the wisdom of unfettered hegemonic power. This at least temporary shift in global outlook could, in time, lead to a rethinking of how the world governs itself.

The 2008 election of Barack Obama partially restored global confidence in America, a confidence that has again waned since the 2010 reentrenchment of conservatism and the ensuing legislative gridlock and a continuing global inability to act decisively regarding climate change and other global concerns. This ongoing reality reminds the world that extreme conservatism could again come to power in America. Rethinking a world dominated by an unpredictable hegemonic power is now essential.

This rethinking is necessary because our world is stunningly good at forgetting the past, even one so recent. American conservatism, for example, has adapted little since the Bush years and America's media sometimes report as if those eight years, and the intense global reaction to them, never happened. Mitt Romney's presidential candidacy was as belligerent regarding the Middle East as the Bush administration had been. Indeed his foreign policy views were guided by many of the same people. Romney was, in 2012, more inclined to climate change denial than Bush had been despite Romney's own quite decent climate record as governor of Massachusetts. As well, Romney's economic and social policy assertions during the campaign made Bush's inaction in New Orleans during Katrina look like the humane ministrations of Mother Theresa.

Doubts regarding hegemonic power have emerged in this still new century, but what alternatives are possible? One this book will explore is the possible emergence of a new actor on the global stage: a global citizen's movement, inevitably a long process, but one entity that could spur interest in collective global action on urgent matters. If trust in such a movement were to build, perhaps even global security could in time be dealt with cooperatively. Before any inquiry into how citizenship might evolve in the face of global economic integration, we need to explore hegemony and the risks associated with highly concentrated global political power.

Sometimes in global affairs, as in everyday living, we must experience the consequences of getting things wrong in order to slowly begin to imagine how they might be better. After eight years of Bush and Cheney many, including a majority of Americans, came to appreciate where they did *not* want to go. The Bush years and since have been full of horror and hope. The hope is very far from realized, but it remains alive.

Obama's election was a great relief to the world, but hegemonic power on his watch has only been able to haltingly respond to the problems the world faces: climate change, rising inequality and the many environmental and economic problems rooted in the deregulatory mindset. Not that the Obama administration has not tried, but at best only very small steps have been taken. The clear reason is that American government is designed to avoid an undue concentration of internal power in the hands of public officials and in this it is a brilliant success, too brilliant at times. Presently in America policy paralysis seems the only alternative to something much worse.

Before Obama was elected, the view of America from within and the view from without seemed very different. It was difficult for Americans to see how they were seen from the outside and why they were seen that way. For those outside it was difficult to appreciate that America is highly complex and that individual Americans, even some arch-conservatives, are decent people. To the world's credit the 2008 election was followed intently across the planet and Obama's victory was celebrated widely. The world's citizens had not given up on the possibility that America's better nature would reemerge.

Today many Americans see that powerful nations are not exempt from global obligations and no nation, in the end, is uniquely capable even if it is exceptionally rich and powerful. The illusions of some regarding the meaning of American exceptionalism arise out of a distinctively American blend of self-confidence and insecurity and, for many, a lack of information regarding the rest of the world.

Exceptionalism as a dominant American worldview has faded somewhat. Yet many Americans are still prone to forgetting that no other nation has ever held global hegemonic power and that maintaining that power may prove even now to be unaffordable. The 2008 election responded to the overreach of the previous eight years, but did not rise to the level of national reflection. Since, however, more and more Americans have begun to tire of unfulfilled domestic needs which grow all the more striking in contrast to vast continuing expenditures on military power.

Some understand that imperial power and long occupations have become impossibly expensive and that within a global economy that is thoroughly integrated may be unnecessary. This combination creates real limits to, and for, hegemonic power. It illuminates the need for new thinking about international affairs and new ways to establish global security, stability, policy, and law.

The Bush administration failed profoundly because they could see nothing but hegemonic opportunities arising out of the collapse of the Soviet Union. They assumed that American global dominance could be asserted as if nothing else had changed. They could not have been more wrong. The real global challenges of the twenty-first century cannot be readily resolved through military power and indeed excessive military spending may assure that they will not be resolved. Moreover, global economic integration turns potential rivals into business partners. Many understand that—but few yet see a new way forward.

This chapter explores the limits of hegemonic power in this context. The book as a whole considers what may initially seem an improbable alternative to hegemony—a more globally oriented sense of citizenship and explores the circumstances that might make this a real possibility.

Hegemony in a Postcolonial World

What is hegemony? A hegemonic nation is not just the most powerful nation; it has overwhelmingly dominant power. At present, and for the foreseeable future, America will hold a preponderance of military power. America's military expenditures are eight to ten times those of Russia or China, the next two leading military powers. Indeed, American military spending approaches that of the rest of the world combined.[1]

Most striking is the contrast between US military spending and that of those nations that America considers leading threats to global stability: Iran, Syria, and North Korea. American military expenditures are *50 times* Iran's and as much as *500 times* those of Syria.[2] Indeed US military expenditures are larger than the *economies* of Syria and North Korea. Since the collapse of the Soviet Union, it is a cliché to say that the United States is the world's "sole superpower." But what does this massive advantage in military might actually achieve?

To put the question bluntly: is hegemony worth the money and the trouble? Is it a cost-effective expenditure of taxpayer dollars? Curiously, few within American foreign policy discourse explore such questions. In such an inquiry one might ask why hegemonic power is increasingly challenged to affordably occupy nations with what seem to be relatively inconsequential military capabilities. The answer is *not*, as Henry Kissinger has asserted, that there is an unwillingness to fight protracted wars on the part of Americans (or liberals, or Democrats).

Kissinger's argument is absurd on its face (and needless to say self-serving with regard to Vietnam). America is as willing to fight wars as any nation save perhaps Afghanis for whom war is almost a hobby. The United States dropped more bombs on Vietnam than were dropped on Europe in World War II. The wars in Vietnam, Iraq, and Afghanistan were each longer than the involvement of United States in World War II. These recent wars had a less comprehensive mobilization and less solidarity for a reason: popular support faded when it became obvious that they were both pointless and could not be "won" in any normal meaning of the word.

It is time to realize that the "problem" goes beyond an "unwillingness to fight" or a lack of enthusiasm for war within democratic nations generally. It also goes beyond the massive incompetence in the early days of the Iraq occupation. The problem is this: global hegemonic domination may not be impossible, but it may no longer be affordable without abandoning nonsecurity societal priorities.[3] Historically, hegemony failed because other nations of roughly comparable wealth and power were willing to compete. It is limited today largely as a result of two developments: wars of national resistance and terrorism (violence primarily waged against civilians).

China can conquer Tibet and America might occupy nearby nations of limited size, but no nation, one might hypothesize, can any longer simply occupy another substantial nation at a distance for an extended period without broad support within the occupied population. At least it cannot do so without massive costs. Russia could not successfully occupy Afghanistan; the United States could not successfully occupy Vietnam and spent trillions trying to remake Iraq. Despite the staggering cost and a withdrawal of US ground forces, the long-term outcome in Iraq remains far from certain. Occupations sanctioned by international agencies or supported by most nations might succeed in some circumstances, but even that is uncertain.

The occupation of Afghanistan, a nation on which it bordered, contributed greatly to the demise of the Soviet Union. The attempt bankrupted a superpower and ended the Cold War. Interestingly in this regard, Lawrence Korb, an assistant Secretary of State in the Reagan administration, asserted that America was in a position to win the Cold War at that point only because it had previously *exited* Vietnam.[4] Contrary to the domino theory, then, America's enemies were *not* emboldened by withdrawal and great powers may be as likely to be weakened by the *initiation or extension* of occupations as with their end.

One might hypothesize that hegemonic powers are more vulnerable when they repeatedly use force rather than acting with restraint. Blood begets blood (and great expense) and there may well be less risk in being seen a paper tiger than Dick Cheney or other macho neo-conservative strategists would allow. When terror and guerilla war capability and feelings of national autonomy are widespread, the clear advantage rests with those that choose to *defend* against foreign occupiers and not with those who occupy hostile foreign territory. The defenders will not always win, but they can make many occupations more expensive than they are worth.

A corollary to this is an even more provocative possibility: military power, beyond the capacity to literally defend one's own territory, is just not as consequential as it once was. War between nuclear nations is not a possibility that any sane nation would wish for, nor could a nuclear attack against a non-nuclear nation produce a net benefit for the attacking nation. The world's nonmilitary reaction alone would undo that nation. In a globally integrated economy where most nations are highly trade dependent the resulting economic damage might well exceed any strategic benefits the attack could produce. For isolated states like North Korea, the response would likely be brief and terminal.

A powerful nation might defeat another nation's standing army, but there are now few circumstances where, on offense, military success is likely to be of net benefit if the act is perceived to be unprovoked and the match highly disproportionate. The blow to US prestige inherent in the invasion of Iraq was considerable. Most circumstances like those Iraq was said to embody (illegal possession of nuclear and/or chemical weapons) could be more effectively handled by international organizations. Indeed Iraq's alleged possession of weapons of mass destruction (WMDs) *was* handled effectively by international agencies and assertions to the contrary were false.

Nor does military strength *alone* provide an effective defense against terrorism. Technological, investigatory, police, and legal techniques are usually more important than sheer military capability. Some may have actually believed that the war in Iraq was part of a global war on terror, but that illusion has been dispelled for anyone that has not been in a coma since 2001. Moreover, the notion that Iraq, Iran, North Korea, or Syria or all of them together could or would attack the territory of the United States is absurd and would still be absurd if America were to abruptly cut its military budget in half.

Terrorists might enter the United States disguised as illegal immigrants (as some political figures have fantasized). Those agents might then acquire weapons sufficient to kill hundreds of Americans, but they could do such things regardless of who governed Iraq, or any other nation. And, if this scenario was plausible, why would the Bush government *for years following September 11* have allowed millions to illegally cross the border and go to work without significant interference? Or for that matter, why is it that even today virtually anyone, including hypothetical terrorist infiltrators, can buy automated weapons at gun shows anywhere in America?

Prior to 2014 the war in Iraq was about conquest, not terrorism or dictatorship. It was also a Machiavellian illusion, a belief that being more feared than loved has practical value in a postcolonial age. It was also, for some centrally involved in its planning, about exorcizing the ghosts of Vietnam. It was a delusional dream that if only the American public did not see bodies and atrocities on television that they could be persuaded to accept a war of occupation and conquest. They *were* persuaded, but only for a short time.

The question remains: does it not now make sense to foreswear unilateral invasions and occupations? Since it may now be impossible to control a distant occupied nation without spending trillions of dollars and many lives this conclusion would appear to be the very essence of American pragmatism. One might even imagine that most Americans will come to see why the UN Charter that they themselves wrote long ago (and then disregarded) is so important.

A hegemonic power, above all others, needs the United Nations because vast power is instinctively distrusted. More than that, a hegemonic power, unless it is driven by greed or madness, should prefer the status quo and stability.[5] Only a rogue hegemon would not. A hegemonic power almost by definition should prefer the world as it is, where it has won the game in terms of wealth and power. Why would it want to change the rules under which it attained a dominant position?

Obama's election was a political reaction to the events that unfolded during the Bush years, in part a recognition by a majority of voters that defying world opinion is not an astute long-term geopolitical strategy. It perhaps even reflected a realization by some that hegemonic power has limits. That latter reaction may gradually grow into introspection and reform, or it may be pushed aside by future events.

What *would* trigger nonsuperficial reflection on the cost, conduct, and efficacy of hegemonic power? Would reflection lead to more

Americans seeing their nation as others see it? Future approaches to global challenges may depend on the answer to those questions. Hegemonic attitudes are deeply entrenched and global voices should encourage reflection of this sort.

Hegemonic power is, however, every bit as mesmerizing to the leaders of other nations as it is to those who govern the hegemonic nation. Once Bush and Cheney were gone leaders of other nations could just breathe a sigh of relief and proceed as if the Bush administration had been an aberration, a largely accidental deviation from a comfortable norm. That may be the case, but only time will tell.

The rest of the world should encourage self-reflection in America and more actively celebrate the political adjustments that have taken place. Truly rethinking hegemony and creating a role for citizens in global governance will almost certainly require citizen mobilization on a global scale. A global citizen's movement would need to create a capacity for coordinated collective action within most nations. Today's restoration of relatively benign hegemonic power should not be an excuse to lapse into endless waiting for America to find solutions to the globe's problems. It is too easy to avoid summoning the political courage necessary to take *collective* responsibility and to place the burdens on a hypothetical "they" that is willing and able to lead.

The threats facing humankind require not only significant political change within the United States, but also new perspectives in the rest of the world. As we will see in later chapters neither will come easily. Hegemonic powers, perhaps especially, can be like donkeys in terms of noticing what the world needs them to do. Given internal and external inertia, hegemonic powers are also like massive oil tankers needing course correction even when they have excellent and well-intentioned leadership.

Hegemony, Arms Races, and the End of Oil

Some new political force must emerge to countervail the internal and external political base of hegemonic power. That base is powerful and self-maintaining. It can overwhelm any possible waning of the advantages that hegemonic power embodies. Nations like South Korea, Israel, and Kuwait can be protected, but installing compliant governments at will no longer comes easily.[6] Yet few Americans doubt that hegemonic power is essential to America and to the world.

One reason national military power itself is no longer all-determining is that the capacity to resist occupation or foreign-sponsored governments is now nearly universal. Guerilla war tactics, terrorist bombings, suicide bombings, improvised explosive devices (IEDs), and universal access to AK-47s have changed the way wars are fought and alter hegemonic capabilities. American neoconservatives including the Project for the New American Century (PNAC) do not fully grasp this new reality.[7] Though they might deny it now, neoconservatives imagined a cakewalk when they advocated invading Iraq.

As the *Washington Post* noted regarding AK-47s: "The AK-47 has become the world's most prolific and effective combat weapon, a device so cheap and simple that it can be bought in many countries for less than the cost of a live chicken."[8] IEDs are even more readily available almost everywhere. Hegemonic powers can destroy the world many times over, but they cannot easily occupy even a medium-sized nation indefinitely. Even if Iraq is more peaceful than it was in 2006–2007, America has already borne a cost that exceeds any strategic gains stability might hold (especially allowing that it might have purchased whatever Iraqi oil it wanted in any case and for much less than the cost of the war).

What this means is that in today's world *defense* (against occupation) is far cheaper than *offense* (establishing and holding an occupied territory). It is also the case that while powerful nations, given urbanization and global mobility, are vulnerable to terrorist attacks, a truly defensive defense of a nation's territory does not necessarily require either high-tech offensive weapons (beyond the capacity to retaliate against attacks) or massive armies posted outside one's own territory.

If more Americans had a better sense of the limits of hegemonic power, they might be less enthusiastic about paying its high cost. Yet at the same time, ironically enough, if they could appreciate the limits of hegemonic power in today's world, America might continue to hold a far less expensive leading role within a new architecture of international relations. That is true in part because citizens of nonhegemonic nations would react less negatively to American power were there a widely accepted set of internal and external checks and balances on that power.

To be more widely accepted externally, hegemonic power must be profoundly stable internally (and that stability must be democratically rooted). As well, to be trusted externally a majority within the hegemonic power must hold visible reservations about the self-interested use of military power. The hegemon must use hegemonic capacities to further global stability rather than exclusively and aggressively in the pursuit of disproportionate national advantages.[9] There would also need to be some means of recourse should the hegemon betray over any extended period the global trust, or should it elect a government widely perceived to be dangerous.

Thus, while hegemony may always be seen by some as a threat, a dominant power could be a part of a widely accepted global future. To understand this we need to consider three possible routes out of a hegemonic system. They are: (1) the collapse of the hegemonic power; (2) the gradual decline of the hegemonic power and/or the emergence of one or several competing powers; and (3) the evolution of hegemony into a system of global governance (including perhaps the continued existence of a dominant power *within* that system of global governance).

Collapse of a hegemonic power, the first change scenario, is always at least a remote possibility. Since the dramatic economic downturn of 2008, and the continuing proclivity within American politics for government shutdowns, financial deregulation, austerity, and irresponsible tax cuts, this possibility remains plausible. Beyond that, the high cost of hegemonic power may simply become unsustainable. Indeed, a high rate of economic growth is not easily maintained in mature economies with aging populations, especially when accompanied by unabated military procurement.

The post-2008 recession was the fourth or fifth event in a series of deregulatory-inspired corporate and financial malfeasance: the savings and loan crisis, the Enron/Worldcom scams, the dot.com crash, and then successively a housing bubble, and a financial sector collapse. In addition is the 2013 self-inflicted debt crisis, not unrelated to military spending.[10] Largely unseen, but also underlying these troubles, is an ongoing need to transform the energy basis of the national and global economy.

Even without rebuilding America's infrastructure, adapting to climate change and accelerating the development of a postcarbon energy, America is prone to four kinds of debt: public deficits, consumer debt, low savings rates, and the balance of trade.[11] Reduced oil imports aid with correcting the balance of payments, but may ultimately require additional public expenditures on transit, research, and tax incentives. These costs could be offset by carbon taxes or reduced subsidies to the fossil fuel industry.

George Monbiot and others have detailed the transformation that dealing with climate change is likely to require.[12] Even in Britain (which is significantly more energy efficient than North America) much would need to change. Monbiot foresees a revolution in how houses are built, in transportation and energy supply systems, and in most consumer products. The changes would affect land use patterns, reconfiguring both cities and countryside. The changes Monbiot envisions also included changing what Britons eat and how they live their daily lives.

Yet some "peak oil" analysts criticize Monbiot as understating the changes that are necessary (and, fun people that they are, doubting that those changes will be possible).[13] I note this view to observe that Monbiot does not hold the most extreme position regarding the energy future, far from it. Some see economic collapse as almost inevitable, a collapse more dramatic and long lasting than that which began in 2008. The reality, however, may be less bleak than either they or Monbiot would have it, but at the same time it is staggeringly naive to imagine that new technologies will just conveniently arise as and when we need them and at a cost that will not affect some aspects of how we live.

Whether or not climate change or peak oil will produce an economic collapse remains to be seen. What we *do* know is this: neither avoiding these risks nor enduring them will be inexpensive. The energy-related capital demands of the coming decades will be massive even to *maintain* present levels of global energy consumption, especially if we are to simultaneously attend even semi-adequately to *mitigating the effects of* climate change—for example, delivering water where supplies are diminished, protecting coastal cities and beaches and changing agricultural practices and locations.

Monbiot describes a low carbon future Britain in great detail. All organic waste is converted to fuel. Massive windmills extend along the Scottish coast and the power of the waves is harnessed with as yet not fully proven technologies. The transmission grid and the transportation system are transformed. Most home furnaces are replaced by new technologies like ground source heat pumps and most existing appliances and machines are replaced. These and most buildings, especially new buildings, meet much more stringent energy efficiency standards.

Change in North America will likely be broader and deeper since North Americans use nearly twice the energy per capita. Both, however, entail large capital expenditures—made simultaneously by businesses, governments, utilities, and individuals. The transition is thus both a financial challenge and an opportunity to create jobs and economic growth. The costs are big enough to impact expenditures on the military and even perhaps the strategic relationships among nations. North America is particularly vulnerable to losing ground if energy prices rise rapidly prior to change taking hold.

The longer the delay in starting, the greater the risk that we will simultaneously face insufficient energy supplies and growing climate impacts. Whatever wariness one might feel about hegemonic power, a deep economic downturn within America's energy inefficient economy is *not* a desirable alternative. The possibilities associated with precipitous American decline include global economic contraction, international instability or a sharp turn to the right within US political life.

Later chapters will note some anti-democratic political forces within America, forces that have been balanced thus far by America's pragmatic inclinations, durable political institutions, and long-standing democratic political culture. These darker forces could, however, grow during an extended economic downturn. Romney's 2012 behind-closed-doors "47 percent" speech to wealthy donors is the kind of thinking that might rationalize anti-democratic actions including vote suppression.[14]

The political risks associated with economic downturns are a key reason why action on an energy transition is such an urgent matter. The political impact of severe economic contractions are also why unchecked hegemonic power is also problematic. Hegemonic powers are not automatically stable and there would be no easy way to rein in such a power were uglier forces already visible to gain ground.[15]

What then of the *second* path out of hegemony—the gradual emergence of competing powers? China, Europe, Iran, India, Brazil, a reestablished and energy-rich Russia are among the candidates for emerging (or reemerging) great power status. Might the rise of one or several of these nations help to restrain possible future unilateralism?

Unfortunately, national rivalries in the absence of new ways of conducting international affairs would likely be a contest of military capability. To not put too fine a point on it, a return to rivalry in military spending and weaponry development in present circumstances puts lives at risk as a result of unmet needs in lieu of arms spending. That is why the war in Iraq was so wrongheaded—it encouraged arms build-ups and accelerated new quests for nuclear capability, quests that may still be with us.

A full-blown arms race would be at least as dangerous as today's international system. The rivalry could lead to war, but just as critically the *extreme cost* of the race would diminish both the prospects of a timely transition from oil and opportunities to mitigate climate change impacts. The world may well not be able to afford all three sets of expenditures simultaneously. Indeed, a successful transition from oil would be much easier if the world would redirect a share of *existing* military budgets to the task.[16] There are at least three reasons for this latter conclusion.

First, timing is the key. Increasing military budgets might delay an energy transition to a point at which slowed economic growth resulting from energy curtailment, climate impacts and rising energy prices in combination constrain timely solutions.

Second, the transition from carbon-based energy will involve a big share of the world's capital and industrial capacity for decades.[17] Few nations will act with the dispatch that Monbiot and others advocate, but even with a quick start, the challenge will be large enough to provoke this question: Can the world afford both a major arms race and a timely energy transition when the nations needing to make the deepest transition and most able to lead it technologically are also most likely to be engaged in the arms race?

Third, the sources of capital for the energy transition almost all have a strong political constituency. For example, Monbiot envisions a future where bus travel eclipses travel in cars and most goods are moved on trains not in trucks. However, few will be willing to do without cars, or even leave them in the garage other than for special trips, unless and until convenient and comfortable alternatives are thoroughly established. North American's resistance to any such shifts aside, modal shifts in transportation will require dual systems for a considerable time and thus during the transition there would be little capital freed up, only additional capital demands.

Shifts in the energy system would be similar—only on an even larger scale. Oil companies will continue to expend capital looking for the last drops of oil unless and until the market redirects more of that capital or the government captures more through taxes on fossil energy and redirects it to investments in energy efficiency and alternative energy.[18] Needless to say, moving capital from the private to the public sector and from short-term to long-term objectives is a political and economic challenge.

Nor can one be entirely confident that the public sector will allocate sufficient money to energy transition, or do so efficiently. Insufficient allocations would be especially likely were a nation locked in an arms race during economic turmoil.[19]

If a new arms race is unaffordable, what of the third route from hegemony: more open, citizen-based global governance? Is there an international relations architecture that would foster that outcome? Though it seems counterintuitive, one possible arrangement (perhaps the only one that is feasible in the short term) might be continuing hegemonic power—offset and constrained by a global citizens' movement, nonhegemonic governments and international organizations. Since *either* the abrupt hegemonic decline or a new arms race are problematic, it is worth considering ways to live with hegemonic power within a (very American sounding) global system of checks and balances.

Such a possibility will not emerge easily or quickly, a global movement of citizens, even with help from many nations, will not influence hegemonic power regarding strategic interests without first gaining broad influence. The idea seems hopelessly idealistic. Hegemonic power is not assigned by a global committee; it exists by virtue of vast national wealth and a willingness to spend much of that wealth on weapons. Or is it? Hegemonic power is also *bestowed* by those nations that implicitly choose not to challenge it.[20] The *accession of the unenthusiastically willing* is as much the basis of power as, pardon the expression in this context, the triumph of the will.

Until the invasion of Iraq, in defiance of the UN Charter, and the atrocities in Abu Ghraib in defiance of the Geneva Conventions, the United States could be said to have been a *designated hegemon*. Under Obama or a president of similar outlook, most nations, and a good proportion of the world's citizens, may again become comfortable with that status. Before Iraq, American power was generally acceded to by Japan, Australia, Canada, and the nations of Europe, by rising powers like Brazil and India, by nations protected by America like Israel, Saudi Arabia, South Korea, and by many others.

However, this underlying trust was undermined during the Bush years. It probably can be restored, but should it be (given that America could lapse back into neo-conservative governance)? The extent to which global trust was undermined was visible in the world opposition to the invasion of Iraq.[21] It could also be seen in the disparity between press attitudes toward the Bush administration within and outside America.[22] Above all, it was visible in public opinion data from around the world.[23]

The questions really comes down to these: Will a global majority again be truly comfortable with the dominant power of the United States or might that majority prefer a restructuring of the international system? The answer might lie in another question. Could there be real checks on or balancing of hegemonic dominances while a hegemonic power maintains its position? There are at least six components to a more balanced international system that includes a democratic hegemonic power.

One, there would need to be a community of nations possessing the courage to act as a "loyal opposition" to the hegemonic power—supportive in broad terms, but with a self-consciously different approach to global affairs. That "loyal opposition" would need to be willing to openly express disagreement and to use soft power to counter blatant acts of unilateralism. Such open criticism might be forthcoming were national leaders pressed by a citizen's movement oriented to global concerns.

Nonhegemonic nations may well be inclined to multilateralism, but they should be more forthright in calling out and responding to negative hegemonic tendencies regarding international cooperation. Objections emerged during the Bush years, centered in continental Europe but including Canada, Australia, Japan, and other nations, but their tone was typically muted. A loyal opposition must oppose, collectively and firmly, when opposition is warranted.

Two, the nations within this loyal opposition should limit their own military expenditures and seek to dissuade other nations from increasing arms spending and encourage quid pro quo spending restraints in the United States. Many forms of nonmilitary public spending produce greater economic stimulus. The combination of modest military expenditures elsewhere and internal economic constraints could push America toward rebalancing its priorities.

Three, more matters of global consequence need to be resolved within international institutions. That is why Kyoto and its successor agreements and the International Criminal Court are so vital, as is the broadening of international trade arrangements. Trade arrangements could incorporate such things as a global minimum wage formula and global environmental and labor standards.[24] These are potentially key components of a system of global governance that moderates the neoliberal "free trade" approach to global economic integration. Citizen-centered economic integration would build support for the international system generally. A global citizen's movement could push for it.

Four, now is the time for the emergence of that global movement and for public discussion of global governance. It is increasingly clear that the United States, even with a president disinclined to unilateralism and accepting of the realities of climate change, is constrained by domestic political forces. Moving forward on global concerns is easier while America's government is relatively benign, but advance on global needs will not happen without citizen activism and leadership.

Why now? When hegemonic power is relatively benign, questions about creating a global capacity to constrain or respond to unilateralist hegemonic power are not, to say the least, easily broached. Such questions arose widely during the Bush years, albeit sometimes as they say, in quiet rooms. An unquiet global citizen's movement today is essential to achieve any action on either increasing inequality or climate change, let alone both.

Ultimately, the really hard questions might or might not ever arise. Those hard questions, just to be clear, would include how to countervail hegemonic power (nonmilitarily) should that power return to arrogant unilateralism. Soft power, as the United States itself is beginning to appreciate with regard to Iran, for example, need not be all that soft. In extreme circumstances such not-so-soft soft power could be used by either nations or a global citizen's movement (or both).

Beyond diplomacy, soft power can include: trade penalties, restrictions on assets, the reduction of debt holdings or the threat thereof, and reduced access to crucial resources (most notably, of course, oil). Coordinated use of such capacities could potentially offset military power. Hopefully such options will never need to be considered much less used to countervail rogue hegemonic power. A global citizen's movement might be mindful that such considerations could arise in the future, but should work, thankfully in the absence of such circumstances, to slowly build the postfossil, less militarized, more equitable world where such matters are less likely to arise.

Five, consideration of countervailing power should never arise unless America, or any future hegemonic power, fails to maintain a commitment to human rights, international law, and internal democracy. America is the longest standing continuous democracy in the world. It has been a leading (though inconsistent) champion of human rights. There are as well recent concerns regarding the quality of American democracy.[25] The hope remains that these concerns will be rectified and that there will be no relapse to the posture that prevailed during the Bush years.

Six, there would ideally be a willingness on the part of Americans to eschew using military power in blatantly self-interested ways. Obama and many other American presidents have understood this. Of course a hegemonic power would protect its territory and expectations are that it would also prefer global political and economic stability. Its leaders need to appreciate that the stability is in part conditional on restraint in the use of its power. Many Americans understand that.

Americans need to better appreciate that citizens of other nations might reasonably fear the mere possibility of a rogue hegemon—a nation that cannot easily be prevented from simply taking what it wants. Effective democracy in America is thus a *global* concern. So is some semblance of national humility. That is why the world so comprehensively welcomed the electoral outcome of 2008—not just the election of Obama, but the clear rejection of a national posture of unrestrained arrogance.

The open rejection of multilateralism and international law by the Bush administration may ultimately move the international system forward. Global leaders may conveniently forgive and forget the Bush years, but the distrust should not just be forgotten by citizens. Tony Blair as well should have known better and behaved differently.[26] There is no quick solution to this dilemma, but we should be aware that it is a dilemma.

The world owes something to itself, to the dead of Iraq, and to future generations. It needs new cultural and structural realities—perspectives and institutions that make a return to hegemonic unilateralism far less likely. We also need to move nations including reluctant hegemons to develop a *collective* capacity for resolving global challenges.

It's Hard Out There for a Hegemon

Americans have sacrificed to outspend the world on armaments. Even after the hardfought passage of health care reform, America remains the only wealthy democracy without some form of universal health insurance. Some of the 40 million Americans not previously covered by health insurance are only now able to take their children to a doctor. However, infant mortality likely remains more common in America than in, for example, Costa Rica. Many other public needs remain underfunded—from levees on the Mississippi to prevent flooding to public transit and bridges, water and sewer systems, early childhood education, and environmental protection.

Yet security achieved by spending on military prowess is a long way from invincibility though an illusory invincibility is asserted frequently, as in the noted PNAC document. National invincibility is a myth—all the more in the age of terrorism and universal AK-47 access. As Canadian columnist Lawrence Martin put it: "When you're equipped with the greatest arsenal ever known and you are taken down by a bunch of goat-herders with pen-knives, you have to forever prove your manhood—even if the new tonnage in armour is barely relevant to the fight."[27]

Martin's observation sums up a core dilemma of hegemonic power. It is staggeringly expensive and the cost in terms of unmet needs is very real. Yet it does not work all that effectively and the expenditures breed further expenditures through the political empowerment of the military–industrial complex.

Another key dilemma is illustrated by the Iraq war—one well beyond being unable to affordably contain a civil war/insurrection led by "goat herders with pen knives." Nations that spend so much on military power are under continuous pressure to demonstrate that they are willing to use it.

President Obama seems to understand that the best way to counter terrorism militarily is to act only when and where real enemies pose a genuine threat. As well, he has generally sought multilateral support when he acts. Defeating terrorism requires international support and bringing moderate Muslims to oppose terrorist violence. Moderate Muslims are in the overwhelming majority and some may have knowledge of those who support terrorism. These forces of moderation are far less likely to feel comfortable opposing terrorism in the face of unilateral wars of aggression.

It is for this reason, keeping moderate Muslims from feeling divided loyalties, as well as for the betrayal of American principles and the First Amendment to the US Constitution, that the 2010 Republican and conservative campaign against mosque construction was so staggeringly wrong-headed. Threatening and intimidating moderate Muslims plays into the hands of the terrorist micro-minority and aids their cause just as the bombing, invasion, and occupation of Iraq did.

More broadly, the mere fact of hegemonic power may promote resistance, but using that power may enhance resistance. This instinctive distrust of overwhelming power is seen by neoconservatives as an automatic target on the back of America. This fear produces political and psychological pressure to *use* the weapons the nation has sacrificed so much to obtain. Neo-conservative paragon Dick Cheney welcomed the world's animosity as confirmation of America's status as the world's most powerful nation. It also underlies neo-conservative claims that Europeans condemned American unilateralism in Iraq only because they themselves lacked courage and/or did not have adequate military forces.

Politically, those that sought to remake the Middle East exploited these attitudes, as well as post-9/11 fears, as they launched the war in Iraq. Stirred fears add to the political support for war that is always there from arms manufacturers, military contractors, and those who always readily rally to the flag. Economically interested supporters of war know that without enemies against whom to direct military might, other unmet needs might generate sufficient political pressure to reduce military spending.

Thus supporters of military spending need threat perceptions that can at least be made to appear consequential. Small isolated groups of terrorists are not, in and of themselves, sufficient because against them missiles, antisubmarine weapons systems, tanks and antitank capabilities, weapon-laden space platforms, aircraft carriers and stealth bombers are generally ineffective (though drones would later prove to be). Iraq was thereby, in the moment when neoconservatism was ascendant, a designated nail for what was seen to be an underutilized American hammer.

Without demonizing Saddam as a threat to America (not that he needed demonizing otherwise) it would be apparent that much of that weaponry was of little use against America's actual enemies. The risk was that many Americans would conclude that more of the defense budget should be used for antiterrorist *defensive* measures like improved port security, additional protection for chemical or nuclear plants, or for infiltrating terrorist organizations. Thus politically it was important that these systems be seen as important to a "global war on terror" and that antiterrorism be seen as a "war" in the conventional sense.

The psychological aspect of the need to *use* existing weapons is more complex. Some political pressure emanates from those that compensate for personal insecurities and self-doubts by basking in their "greatest nation on earth" status. In 2008 such people fretted that Barack Obama might not have sufficient experience to suddenly be "leader of the Western world." This assessment blithely ignored the fact that few nations were any longer willing to follow America's lead by that point. The collective sense of mightiness is important to many; it is ingrained in the makeup of some in myriad ways.

National power may compensate for a lack of personal economic security or a sense of success in life—a reality that makes periods of economic crisis so dangerous. That sublimation is subtly yet powerfully addictive. The nation's role in global events is magnified in importance and many feel that they are somehow personally a part of that importance and global leadership. This pattern holds even when the national mantra about being the greatest nation on earth was wearing a bit thin in the face of rising national debt and a declining manufacturing sector.

Ironically, such feelings may be especially important to some of the people whose jobs are made more vulnerable by a high dollar caused by oil imports, corporate foreign investments, foreign wars, and foreign military bases. The psychological impact of job insecurity is intensified when one's society is obsessed with everyone "standing on their own two feet" and not being "dependant on government." Today's economic realities are not easy for most Americans, especially those with family medical needs where job loss can mean a loss of quality health insurance.

Humans are social animals—they *need* family, community, and a sense of security and comfort. America, the world's first truly hegemonic power, is intensely focused on protection from foreign enemies. The sense of insecurity has, in effect been in part "nationalized" and directed at foreign enemies rather than understood primarily as an insecure job market or an inadequate social safety net.

Military power thereby compensates for the inadequate public services (family leaves, universal health care, and affordable postsecondary education) that sustain families in other wealthy nations. That is why Obama's election was so important—a majority of Americans chose to reject foreign wars partly to rebuild America, including more affordable health and education. Americans were deeply frustrated in this regard even before the abrupt 2008 downturn.

Even as Obama's support declined during his first term, Americans remained resolute in their doubts regarding foreign wars. A Columbia Broadcasting System (CBS) poll in August 2010 indicated that only 25 percent of Americans believed that the war in Iraq had made them safer and 53 percent in a Gallup Poll in the same month believed that the war would be judged a failure in the long run.[28] As well, only a small minority felt that the war had made the Middle East more stable. These findings suggest that there has been broad learning that may make a return to an aggressive posture harder.

Hegemonic power has encouraged Americans to see the government as a "protective father" and to be offended by the very idea of government as a "nurturing mother." In the absence of the latter, the need for the former becomes more urgent. There is a need to *control* a world perceived as hostile, in part because American society has been so divided against itself and so unwilling to nurture citizens using public resources.

Thus being a part of "the mightiest nation in the world" has become a deeply and widely felt need. Steps toward breaking out of that perspective have thus far been tentative, but real. Hegemonic power is both the end result and the principal cause of that need. Escaping from this pattern will not be easy. One possible way to alter the pattern is to rethink the meaning of the words *defense* and *security*. Americans should focus their legendary pragmatism on opportunity costs—on what else they might get for what money is spent on defense (at least to some extent unnecessarily).

Defensive Defense

There are presently three territorial threats that nations must defend against: WMDs (essentially nuclear weapons), invasion (or hostile actions short of invasion like blockade), and terrorism. Threats to a nation's "interests" elsewhere are not, in the strictest sense, *national* defense—they are the defense of a forward position, usually an offensive forward position if those interests are military assets.[29] Such attacks are relatively rare if one excludes attacks by terrorist groups.

Violent attacks on citizens or property abroad are almost always attacks by nonstate organizations—few *nations* would single out another nation's citizens or property in a third nation. There are notable recent examples where that has happened (including the Libyan downing of a Pan American Airways plane over Lockerbie, Scotland), but most have been associated with border disputes. On the other hand, one objective of terrorist violence is to feed paranoia.[30]

One reason that nations rarely attack another nation's citizens or assets abroad is the integration of the global economy. Attacks on another nation's property or citizens elsewhere invite attacks on one's own citizens and property. Most state-to-state attacks are related to border disputes or the protection of self-defined national or ethnic/linguistic allies within nearby states.

In reflecting on these matters it is also interesting to realize how few nations other than the United States have military bases outside their own borders and how widely the United States has positioned military assets. It has military bases on every continent and in scores of nations. This global distribution of military assets is part of the definition of hegemonic power.

In sharp contrast, a defensive orientation to defense would focus on the three threats identified above and would thereby imply a more limited global role for even a very powerful nation's military forces. Such a shift in the case of the United States would take a long time to effect even if all concerned were prepared to see it happen. I am not necessarily suggesting that America should draw its forces inward into a more defensive posture *in all cases*; I merely want to explore here what a defensive approach to defense policy might look like for any nation, including the United States.

The only effective defense against weapons of mass destruction presently available is deterrence, usually understood to be the threat of retaliation in kind (nuclear retaliation against a nuclear attack). Deterrence for some also includes using stronger retaliatory threats against weaker initial actions (nuclear retaliation against conventional invasion, for example). Israel's unspoken threat of nuclear deterrent against a major territorial incursion is an example of this. Another variation on deterrence is the threat of dispersed retaliation against a direct attack (e.g., Iran's 2007 threat to attack US assets around the world should the United States bomb Iran).

Deterrence may also involve the creation of technologically advanced defenses against any and all possible attacks from the air or space. Interestingly, outside of the Middle East, and excluding the use of missiles by the United States, there have been few instances of missile use against the territory of other nations. Indeed, again outside the Middle East, missiles have rarely if ever been used against nations that themselves possess such weapons. Deterrence is, of course, far from a perfect defense, but it is generally effective (albeit dangerous).

Deterrence itself, however, could be undermined by technologically advanced missile shields and/or the weaponization of space. American exploration of anti-ballistic missiles late in the Bush administration raised concerns in both Russia and China. These concerns led to a Russian objection immediately following Obama's election (seemingly almost in lieu of a congratulatory message). As well, China, during Bush's second term, shot down its own satellite to demonstrate that it can do such a thing—presumably in the hopes of achieving a restoration of the agreement that no nation will place a weapons system in space. Resolving such issues might help to avoid future arms races.

More than that, it could be argued that domination using antimissile defenses and the weaponization of space poses threats to everyone, including the dominator because they undermine the effectiveness of deterrence. Hostile intent on the part of the initiating power will be widely presumed in such situations. Alternative means to deliver weapons of mass destruction, possibly those that involve large numbers of dummy warheads or do not involve missiles at all, will be sought. That is a form of destabilization that no one could wish for, other than madmen.

Beyond deterrence, which America and others already have in place hundreds of times over (without antimissile capabilities), effective defense has two aspects: defense against invasion of one's territory and counter terrorism. Here, reflecting on the defense of the United States, the possibility of an actual invasion is absurd in any conceivable circumstance. Prior to the Iraq war the Bush administration hyped the risk of attack on America by Iraqi drone aircraft, aircraft that had a range of only a few hundred miles. The claim would have been humorous had its ludicrous audacity not punctuated an imminent attack on Iraq.

Since an invasion of the United States by Canada or Mexico is rather unlikely, the invasion would have to come by air or sea. That is implausible since no attack (other than terrorist infiltration, considered separately below) could take place undetected. Any nonmissile attack force would be obliterated before reaching the continent. High-tech defenses aside, it should always be remembered that Americans are numerous and so well armed that they could probably eventually defeat any invading army even if America had only a modest standing army.

Canada is probably defensible through size alone, assuming that the invaders did not freeze to death or end up with stalled vehicles before capturing anything of consequence. If there were concerns about any such possibilities an effective defense could be mounted through the training and equipping of citizen militias. For that matter *no nation* (other than the United States) has the capacity to quickly transport a large equipped army of any size across the oceans.

What is left then is terrorism, a threat that is all too real. The risk of terrorist access to WMDs was, of course, used to sell the invasion of Iraq. This was a dubious claim not just because those weapons did not exist and the alleged connections between Iraq and terrorists were unfounded. There are other reasons why this assertion made no sense as a basis for invading Iraq.

One reason is that other nations would seem to have been more credible threats. Pakistan, for example, was vulnerable to seizure by terrorist elements and had both nuclear weapons and a history of supporting nuclear proliferation. Second, while the Bush administration was voicing concerns regarding WMDs in Iraq it opted not to place a priority on port security to block the only way such weapons could enter. Third, the occupation of a nation in the heart of the Middle East was likely to encourage support for terrorism, not weaken it.

The Bush administration called the Iraq war the central front of the global war on terror, a phrase repeated endlessly on American media. It is unlikely that the US military, or even the Bush administration, was foolish enough to think that this characterization was valid. Whatever the reasons for attacking Iraq, it had little to do with terrorist threats.

Terrorism is a quasi-military response to asymmetrical power—attacks on civilians by groups other than national militaries when attacks on "hard targets" are too difficult. *Brandishing* asymmetrical power in a cavalier fashion can increase the appeal of terrorism as a strategy and that is exactly what the war in Iraq, from shock and awe onward, seemed designed to do. Attacking nonterrorist targets created resentment and may have aided terrorist recruitment in part through justifications of the war that credited terrorist organizations with greater global capabilities than they had.

In early 2007, President Putin spoke of two other negative effects of American military action in Iraq. Putin noted that the invasion had provoked additional nations to seek nuclear weapons—nations that felt threatened by America's new propensity for aggression. Putin also said that the war made it more difficult to settle outstanding disputes diplomatically. He presumably was referring to North Korea and Iran in both instances, nations that were singled out and glibly branded as part of an "axis of evil" even though they had no connection with each other or, in the case of Iraq and Iran, were historic enemies.

The Bush administration's global war on terror had, then, little to do with defense. A *defensive* defense against terrorism would begin with policing and a multilateral effort to locate individual terrorists and terrorist organizations and to bring those captured, including those that knowingly provide those individuals and organizations with material support, to swift trial.

A defensive defense against terror would also emphasize weapons detection and easy availability and the protection of vulnerable targets. In addition it would block the flow of funds to terrorist organizations and deny access to explosives or materials that could be fashioned into weapons. These efforts might well involve a range of secret activities, including infiltration and penetration of closed networks. All of these things are being done, but at the time of the invasion of Iraq were not done as systematically as they might have been if anything approaching the additional resources poured into conventional warfare were applied to the effort.

It is also important to avoid the language of war in relation to terrorism and to identify terrorists as what they are—deranged criminals and nothing more. Why not avoid glorifying them and their activities and minimize actions that might aid terrorist recruitment? The Bush administration seemed oblivious to such considerations. As former Senator Gary Hart put it, "First, treat jihadist terrorism more like organized crime than like traditional warfare. By declaring 'war on terrorism' we made the fatal mistake that it could be crushed using conventional warfare and massed armies."[31]

A comprehensive campaign against terrorism would also address the underlying tensions between Muslims and non-Muslims and among Muslims. Ending the Iraq war was important regarding the former. The next priority would be a resolution of the Palestinian question. Third would be a major effort to encourage diversified economies in the Middle East to reduce unemployment. Fourth would be a greater effort by Muslims, Christians, Jews, and other religions to reduce fundamentalist currents within all faiths—this would be a long, slow but overdue process.

In summary, deterrence and a strictly defensive defense of national territory will and should remain largely in national hands. Many other aspects of defense could, however, be collectivized to a greater extent than they have been. Antiterrorist actions are inherently multilateral. Military incursions should also be collectivized, regionalized, and minimized to the greatest possible extent. Were this to happen, global governance would be seen in an entirely different light.

One of the best things America could do for its defense would be to get out of the business of single-handedly invading other nations. Military actions of any kind by any nation should be avoided except when allies are under siege, action is essential to save civilian lives, or the action is sanctioned by international bodies. Involving truly multinational forces in most situations (as President Obama did in support of the overthrow of Gaddafi) is not a threat to American influence or power, indeed exercising power collectively and judiciously would help to maintain America's global position. That is true both in terms of the global reaction to hegemonic power and the high cost of that power.

Hegemony taken as a license to act unilaterally is hegemony destined to decline. Hegemonic power is thus nothing if not ironic.

Can Hegemons Adapt?

The dominant strains of international relations discourse are idealism and realism. Most strains within American foreign policy debates assume that American hegemony is both secure and desirable and most see the hegemonic challenger on the horizon to be China and view that possibility with alarm.[32] Little attention is paid to the fact that America and China are each others primary source of economic support and that therefore there are real limits to military rivalry. Within most foreign policy discourse everything is seen as necessarily a competition between rival powers. The prospect for growing out of militarism in an economically integrated world is rarely contemplated.

During the Bush years a group of neoconservative foreign policy idealists including Paul Wolfowitz, Robert Kagan, Richard Perle, William Kristol, and others actively promoted the war in Iraq.[33] Long before September 11, this group advocated an invasion, ostensibly to "sow seeds of democracy" in the Middle East and, less often publicly asserted, to transform the balance of power in the oil-rich region and to protect Israel. With help from a supportive media, this group sold a series of fantasies to Americans and the administration regarding the ease with which such a transformation might be accomplished.

Another school of American foreign policy analysis, conservative foreign policy realism, as practiced by James Baker, Brent Scowcroft, Henry Kissinger, and others is less concerned with remaking the world in America's image and more concerned with simply using American power to maximum effect.[34] Conservative realists focus on protecting the United States and its interests. Spreading democracy is seen as either impossible or of lesser importance. Using power in this view is why one creates power, though they prefer being prudent and avoiding using power counterproductively or foolishly.

The Bush administration also included a third group of foreign policy actors led by Cheney and Rumsfeld. They practiced a hyper-ambitious realism believing that nations have power *only* if they are willing to use it. Cheney and Rumsfeld could never be accused of being either subtle or prudent. As celebrants of American hegemony, they sought above all to purge the ghosts of Vietnam, which they saw as having rendered America reluctant to exercise military power. They sought domination and imagined that that was leadership.

Where it might have seemed reasonable to see the end of the Cold War as an opportunity to improve international cooperation and reduce military spending, the hyper-realists saw it as an opportunity to wield unchecked military power and to remake the Middle East. They convinced key power sectors within government (especially the military, the Department of State and the CIA) to *use* American military capabilities. The central lesson of Vietnam, in their view, was the need for media and message control to keep unfavorable publicity from undermining the war effort.

As a result, bodies of the dead were not shown on American television—neither enemy bodies, nor American bodies. Even wounded American soldiers were rendered invisible and military coffins were kept from view. No administration official was ever seen at a gravesite or a funeral. To this end a consistent political line was followed for the first several years of the war: anyone who expressed doubts about war was branded a traitor. In the early years of the war, few elected representatives in either party dared to express their doubts (notable exceptions being Senator Chuck Hagel [R-Iowa], Senator Russ Feingold [D-Wisconsin], and Representative John Murtha [D-Pennsylvania]).

While television images and messages were controlled quite effectively throughout the early years of the war, mobile telephones with cameras left the hyper-realists outflanked in a futile campaign to control the *last war's* media landscape. With the sudden appearance of Abu Ghraib photos on the Internet and then on national television, message control was lost. Support for the war quickly faltered. Shortly thereafter, the botched response to Hurricane Katrina further undermined administration credibility and washed away their efforts with regard to a wide range of issues.[35]

Support for the war in foreign policy circles nonetheless held firm. Virtually *all* major American variations of foreign policy analysis continued to favor hegemonic power and few media-visible analysts had the courage to reject unilateralism outright. Conservative hyper-realists and the conservative idealists, without subtlety, continued to celebrate unilateral power. Even today conservative realists remain uninterested in global governance unless it is dominated by the United States. Even many *liberal* idealists and realists in America see multilateralism primarily as a means of gaining broader support for America's pursuit of its interests.[36]

Somehow this hegemonic mindset must be overcome if genuine multilateralism, or any cooperative way to manage global affairs, is to emerge. Such a shift will not come easily even with a progressive internationalist in the White House. Entrenched forces in American society, government and media make any such shift a great challenge. President Obama has not publically considered significantly reducing military budgets even when confronted with painful cuts elsewhere, and has made only limited progress on climate change, yet he is still systematically attacked on conservative media as a threat to "America's position in the world."

Even a president's power is limited in the face of institutions and interests that are deeply entrenched. Much of the rest of this book explores how new perspectives might at least be set in motion that could help to counterbalance such forces.

What, if any, change in foreign policy perspective might emerge from reflection on the Iraq debacle? This is a difficult question since there has been surprisingly little reflection beyond considering the mistakes of execution that were made. Without getting to the implications of hegemonic power all one might hope for is a more prudent version of realism than that which guided the Bush administration. Americans it seems would prefer to simply exit Iraq and Afghanistan without deep reflection.

Without considerable intellectual turmoil the outcome is likely to be a pragmatic, mildly chastened version of what was the norm before Bush and Cheney took America off the rails. Alternatively, some analysts assert, usually in a fearful tone, the danger *to the world* is American isolationism. Either option, it might be said, would be an improvement on aggressive unilateralist hegemony, but other forms of change are both needed and possible.

That deeper change, however, is not likely to arise solely from within America. Deep introspection has not been commonplace in the corridors of power anywhere since Hamlet's day (and that was fictional). But change *is* possible if an emerging sense of global citizenship can make it clear that there are places millions will never follow regardless of which power or powers hold a dominant position in the minds of foreign policy analysts.

Second Thoughts about Hegemony

As noted, using large-scale ground forces against terrorists is costly and often ineffective. Drones have proven lethal but do not discriminate terrorists from civilians. Actual terrorist training "camps" are rare outside of Hollywood movies and thus drones depend on human intelligence and information interception. The drones are less essential than the intelligence capacity. Since terrorists can self-create, equip and prepare themselves anywhere, the most effective information sources are indigenous, using those with links to and knowledge of local communities. These security capacities do not necessarily require massive military capabilities.

Even within failed states massive military capacities are not necessarily the primary need. Consider, for example, a plausible scenario where terrorist elements sought to seize Pakistan's nuclear weapons. Such an eventuality would produce wide support for an external military response. What would be most needed in such a case, however, would be less a large-scale military capacity to roll back the "rebellion" than a limited-size capacity to *instantaneously* intercede between the rebels and the *weapons themselves*.

Specifically, a fast acting on-call force would need to know, or to be told in any crisis situation, precisely where weapons and weapons production capabilities were located. They would, in short, need the trust of the nuclear-armed nation that was under attack. Would such trust necessarily be granted to America or any leading power? Would not most vulnerable nuclear-armed states prefer that a multilateral force play this role? In particular many such states might hesitate to make detailed disclosures if American forces were involved.

Such an on-call force should already exist, but it does not. Again, this force need not be large, just exceeding effective—not unlike the units that killed Osama bin Laden, but a force that would not be impeded by the nation that held nuclear weapons since protection could not be delayed. The best such force would have the support of virtually all nations, a possibility that will not emerge easily, but could in time. The force would be a twenty-first century (age of terrorism and failed states) version of the red telephone hotline. It could protect nuclear weapons in place, or remove them in the event of extreme national emergencies. Should the government of a threatened state be suddenly incapacitated the force should be empowered by treaty to act on a quick authorization from an international agency.

This is an example of a plausible threat to global security that does not requires a hegemonic power. Many other threats do not require massive military capacity, vast standing armies, or large-scale weapons. Any response to events like the hypothetical overthrow of the Pakistani government that depended on massive invading armies would almost certainly be too slow to secure the weapons. It is anathema to the logic of hegemonic power, but armies and large weapons are not necessarily crucial to effectively countering threats to global security.

Are nations thinking in these terms? Many would presumably resist the formation of an on-call emergency military force under the authority of an international body. In America even suggesting it might erode a president's hold on power and generate howls of outrage. America is locked into the hegemonic paradigm and most foreign policy commentators with media access agree that only American military forces can make the world safe.

Too little consideration has been given to the possibility that hegemony inevitably induces both paranoia and hubris. Nor is it often asserted within nonradical American foreign policy analysis that most of the world is quite capable of looking after itself. The possibility that collective strategic forces or defensive defense might be far cheaper *and more effective* has rarely been raised. The notion that the rest of the world needs to be *managed* by American power is endemic.

Some decades ago American foreign policy focused above all on Latin America. It aided and abetted the overthrow of governments. In recent years its focus has concentrated on Asia and the Middle East and what has happened to Latin America? It is almost universally democratic.[37] Most of its governments are mildly progressive. Only a few are notably hostile to America and one might anticipate little future hostility so long as interventionist neoconservatives are not in power. The changes in Latin America pose no threat outside of the imaginations of a few that might have economic ambitions in Venezuela. No one is invading Florida, no nation is at war with any other nation, and Latin American economies are faring better than they did when the American hand in the region was far heavier.

It is time to carefully reexamine the concept of "interests" in an age of global economic integration. National interests discourse clings to definitions forged in a bipolar or unipolar world without collective global challenges. Global integration and global challenges are now comprehensive and center stage. It is difficult to imagine any substantial nation failing economically without many nations being heavily impacted or any surer way to cause an economy to fail than incoming bombs. The "national interest" mindset has not sufficiently adapted to an age of global economic integration.

At the same time, protecting all conceivable economic and strategic interests is impossibly expensive when assets are global. America seems to militarily defend all presumed interests in every last corner of the earth out of sheer habit. One of the costs of hegemony is that it leads to imagining that anything and everything is a vital national interest. One never knows when an old enemy might lapse back into its former ways or a new enemy might emerge.[38] Paranoia goes with the territory and the territory is the world.

The plain truth is that America is so powerful that its territory cannot be significantly threatened militarily by any other nation, or all other nations taken together. Yet somehow many Americans feel perpetually threatened. Hegemony indeed may create enemies, but paranoia and hubris create more. America is beginning perhaps to see its way out of this siege mentality, but undoing a hegemonic mindset is likely a long, slow process. As noted, hegemonic power paints a target on a nation's back. Global economic integration and an endless array of international bases distribute those targets everywhere.

It is a bad time to be a hegemon. No other nation has such disproportionately large military expenditures (and many seem uninterested in having them). This makes it harder to justify America's expenditures and, increasingly, *no* nation can afford the next generation of new weapons systems. An *effective* antimissile system, for example, might well be beyond reach even for the United States.[39] Nor can America afford another lengthy foreign war and more and more Americans understand this.

Moreover, the most lethal weapons in the US arsenal can never be used. The frustration on the extreme right in the United States on this point during the Iraq war was palpable. They simply cannot grasp the advantages of self-restraint. President Bush himself, speaking in Vietnam during his second term, noted (tastelessly) that wars will always be won if one perseveres, as if the United States did not try hard enough or long enough in Vietnam, the longest war in its history to that point, where more total ordinance was dropped than in World War II.

It is clearly time to fundamentally rethink hegemonic power—its costs, its limits, and its dangers. Arrogant hegemony offends and angers just about everyone, and even a benign version does not necessarily produce a net advantage. Impertinent as it may be, someone needs to offer this advice: America, find a shared power variant on hegemony that is both more globally acceptable and more cost effective. Just gradually ease away from a self-appointed role as the one and only global superpower.

Allow and encourage other nations to look after themselves and their neighborhoods, defend your territory, renew your cities, restore your industrial economy, modernize your transportation system and build a new energy system, and improve health and education. In effect trade hegemonic dominance for again being distinctive as an unparalleled land of opportunity. You will be happier for it and the world, with care taken with the transition, could well be at least as peaceful and secure.

Rethinking Hegemony and the Middle East

New York Times columnist Thomas Friedman has discussed the links between oil, terrorism, and climate change. In his "geo-green strategy" he advocated forcing reductions in oil prices at the wellhead (and establishing carbon taxes in America) as a way to undermine oil dictatorships in the Middle East. This perspective came after Friedman's previous support for the Iraq war that continued well after others had turned against it.

Middle Eastern conflict, terror, war, climate change, and depleting conventional oil *are* related. Friedman, however, would have it that high oil prices allow Middle Eastern governments with oil to avoid industrialization and democracy because they do not need to create jobs through industrialization. He believes that high oil prices help Middle Eastern autocrats buy off political opposition and avoid modernization. This may be partly right.

Oil and democracy do not mix easily. One reason is that oil can be produced without much labor. It is wealth without jobs—oil generates little broad-based distribution of income through mass employment. Wealth in oil states like Saudi Arabia is skewed radically. What Friedman had right is the need to gradually increase fossil energy prices to encourage conservation and alternative energy. What he had wrong is the likelihood that wealthy Middle Eastern elites would do any more for their citizens under less prosperous circumstances. Why does he imagine that they would, or could, promote democracy or industrialization if national income were to decline? The Arab Spring suggests that democratization is at least possible in the Middle East, but it will be brutally resisted regardless of the price of oil.

Sheiks buying real estate in London and New York do little to advance modernization in the region, but placing that same money in the hands of Western oil companies would do even less. A better scheme might combine tax-induced demand reduction in the West with improved economic aid and preferential oil purchases from those exporting nations that invested oil revenues in broad-based national development—health, education, and economic diversification rather than in private jets with gold-plated toilets. Such an approach, of course, flies in the face of both foreign policy "realism" and conservatism of all stripes.

Friedman sees the linkages between oil and Middle Eastern autocracy, but he and most others with influence are not prepared to countenance nonhegemonic options or to fundamentally rethink foreign policy instincts and habits.

One Nation among Many Is neither Isolation nor Weakness

Since September 11 it has been a widely held American sentiment that all US military expenditures are warranted. This view is shared even by many critics of the war in Iraq. They want to spend smarter, but not less. Obama has not reduced military spending, but he has worked hard to end ten plus years of war. Some across the board spending cuts came, but primarily as a lever to get Republicans to accept tax increases, not as part of a plan to reduce weapons spending. Perhaps the end of the Bush-era wars and the passage of time will create a climate where shifts from military to domestic spending will find a way onto the national agenda.

The core of the issue is opportunity costs. What might be done with the money spent on defense were it spent on other things, starting with a more defensive approach to security? A national discussion of how much defense spending is enough and in relation to other needs and priorities is essential. Such a discussion could be linked to Michael Porter's concept of a Social Progress Index, which shows that America does less well in many important areas than it might, given its wealth.[40]

That discussion will happen only when more Americans think outside the box about both security and domestic policy priorities. For example, what if even a modest proportion of America's military budget were diverted to micro-loans to families and small firms in both America and in weak states around the world? Which expenditures would be more cost effective in security terms especially if the foreign spending were concentrated in locations that threaten global peace?

Palestine is an important contributor to volatility in the Middle East. Somalia has been in chaos for a generation. What could be done in such places for a fraction of the cost of war? Truly innovative and effective development efforts might attract additional support from Europe and the Middle East. Hamas and Hezbollah gain popular influence primarily by providing social services—they could be outspent for a minute fraction of the cost of war. Why does this not happen?

It would be naïve to think that such initiatives could come overnight or that there would not be those that would attack such efforts or that corruption that might not siphon off some of the funds. But where such efforts fail, efforts could be redirected to places where they work. If Gaza is presently unreachable funds might go to the West Bank or Jordan or Lebanon. It is hard to imagine that they would not be more effective at "changing hearts and minds" than arriving in the region looking like Star Wars storm troopers decked out in night vision goggles with communications devices that spout English. Mercifully those days appear to be over for now.

Fear begets hate, not obedience (unless it is grudging and fleeting). The reaction to the "shock and awe" campaign and the extended occupation of Iraq will not fade quickly in a region that still remembers the Crusades and lives are lost daily over the ancient rivalries between Sunnis and Shias. The shock and awe clearly did not have the intended effect on the Iraqis who fought the occupation for years. It is past time for new perspectives.

Even this reflection does not fully expose the amount American taxpayers paid for the counterproductive lurch into unilateralism. Most of the costs were covered with *borrowed* money. The compounding interest rendered America less able to deal with ongoing post-2008 economic difficulties and America's struggles have undermined the *global* economy. Moreover, from a purely American perspective, much of the borrowing for the war was not internal debt. It added to trade imbalances compounded by the spike in oil prices that was provoked by the incursion into Baghdad.[41]

Another rarely examined effect of excessive dependence on military solutions is the impact of arms sales. America, Europe, and Russia sell weapons to nearly every nation on earth. While arms sales are lucrative, America's profits from those sales may be less than the cost to America of constraining their use. Arms producers win this game and taxpayers lose. Iraq today is still awash in weapons and explosives. Most of the weapons in Iraq were not produced there. The explosives in improvised explosive devices and car bombs were imported from the old Soviet Union, America or Europe.

America is first among arms exporting nations with Russia following closely and France, Germany and the United Kingdom coming next at some distance.[42] The leading importers are China and India, but the list of importers prominently features Middle Eastern nations. Arms sales are tempting not just because they are highly profitable but also because they can lower the cost of developing weapons systems through savings of scale. But that straightforward calculation does not take into account the cost of facing one's own weapons or needing to separate two sides after one has armed both.

These unintended costs of military spending are not publically debated. Nonetheless, most Americans have become far less aggressive in outlook compared to the Bush years. In a review of American polling data compiled by Pew and others, Jonathan Rauch of the Brookings Institute observed: "A sizeable majority is worried about the decline in America's image overseas, and it blames the Iraq War for much of the decline. Two-thirds of the respondents told Pew that America is less respected now than in the past and 43 percent of the public (not just of the two-thirds) calls this a major problem. And what is it that has caused America's decline in the world's eyes? A heavy majority, including almost two-thirds of Republicans, points to Iraq."[43] This reality was important to Obama's election and were also reflected in his notable 2012 caution of Mitt Romney during the Presidential foreign policy debate.

The Perils of Hockshop Hegemony

The debt financing of US military spending by foreign governments is a variant of "too big to fail"—the principle that keeps governments from allowing major banks or corporations to collapse. America can import oil and manufactured goods and deficit finance wars only because lenders and sellers are willing to buy US treasury bills and other dollar-denominated financial assets. American military dominance might be called hockshop hegemony. America manages huge budget deficits only because China, Japan, and Saudi Arabia are willing to hold American debt. China alone holds more than a trillion dollars.

These debt-holding nations would not want the US dollar to fall precipitously or to see the American economy falter. Were that to happen, America could not import as much Saudi oil or Chinese manufactured goods. Lenders also assume that scale creates stability. In effect, since America could adjust, it does not have to. The Bush administration, however, took American public debt into the realm of riverboat gambling and did little to discourage loading the dice within the financial system. Yet somehow the widespread faith in American economic stability was not questioned even after the city where riverboat gambling was born drowned.

The multi-century total federal debt more than *doubled* between 2000 and 2008 and America's balance of payments shortfalls were never larger. Massive tax cuts were enacted in the face of wars and runaway oil imports. Lenders continued to pick up the tab for hegemony *and* for gambling with the world's economic future. Nor did many note that at the same time the *citizens* of the United States were establishing new ground in terms of low savings rates. Everyone wanted to avoid breaking the spell under which the global financial system and the global economy were held together.

In the year 2000, individual Americans had a savings rate near to zero. Most spent what they earned and many spent more. Yet by 2005 consumer spending had gone up considerably while median *wages* had not gone up at all. There was no income growth and no savings, yet there was consumer-led economic growth. On the face of it this would not seem possible. Where did the money come from to finance consumer-driven economic growth? Primarily from mortgage borrowing on rising home values spurred by the, until then, lowest interest rates in history. The borrowing also included risky sub-prime mortgages and a wondrous array of financial instruments that soon would collapse the global financial system.

Back in 1998, when Russia appeared to be in over its head, many investors assumed that the "mere" possession of nuclear weapons put a floor on the value of Russian bonds. The thinking went that neither Europe nor the United States would allow Russia to plunge into economic misery and default. Thereafter oil and metals prices rose and Russia climbed out of its hole. America received even more leeway because an American recession would guarantee global-scale trouble. An irritating rogue hegemon was less problematic than a foundering hegemon and no one blew the whistle on irresponsible banking practices or on the far-too-low-for-wartime interest rates that spurred the bubble.

The Bush administration blithely took advantage of America's economic position and used this leverage freely, giving new meaning to the game of chicken. The world should have learned that hegemonic power should not be used as a chip to gamble with the world's economic future. No one, however, has yet said: "America, pay for the next self-declared New American Century yourself."

In the future global citizens in both America and lending nations should demand responsible behavior from both sovereign lenders and hegemonic borrowers. Asserting that one nation has the right to manage the world is one thing; borrowing the money to do so definitely pushes the envelope.

This will not be easily accomplished. The Saudis and others get to sell oil and to buy the weaponry necessary to discourage any emerging demand for democracy. China gets the economic growth it needs to avoid unrest, trade unions, a free press, and all manner of other things. Japan gets strategic protection, a strong balance of payments and only limited pressure to increase the value of its currency. Hopefully, more nations, including the United States, next time, if there is a next time, will learn to recognize hockshop hegemony for what it is. If they do they may even have the courage to sometimes ask for hard cash for what they are selling. One might say, as will be discussed in later chapters, soft power is not necessarily soft.

The Last Temptation of Hegemony

Hegemonic powers will always be tempted to use their military capacities to pursue national advantage and to deepen their domination. Their leaders may imagine that they are merely protecting national well-being or collecting their just due. They may even believe that their nation alone can keep the world secure, or even "protect civilization." The temptation to use hegemonic power to national advantage can create tensions between hegemony and liberal democracy. As Rawls put it: "A liberal society cannot justly require its citizens to fight in order to gain economic wealth or acquire natural resources, much less to win power and empire."[44] As well, leaders of hegemonic powers can easily forget that in the end their power exists through the tacit consent of the rest of the world.

Hegemonic power exists only if much of the world trusts or in some cases admires the hegemonic power. That trust may assume that the hegemonic power prefers stability and peace. Why would it not? Almost by definition a hegemonic power should find the status quo acceptable; they are on top of the world in terms of both wealth and power. The last great temptation of hegemony, the one into which

America lapsed during the Bush years, is to imagine that one's nation is not only fortunate, or even exceptional, but *above* the rules of conduct which most other nations accept.

In an age of global economic integration, the rules of conduct must be broadened and deepened, especially in the economic realm. The rules could ultimately include some harmonization of labor and social policy as citizens defend social programs against the absence of equivalent arrangements in trading partners, rather than abandon their own as many will counsel.[45] More environmental policies may also become global. Responsible states work to improve global rule-making rather than presume that they are exempt.

For example, participation of the richest and most powerful nation in global climate action is not just appropriate hegemonic behavior, it is part of what global leadership means and it is essential. Standing apart claiming an exemption is not just arrogant, but doing so all but exempts other states from acting. Global leadership depends more on developing global cooperation than it does on military might. *All nations need to learn how to collectively and democratically manage our increasingly collective global existence.*

Hegemonic power rests in part on the absence of widespread opposition to hegemony. No nation has ever been sufficiently powerful to stand against, let alone control, the rest of the world if that world is determined to oppose it. The PNAC's dreams of domination were precisely that—dreams. If a purportedly hegemonic power consistently and insistently pursues its national self-interest over the global interest, it will rouse resentment and eventually create some form of countervailing power. Divide and conquer has its limits in an age of instant global communication with a potential for citizen action on a global scale. Many are beginning to understand this.

Letting go of or adapting hegemonic dominance might even be especially beneficial to the United States, providing a way to lessen increasingly unmanageable burdens. It might also help the world to avoid a deeply tragic *politics of hegemonic decline*. The Bush years seemed at times to be a precursor of such politics—one where the costs of maintaining hegemonic power undermine many positive aspects of American society. All, including basic social equity and economic growth, was sacrificed to preserve an illusion that America is the most powerful nation on earth now and forever.

Even relatively benign hegemony may arouse instinctive distrust or lapse into less benign forms that not be easy to contain or counter. Chapter 2 reflects on events during the administration of

George W. Bush, events far enough in the past to permit reflection, yet recent enough that they will be familiar.

We look at three sets of events. The first are related to the Kyoto Accord, a flawed attempt at global governance. Cooperative global governance, as noted, is a possible alternative to hegemonic dominance. The second set of events are those that took place in Iraq, especially Baghdad. These events are illustrative of hegemonic dysfunction, they remind us that hegemony is not necessarily an inherently stable system. The third set of events are centered in and around New Orleans during and following Hurricane Katrina, which rendered visible to America and the world some of the opportunity costs associated with maintaining hegemonic power.

Taken together I believe that these events open a set of questions about the permanence of hegemonic power and suggest in broad terms an alternative pattern of global governance, one more open to citizen influence. In later chapters a case is made that citizens and citizen organizations could in time help to democratize international relations and to raise questions regarding the assumption that global politics must be dominated exclusively and eternally by nationally based economic and military power.

2

A Tale of Three Cities: Kyoto, Baghdad, and New Orleans

The period from the late 1990s until the end of 2008 was tumultuous. The events noted in this chapter illuminate the global political system led by American hegemonic power. The system itself has become dysfunctional in several ways and unable to address key global problems. Moreover, America for a time proved unable to resist the temptation to use hegemonic power in self-serving ways—and unable to avoid imposing the costs of hegemony on its own economy and citizens. The systemic flaws described in this chapter led to the election of Barack Obama, but none have been comprehensively or permanently corrected. There has been change, but nothing like the needed transformation of the system either within the United States or globally.

This chapter offers a bridge via this recent history from a reflection on hegemony to tomorrow's possibilities for a more democratic global system. That system, one hopes, will be one more able to deal with climate change (discussed in relation to Kyoto immediately below) and rising inequality (discussed in relation to events in New Orleans during Hurricane Katrina) and better able to avoid war and excessive military spending (discussed in the section of the chapter on Baghdad and the war in Iraq).

The political tone of this chapter may seem harsh to some. It expresses a perspective on events that is largely outside that of any particular nation. I cannot claim that my perspective is global—I am rooted in my American upbringing and Canadian citizenship and experiences. I believe that the period considered here illustrates the limits of a hegemonic system and provides a glimpse of the challenges that will be faced in a necessary, but at most possible, transition to one rooted in a politics of transnational cooperation and global citizenship.

Kyoto: Cooperative Global Governance, a Failed Attempt

Kyoto largely failed, but at least it was an attempt at cooperative, transnational global action regarding a problem of staggering proportions. It was an essential first try, even if sputtering and inadequate. Had it succeeded, the Kyoto Protocol might by now have helped to establish an effective system of global cooperation regarding a wide variety of problems. Such a system would not be, as today's American conservatives might have it, a nefarious foreign plot. It is simply necessary given a globally integrated economy, a new human capacity to threaten ecological viability, and a global interconnectedness that encourages inequality and undermines effective public initiatives including reasonable regulatory initiatives. Kyoto did not succeed and no reliable global system of decision making exists, but it can, and in my view—given the above concerns—emerge through citizen-based efforts.

The Kyoto agreement was flawed, but it addressed a fundamental threat to the living world, a threat that can only be resolved by cooperative global action—something beyond rare in human history. The threat that led to Kyoto and to long and thus far futile discussions in Copenhagen, Durban, and beyond will require both technological and behavioral changes within most nations, changes that will affect individuals and communities everywhere. Twenty years after the attempt in Kyoto, the goal of an effective global climate change effort still seems out of reach.[1]

There is no need here to repeat the easily available details of the Kyoto Protocol or the mounting and familiar evidence regarding climate change.[2] Nor do we need to chronicle the array of already visible and possible future climate change impacts.[3] The broad outlines of this negative future are well known though we still do not know, of course, precisely how climate change will progress if for no other reason than we do not know if nations will consistently engage in an accelerating transition from fossil fuels.

What climate change does create is ecological mistiming—animals fall out of temporal step with food sources at critical times, especially in breeding seasons. Bird eggs hatch before or after caterpillars are most abundant, caribou arrive at calving grounds before key forage plants are available. As Naomi Klein points out, human societies too have also crucially mistimed things in relation to climate change: "Climate change is a collective problem demanding collective action the likes of which humanity has never actually accomplished. Yet it entered mainstream consciousness in the midst of an ideological war being waged on the very idea of the collective sphere."[4]

What is also crucial is realizing that even if climate change was not a great threat, a global effort to reduce fossil fuel dependence would *still* be vitally important. The global supply of oil is limited and the time necessary to end dependence at a pace that avoids economic disruption will be long. Therefore the only prudent course is to stretch existing supplies, and to open the possibility of making the transition rapid, but nonetheless as gradual as possible, by beginning now in earnest.

However, were there no climate change, declining conventional oil reserves could lead to a rapid turn to coal or other carbon-intensive fossil energy options. These options are, in many ways, not part of a desirable future. Coal not only emits more carbon per unit of energy output, but creates acid precipitation, airborne mercury pollution, and either black lung disease or mountaintop removal, as well as massive air pollution. Even the waste from scrubbers at coal-fired power plants is a high risk material often handled unsafely. Whether or not we continue to use coal in limited ways, few outside the coal industry think that coal can serve as a replacement for conventional oil. Indeed recent estimates regarding climate impacts and calculations regarding the total amounts of fossil fuel that can be safely burned that it simply makes sense to leave most coal in the ground forever.[5]

Kyoto was a remarkable achievement in the sense that it allowed most nations to begin to cooperate on climate change (and thereby on the transition from oil). Alas the effort was largely unsuccessful and little has been accomplished since through international diplomacy (though there have been notable initiatives at the local level in many jurisdictions) and nations like Germany and Denmark have made enormous strides on renewable energy. As well, during the Obama administration America has at least gotten into the game.[6] More recently Saudi Arabia, China, India, and other nations are beginning to step up as well regarding renewables.

At the same time many nations have failed to live up to what they agreed to in Kyoto. Canada, for example, has not even tried to do so. Moreover, the agreement has been outdated by the ongoing transfer of industrial capacity from North America and Europe to other nations. It is now likely impossible to reduce global emissions without at least slowing the rate at which emissions are increasing in rapidly growing economies. Under Kyoto that matter was temporarily put aside in the hopes of getting action from the large per capita emitters of the West while drawing all nations into participation in the process for the long term. The long-term process has stumbled forward since though there are recent signs that at least some nations are finding other reasons to act.[7]

As David Orr put it: "the continuing failure to anticipate and forestall the worst effects of climate destabilization in the face of overwhelming scientific evidence is the largest political and moral failure in history." Orr argues that paralysis on the issue is a result of a number of sheer difficulties associated with it: "Climate change is scientifically complex, politically divisive, economically costly, morally contentious, and ever so easy to deny or to defer to others at some later time."[8] Regarding denial, some American political and media figures seem to imagine that America is so exceptional that it is exempt from the laws of nature.

Too few even now fully grasp the threat to human prosperity and well-being that climate change poses.[9] This matter should be especially important to a hegemonic power. As noted, such powers typically favor stability instinctively. The threat of climate change to stability has been well-documented.[10] Renewable energy sources like wind, biomass, and solar are a benign substitute for fossil fuels. Nuclear energy might also be part of the solution, though especially after the horrendous recent events in Japan it is only reasonable to be concerned about the environmental implications (as well as the potential link between nuclear energy and nuclear weapons).

Given that climate change excludes using coal as a substitute for oil it is not certain that the array of alternative sources of supply can replace *all* of the energy supplied by oil and coal (especially in energy gluttons like Canada, Australia, and the United States) or sustain a comparable (energy glutton) level of per capita energy demand in densely populated nations like China and India where only limited amounts of land are idle.[11] Energy efficiency can, however, be advanced considerably; we can get more light, work, and heat from less energy.

Some behavioral adaptations might also be necessary, especially wider acceptance of less travel and more modest and conveniently located living spaces. Few want to say it, climate realities require increased energy efficiency and rapidly expanding alternative energy supplies, but may also necessitate a somewhat more energy-modest way of life for some. *Sustainability*, that now perhaps overused word, implicitly underlies what was agreed in Kyoto and in the many attempts to extend that agreement. Sustainability is a one-word shorthand for the future viability of human civilization. It does not imply massive stringency, especially if undertaken soon enough to allow it to be undertaken gradually.

Even without climate change all nations and peoples will need to learn how to keep future generations sheltered, nourished, and prosperous using less energy. Fossil fuels supply the bulk of the energy presently consumed and some alternatives, including yet-to-be-proven options like biomass-based alcohol, are expensive and some are environmentally problematic in other ways.[12] Solar and wind energy are improving rapidly in terms of efficiency and spectacularly in terms of price, and other possibilities may emerge, but we need to avoid the assumption that some magic bullet will be found.

There is also another concern, one tied closely to our discussion of the instability of a hegemonic system, one that is not often discussed outside the relatively closed world where military strategy is considered. This is, in my view, a crucial reason that new agreements are needed to get humankind through the twenty-first century.

In an armed-to-the-teeth terror-infused world, climate change and associated water shortages, flooding, and crop failures are a virtual guarantee of mass refugees, governmental instability, and a felt need for military action. Avoiding such a future will require two things, assuming that deep disarmament is not likely in the short term. One is a well-established set of global rules for allocating fossil energy *and/or* a way to manage global energy prices more effectively than the market alone seems capable of doing absent a significant price on carbon. Second is an accelerated effort to develop alternative sources of energy and worldwide infrastructure improvements to make every nation less fossil-energy dependent. Acting decisively on climate change will help to ameliorate instability and that alone will have significant economic, political, and social benefits. And, most climate change solutions would be essential even if there were no climate change.

The attempt at global energy policy coordination, even one as limited as that adopted in Kyoto, did not emerge easily. For a time the United States, Canada, Australia, and Japan all opposed effective action while China and many other key nations were not required to take action. Some years later, near to when the Bush administration rejected Kyoto, the Iraq war was, in a sense, a policy alternative to the energy policy adjustments that were embodied in Kyoto (which were seen by some in the Bush administration as a threat to the American way of life).

To not mince words, the decision to invade Iraq was one of the most blatantly illegal acts by a major power since World War II. Before the war ended, if it can be said to have ended even now, it cost many lives, a vast fortune, and a decade of potentially greater progress toward a post-oil world. The Iraq war made it easier to delay finding a cooperative way out of the climate dilemma. Greater global access to Iraqi oil reserves buys some years to get the world off of oil.

Delays matter greatly because collective progress on energy *could* at some point, in a climate-altered future with precipitously declining oil availability, no longer be possible. Rational energy policy will only remain an option if we can quickly now establish a history of visible progress on collective action. We will move away from the possibility of progress if competition for declining oil supplies intensifies. Unless oil becomes just one of many energy sources that competition will become increasingly dangerous. For this reason, and others, the decade lost (from 2000 until 2010) in building an alternative energy future has been tragic. How tragic we will only know some decades from now.

It is not certain that we can fully recover that time. Mercifully, considerable progress has been made in some places and humans are highly adaptable. The strong and healthy among us can survive in quite extreme climactic conditions. We also know that one possible key to reversing the global growth in fossil energy use may lie within the often baffling world of domestic American politics.

The election of Barack Obama and the global response to that election suggested that the animosities stirred throughout the Middle East by the invasion of Iraq could be lessened. Some of that hope has since faded, especially in the summer of 2010, when many Republican candidates campaigned against the construction of mosques in New York and other American cities generating worldwide attention. Nonetheless, America has changed since 2008. The Obama administration, in marked contrast to its predecessor, acknowledges the reality of climate change. Even if it has been unable to take fully effective action, it has produced visible achievements especially regarding automobile fuel efficiency standards and an expansion of renewable energy investment.

As well, following the economic crisis of 2008, many nations, especially in Asia, launched green stimulus plans that expanded renewable energy production. Local governments in many nations, including the United States, have also advanced energy alternatives. Even though he was unable to get an omnibus energy bill through the Senate in 2009–2010, Obama did include energy initiatives in the general economic stimulus bill (the American Recovery and Reinvestment Act of 2009).[13] Indeed, it may be municipal, citizen, and market initiatives that are more important to resolving climate change than treaty-based global regimes.

Yet the Kyoto agreement and the post-Kyoto efforts remain important because limiting human-induced climate change requires reduced *global* consumption of fossil fuels (and, as noted, ultimately requires leaving a significant proportion of those fuels in the ground). This staggering challenge means that all options must be pursued everywhere.

Yet, despite many impressive transformation efforts to date, global fossil energy demand has continued to rise. Delays mean that changes must be more rapid and are more likely to be economically, socially, and politically disruptive. Local initiatives are vital, but they must be very near to universal. That will happen more readily if there are legal requirements, as well as widely imposed moral and market incentives, to act. Crucial as well is nation–by–nation confidence that one is not acting in isolation or in vain. Only governments acting in concert can provide this full array of incentives and the confidence economic actors require.

Climate agreements commit governments to early and coordinated policy action that can help to avoid future economic disruptions. This in turn may thereby also help to reduce the likelihood of future wars.[14] The focus on climate change, alarming as that threat seems, underestimates the complexity of the problem that Kyoto addressed. If the transition from fossil fuels is achieved well before conventional oil and gas supplies are severely diminished, the temptation to use even more environmentally doubtful options is diminished. Other fossil options (oil sands, oil shale, and coal) are more, not less, carbon intensive. Most also carry other significant environmental threats. Accelerating the process of change is thus crucial.

Even in the face of escalating oil prices during the early and intense phases of the Iraq war, global demand for fossil fuels continued to rise. It only slowed, and only modestly, during the deep and lingering recession that followed the 2008 financial crisis. In recent history, the only other time fossil energy demand has actually declined was the early 1980s, in the face of simultaneous abrupt oil price increases and severe recession. Few have faced up to the implications of this fact. It suggests that without intervention, markets will not wean us from oil addiction as quickly as we need to be weaned (in part because those markets are embedded in political systems influenced by the political power of fossil energy companies).

We need to carefully consider this complex dilemma, but in North America few seem to do so. In a century, humankind has used about half of Earth's store of conventional oil (though less than half of all fossil fuels).[15] In this time, we have had enormous increases in wealth and in human population. Some assume that considerable oil and gas remain to be found; others that there is less than is claimed, especially in Saudi Arabia.[16] In recent elections, Republicans repeatedly claimed that America could solve its oil shortfalls by more conventional drilling within its borders. But in the summer of 2010, in the Gulf of Mexico, the cost of drilling in ever more inaccessible and ecologically vulnerable locations became dramatically more visible.

It matters little precisely which estimate of global oil reserves is correct. The maximum difference between the various estimates of conventional oil reserves is no more than a decade or two, and humankind faces three threats that can only be lessened by slowing fossil fuel use. The triple threat is comprised of climate change, the risk of war, and the risk of economic disruption should we ever need to *abruptly* reduce energy use. Only a profoundly uninformed or suicidal species would not begin immediately to *gradually* reduce fossil fuel use.

There are, of course, many postfossil options, but even together they cannot *instantly* replace fossil energy. The transformation will take decades because it involves significant changes in the way people live and work, including things as basic as how we array ourselves on the landscape.[17] It is crucial that the process is gradual, given the costs and given how violently our species typically adapts to economic and social dislocations. Again, it is crucial to avoid assuming that there is some as yet unknown new source of energy or technological climate fix available in some hypothetical future. Imagine away, but do not just blithely presume that such things will actually happen.

The rate at which we reduce dependence on fossil fuels *before* most people cannot afford them is crucial to climate change progress *and* to future peace and prosperity. Thus what the Kyoto Accord and potential successor agreements require of nations, or elemental prudence and duty require of us as planetary and national citizens, is necessary in any case. Postfossil initiatives do not depend on ironclad proof of climate change; they do not even depend on the *possibility* of climate change.

The transition will require both time and vast amounts of capital. At present (in mid-2014) capital is as inexpensive as it ever has been.

However, the transition from fossil energy could be prohibitively expensive in a future where capital is costlier and we may face serious economic dislocations. Inaction now thus risks long-term economic decline. Continuing to postpone gradual reductions in global fossil energy demand risks future spikes in energy prices and simultaneous demands on capital markets that will drive up interest rates precipitously. That combination is the equal of climate change as a looming problem. Such a double spike could overwhelm *our collective capacity to make the very transition that might have avoided both climate change and the spike.*

Why do we seem to fear peering into the future that is written all over the present? Without reducing global demand for fossil fuels, *sometime* soon our climate will be significantly altered, oil supplies will peak, energy prices will spike upwards, interest rates will soar, and stock markets will plunge simultaneously. In the face of that at least some societies would come apart.

The only transition from fossil fuels that will work is a gradual transition, what James Howard Kunstler calls a long emergency.[18] However, the sooner change begins the sooner many things seemingly unrelated to climate change improve as well. Air and water will be cleaner and as in Germany, many people, businesses, and institutions such as schools and churches everywhere will become energy producers as well as energy consumers. Like Copenhagen and Amsterdam, most cities will have diversified transportation and be safer and easier for cyclists and pedestrians. Locally produced food that is fresher, healthier, and tastier will be available in more places. Many of these changes will create more jobs than they cost.

Thus assertions that we must wait for additional proof of climate change is wrong-headed (and denial that it is happening is madness). The reality of human-induced climate change is as certain as science gets, but it is hardly the only reason to move rapidly toward a post carbon future. By the time climate change is *experientially irrefutable* for everyone it will be too late to ameliorate its effects or gain all the side-benefits of avoiding them. Soon it will be too late to achieve an energy transition without energy curtailment. A gradual transition from fossil fuels spread over decades is the only positive option. The longer we delay the more comprehensive the disruption.

In a heated world more people will demand air conditioning and the elderly will require it. More places will need irrigation to sustain food production. If conditions are desperate, few will hesitate to use fossil fuels for these purposes or to fight wars to get them.

This is another reason why the invasion of Iraq was such a horrid precedent.

These negative visions are made much more likely when nations like my own (Canada) fail to do what they agreed to do.[19] Since many nations were exempt from immediate action, nations that failed to meet their obligations had the excuse that "large emitters had *no* climate obligations, so why are we obliged to do what we agreed to do."

Significantly reducing greenhouse gas (GHG) emissions is not always easy. But it can be done, as many nations have begun to demonstrate. Climate action may involve modest losses of convenience (walking to a bus stop, turning down the air conditioning, fewer long-distance trips) and might constrain some economic sectors. The negative social impacts are, however, far more modest than the fossil fuel industry would have it. The claim that economic growth would be halted is untrue and there are many economic upsides, especially in relation to early and effective action.[20]

The larger underlying challenge within all nations, perhaps especially a hegemonic power, is *political*. Reducing carbon emissions requires that there be economic winners and losers. Deliberately creating conditions that produce powerful economic losers is always politically difficult, especially in economic hard times and in a nation whose Constitution, concentration of wealth, and political culture conspire to create barriers to a strong democracy.

Mandating economic losers is not, however, impossible—even in the United States. Almost every nation that has signed a trade agreement has knowingly done it, usually with regard to several domestic industries (in order to advantage other domestic industries).

The power of corporate political contributors *was* key to why the United States did not sign Kyoto. Industries that had the most to lose from gradual reductions in energy demand were industries that were at the center of political power (oil, coal, and automobiles). The American auto industry ironically used that political power to commit temporary economic suicide. From 2009–2011, however, a resuscitated auto industry was willing to embark on a new path to the future and agreed to significant increases in fuel efficiency standards, more stringent than those that it had earlier fought tooth and nail.

Prior to 2008 the automobile industry had *twice* come to depend on assumptions about oil prices that flew in the face of economic rationality, petroleum geology, and geopolitical reality. The North American auto industry was hurt badly in the oil price spikes of 1979 because it built only fuel inefficient vehicles. It promptly returned to that same failed strategy when oil prices temporarily fell in 1985. All through the 1990s the industry resisted fuel efficiency standards (and contributed heavily to the Republicans to keep such rules at bay).[21]

Having created a political climate where fuel efficiency and climate change were pushed aside and big cars were yet again the one-note key to auto industry profits, SUV and truck sales began to plummet as the war in Iraq pushed oil prices higher. Toyota became the world's largest automobile manufacturer. Two decades had been lost on making necessary changes within the American auto industry. Those changes are now being made on an accelerated basis following a period of governmental receivership of the once mega-powerful industry. Yet it is somehow still widely believed within American conservative circles that large corporations are *always* paragons of efficiency and savvy market behavior.

A spectacular collective amnesia was necessary to forget that the 2007–2009 decline in car sales of large cars was foreshadowed by the initial rise of the Japanese auto industry in the 1980s and the corresponding setbacks suffered in Detroit.[22] Unvarnished corporate hubris prevailed twice. It was blithely assumed within the industry that political power could trump both climate change and the geopolitical realities of world oil supplies. The price of hubris was the humbling, if temporary, demise of three of the world's great industrial giants. Mercifully for millions of North American industrial workers and the American economy the industry has recovered.

North America's auto industry slipped into the doldrums because even after the experiences of the post-1979 energy crisis it refused to push ahead technologically or structurally. It was cheaper and easier to block effective governmental action and to inspire gluttonous consumer behavior through advertising. Just as the auto sector had put all its capital and capability into tail-finned behemoths in 1950s and 1960s, it did the same thing again after 1985 (sans tailfins).

One reason offered by the Bush administration for nonparticipation in Kyoto was that China, India, and other rapidly industrializing economies should not be exempted from carbon reductions.[23] Though this assertion is a reasonable point, the surest way to keep these nations from acting is nonparticipation by America. China and America have been each other's best excuse (though China could reasonably add that they have historically contributed little to the total anthropomorphic carbon dioxide already in the atmosphere). China did begin to improve industrial energy efficiency after 2009 when it agreed with the United States to do so.

Increased energy use in rapidly developing nations makes even modest global decreases in emissions hard to attain. Indeed, consider that as Canada has shed manufacturing jobs to China, Canadian coal exports to China have accelerated even as Canada, at very great expense, has phased out coal used for power production in Ontario.[24] GHG emissions affect the world's climate the same way regardless of where they are emitted. Mercifully, in 2013 there were signs that China is beginning to step up to the responsibilities of its new status as the world's number one GHG emitter.[25]

With rapidly rising energy prices at the time, a national carbon tax in Canada went down to electoral defeat in the 2007 election. As a result of that election, Canada continued to rapidly expand the carbon-intensive development of Alberta's tar sands and to increase oil exports to the United States. Canada's Kyoto compliance failure is linked to the absence of a firm limit to carbon emissions in both China and America. That is no excuse, but it does show why climate action must be global.

Climate change also poses a considerable moral and strategic dilemma. The carbon from human sources presently in the atmosphere is almost entirely North American, European, Japanese, and Australian in origin. Much of the wealth of presently wealthy nations rests on having in the past unwittingly endangered the quality of the world's future.[26] However, if emerging economies are to get to North American and European levels of per capita wealth, even in relatively carbon efficient ways, the presently wealthy nations would need to *dramatically reduce* fossil energy use if there were to be any hope of slowing global GHG emissions.

What then is fair? Most climate change exemption claims contain elements of fairness and unfairness and all involve political challenges. Since humans have used roughly half of the world's conventional oil, fairness might suggest that the lion's share of the portion of the second half that can be used belongs to those that got very little of the first half. On the other hand, future generations in the wealthy nations did not use any of what originally existed either (though they do participate in the accumulated wealth of their societies). And, prior to about 1990, *everyone* might reasonably plead ignorance regarding GHG emissions since few understood the risks involved.

In both ethical and practical terms then, the bottom line is that global fossil fuel demand must be reduced and at least wealthy nations must reduce demand even if as a result economic growth is slower than it might have been. Luckily, it is not certain that this will be the case and poorer nations can grow their economies while only slowly increasing energy use and generating a disproportionate share of new energy from noncarbon sources.

Paul Krugman estimates the economic growth effect in the United States associated with effective climate action to be a shift from average annual growth over 40 years of 2.37 percent to average growth of 2.32 percent, surely not as significant as the reductions that would result from climate change *inaction*.[27] Poor nations indeed need growth to reduce deprivation, but they can easily be *far* more energy efficient than the wealthy nations were during their period of industrialization. European nations, especially Germany and Denmark, are showing how much can be done to reduce energy demand and to produce energy from noncarbon sources.

First steps in other nations are critical. All nations can reduce demand without necessarily eliminating economic growth. Indeed, for example, electrical utilities in the United States could reduce carbon emissions for $1.00 per ton, a price that would barely dent the spending power of consumers.[28] The Apollo Alliance, a labor-environmental lobby, has long touted energy transformation as the basis for reindustrializing hard hit regions by manufacturing windmills, hybrid automobiles, streetcars, and other green technologies.[29] And, high-growth economies like China can develop differently than the West did by taking advantage of possibilities that were unknown until recently. They can benefit from the mistakes made during our industrialization and suburbanization. Indeed, this seems to be happening to some extent. China is intent on leading the way on renewable energy research, development, and manufacturing.

The BRIC nations—Brazil, Russia, India, and China—can do more than they have. Indeed, climate action is not necessarily an economic threat even to energy-intensive economies. Russia is now reducing waste in its energy sector in order to have more to export; and China is looking to become a leading producer of solar panels. Ironically, had such possibilities been more widely appreciated in Kyoto, a different agreement might have emerged. Had this been the case, oil demand might not have risen quite so rapidly. It is even possible that invading Iraq might not have seemed so urgent other than to those whose ideas were formed and flash-frozen during the Nixon administration.

This is the central lesson regarding the world's energy future: taking modest steps sooner avoids painful steps later. This point has largely escaped the corridors of power, at least among North American and Australian conservatives. Every nation, firm, and individual doing what they can as soon as possible is what makes the global approach initiated in Kyoto crucial. There is no avoiding the transformation of the energy basis of the global economy. Given this need and the failure of governments to meet it, human well-being requires the emergence of a broad-based sense of global citizenship. There is no "they" to see through this transformation, only an "us."

The shift to a postfossil economy will either be gradual and cooperative, using a combination of economic incentives and disincentives, energy efficiency standards, and new technologies, or it will be abrupt and extremely disruptive. Whatever the reluctance of powerful interests, a majority already understands this. This insight is captured in everything from US-Iraq-war bumper sticker assertions like: "Real soldiers died in their Hummers, so you can play soldier in yours," and books like Michael Klare's *Resource Wars*, as well as by the positive global reception for Al Gore's *Inconvenient Truth*.[30] In this same vein many US cities and states adopted climate initiatives throughout the Bush years in part as a response to the federal government's refusal to sign Kyoto.[31] Also, Toronto and other Canadian cities met the Kyoto targets from which Canada's government withdrew.[32]

These actions illustrate the potential power of citizen-driven global action. A sense of global citizenship can inspire individuals, organizations, and communities even when national leaders resist or seek to reverse global decisions. Indeed, the Bush administration's open rejection of global governance (including the United Nations Charter, the Geneva accords, and the International Criminal Court, as well as Kyoto) inspired *global* opposition that included changes of government in Spain, Italy, Australia, and Britain (from Blair to Brown), as well as Republican losses in 2006 and 2008.

Resisting any semblance of global governance, real or imagined, in the name of "American exceptionalism" has been the central unifying theme among American neoconservatives. Resistance to Kyoto was, it turned out, a signal that the United States was soon to relate to the rest of the world in a very new way. The road to Baghdad arguably began in Kyoto during 1997–1998 rather than on September 11, 2001, in New York.[33]

America, but for its politics on the national level, given its economic and technological capabilities and its profligate energy habits, could readily have reduced its global demand for fossil energy. Rejecting Kyoto, however, demonstrated an unwillingness to forego anything now for advantage later. It was as if the only advantages that counted were national and relative, as if one nation could not win unless everyone else lost. Climate inaction on the part of the Bush government demonstrated a limited capacity to think in the long term, as well as a tragic inability to distinguish hegemonic domination from leadership. This narrow view was rejected by a majority of Americans in 2008 and again in 2012, but it has not departed from American political discourse.

In rejecting Kyoto, America rejected obligations that at the time virtually the whole of the industrialized world (other than Australia) was prepared to accept. This decision launched a period of global incapacity to act comprehensively in this matter. There have recently been significant gains regarding renewable energy in many nations, including America, but an American political silence on the subject of climate change continued, for example, through all four 2012 presidential and vice-presidential debates.

The Bush administration sought to expand America's considerable global privileges and to reject many global obligations that the nation had previously accepted. Most dramatic in this latter regard was President Bush's October, 2005 threat to veto a Senate defense appropriations bill that disallowed the torture of prisoners by agents of the US government.[34] The Obama administration altered this approach to international affairs in many regards but has been unable to make significant new commitments within global climate agreements.

The central premise of George W. Bush's foreign policy became transparent from 2001 onwards: if the United States has the power to gain additional advantages, it will use it. "Walk softly and carry a big stick" became "even if what we seek is not in the global interest, that's the way it is going to be anyway." One of the great ironies is that this attitude on the part of the first and only global hegemonic power could in the long run undo global willingness to abide hegemony itself.

Hegemony's costs, limits, challenges, and opportunities are plainly visible in today's climate inaction. The extent of American hegemonic dominance is clear, but it is by turns unwilling or unable to lead on this crucial global issue. The Roman Empire was vast, but hardly global. At any other time dominant global powers have faced one or more rivals. Today's sometimes self-declared greatest nation on earth is militarily and economically dominant everywhere simultaneously, yet seemingly powerless regarding the world's greatest contemporary challenge.

Needless to say, most nations would prefer multilateralism. But nations most inclined to multilateralism—that is, some more equitable form of collective global governance—face a monumental challenge. Unless America adapts fundamentally in an enduring way, those other nations must find ways to limit unchecked American military power without provoking another arms race. Given the cost and complexity of arms today, another arms race could well preclude dealing effectively with the end of oil and many other global challenges.

A foreshadowing of the American rejection of Kyoto preceded the Bush administration. It was apparent in an unanimous (95 to 0) vote in the US Senate taken in the lead-up to the meetings in Kyoto. Then Vice President Gore, in effect, went through the motions of negotiating and signing Kyoto, perhaps just to place America on the right side of history at least temporarily. Given the pre-Kyoto Senate vote, however, there was little point in attempting Senate ratification in the waning days of the Clinton administration. Gore and Clinton must have known that. The world has changed greatly since then, but there remains a seemingly perpetual proclivity in the Congress to resist climate action.

During the Bush years, the United States, the world's then-leading importer and consumer of fossil fuels, granted itself an exemption from climate obligations by denying for years that the problem existed. We forget too easily how at odds with American history this shedding of environmental protection obligations was. For decades America had been the world's clear leader on environmental protection. The stark reversal was only half-heartedly masked by assertions regarding the absence of binding targets and timetables for China and India. It was as if it was just too embarrassing for the Bush administration to say much on the subject.

China's greenhouse emissions have grown rapidly (40% between 1980 and 2003 and even faster in the lead-up to the 2008 Olympics), but the Chinese still contribute no more than about one-fourth America's per capita rate. More than that, China and all other poorer nations combined, it should be noted again, historically contributed a trivial proportion of existing anthropocentric atmospheric carbon. It is on this historical basis that 154 nations signed the Kyoto agreement. No nation other than the United States, the nation arguably most able to reduce emissions, imagined that it should be exempt.

The bottom line is this: the nation that uses by far the most fossil fuels per capita (except for Qatar) *and* that imports the most oil *and* that uses energy as inefficiently as *any* advanced nation (with the possible exception of Canada) did not participate. Too little has happened since.[35] Given this, it is amazing in a way that other nations continue to participate. The Bush rejection of Kyoto really was a "who the hell do you think you are?" moment in global history. Chapter 4 seeks to explain how American domestic politics allows such a perspective to guide American policy making.

How is it possible that so many political leaders in the most scientifically advanced society in human history can deny a scientific consensus that has been in place for more than two decades? The overwhelming consensus is that climate change is real and is caused by human activity. A noted study in *Science* found that all 928 papers on the subject published in scientific journals to that point were within this consensus view.[36] Yet spouting utter nonsense in the halls of power is not seen as outrageous.

Paul Krugman and others have explained how the US media system has functioned with regard to climate change. The oil industry, including the Koch brothers and Exxon Mobil, funds scientists that are climate change deniers. They produce plausible but unverified arguments that often have not been accepted in peer reviewed journals and have not influenced broader scientific opinion.

The climate change skeptics produce "findings" that cast doubt on the consensus scientific view that climate change is real and/or caused by human activities and "the fake research works for its sponsors, partly because it gets picked up by right-wing pundits, but mainly because it plays perfectly into the he-said-she-said conventions of 'balanced' journalism. A 2003 study...of reporting on global warming in major newspapers found that a majority of reports gave the skeptics—a few dozen people, many if not most receiving direct or indirect financial support from Exxon Mobil—roughly the same amount of attention as the scientific consensus, supported by independent researchers."[37]

Most Republican leaders (including senators) absorb media selectively and are out of step not only with scientific consensus, but with what is majority opinion on this issue.[38] Thus climate change is, in much of America's national media, seen as a "controversial" idea despite an overwhelming scientific consensus.[39] As well, the Congress, in terms of comprehensive policy, remains disconnected from both world opinion and scientific fact.

Avoiding the worst impacts of climate change requires large investments today on behalf of future generations, a political challenge that requires strong governmental leadership. It is especially challenging within the system of governance that has evolved in America wherein economic interests hold near to veto power over major policy initiatives through lobbying, political contributions, and media ownership. The Senate, in unanimously rejecting Kyoto, asserted that it was doing so "if the agreement would result in serious harm to the economy of the United States." They were the arbiters of harm and saw the imposition of even short-term costs to powerful interests as evidence of such harm.

In effect the Senate's phrase suggested that in order to avoid small costs in the present they were prepared to incur large costs later. Their goal was to avoid short-term damage to any important sector of the economy, even sectors that might have built their success on a combination of public subsidies and environmental harms. Did they really mean to say that possible short term costs to the US economy today outweighed catastrophic risks to the world, even if much of the world was prepared to accept a collective best estimate of equitably shared costs? Yes, it turned out during the Bush years, was the answer to that question.

The formal rejection of Kyoto was a crack that grew into a multi-issue yawning gulf between America and the rest of the world. A deep political and moral separation was to emerge between America and Germany, France, Ireland, Scandinavia, Spain, Latin America, Japan, Australia, and Canada and another opened between America and most Muslim nations—and yet another between hegemonic America and ordinary citizens the world over. The palpable worldwide relief and excitement at the election of Barack Obama as president speaks to the fact that what drove this gulf was something other than knee-jerk anti-Americanism, as it was perceived to be by American neoconservatives.

The growing gap was on one level about expectations regarding minimal expressions of humility and about the desire for mutual cooperation and the Bush administration's lack of interest in such possibilities. Finally, it was about the global need for dignity and respect in dealings with a hegemonic power and for hegemonic leadership regarding global concerns: peace, prosperity, and security (including, as Al Gore put it at the time, not only terrorism, but also risks to the habitability of our shared planet).[40]

A hegemonic power that refuses to lead other than in purely self-interested ways invites popular opposition globally. A hegemonic power on its best behavior may be prone to having a target on its back, but a hegemonic power that proclaims both that the coming century is theirs and that it has no interest in the concerns of the rest of the planet invites fundamental change in the world order. One might speculate that Obama's election avoided the emergence of a deep, near-universal distrust of the United States.

Thus aspects of the global politics of the day arose out of the failure of Kyoto and the patterns of the future may have as well. The failure of Kyoto was not, however, a failure regarding the possibility of global governance so much as it was a failure on the part of the United States to accept the world leadership that it seems to assume it holds almost inevitably. The Bush years were one faction within one nation's failure to accept a perhaps-flawed agreement as the best that could be accomplished at the time.

Nonetheless, Kyoto may well have been a first step toward the future, a future that might include limits on fossil energy use for virtually every nation, however outrageous that may seem to some. Kyoto was but a first step toward that possibility, a first step taken by all but a small number of nations. The success in getting *any* agreement in Kyoto is breathtaking compared to where the world had been but a decade earlier. Most nations of the world overcame vast diversity to agree to reasonable steps forward despite high costs for some, despite uncertainty regarding the adequacy of the actions agreed to, and despite resistance from two of the world's leading per capita emitters: the United States and Australia, a nation that later sharply shifted its position (and then shifted it back again).

Reflecting on Kyoto while looking backward from events in Baghdad and New Orleans suggests that another possibility regarding global governance may ultimately emerge. In time, the rest of the world may need to find a way to move ahead on many issues even if its leading nation or nations are intent on avoiding responsible cooperation. If many ordinary citizens and many nations can unite on climate change action, they might in time unite on other matters. In the face of global unity, or something near to it, hegemonic power itself might prove to be less consequential and more fragile than its holders and advocates imagine it is.

Baghdad: Dysfunctional Hegemony

The war in Iraq arose out of the same unilateralist mind-set that supported the self-declared exemption from Kyoto. The mind-set, slightly altered, continues within American neoconservatism today.[41] Within the Bush administration this perspective saw an opportunity to sell the invasion of Iraq based on the terrorist attack on New York and Washington. The murderous madness of bin Laden was taken as an opening for misdirected revenge. With evangelical and media cheerleaders in tow, the Bush government invaded the heart of the Middle East.

September 11 and the ensuing occupation of Baghdad politically entrenched the power of extreme neoconservatism in the name of safeguarding America. Cheney, Rumsfeld, and Rove ascended within the Bush administration and the more rational caution of Powell, the CIA, and analysts within the State Department and the military were shoved aside. Most vestiges of prudent conservatism were driven from administration decision centers.

The invasion of Iraq was sold to the American public with the full-throated cooperation of America's media.[42] So thoroughly were the administration's distortions delivered into public consciousness that years later near to a majority of Americans still believed that Saddam Hussein had had something to do with the September 11 attacks. A substantial proportion still even believed that WMDs had actually been *found* in Iraq. For millions assertion and reality were indistinguishable.

America invaded Iraq for many reasons: but those reasons likely included improved access to oil, a better strategic position within the Middle East, and proving that America was not a paper hegemon, unwilling to use its power. For some in the administration it was also about exorcising demons associated with Vietnam. Few in the administration admitted that these were the reasons or acknowledge that they knew that they were.[43]

Media-based mass self-deception meant that for a time less than truthful assertions did not need to stand up to empirical testing and the "reasons" offered for the invasion could shift frequently, as necessary. The occupation could be about "establishing democracy"—even after decades of propping up (or helping to establish) dictatorships in the region.[44] Or the occupation could be justified as necessary to protect Iraqis from al Qaeda (which had no consequential presence in Iraq prior to the invasion). Later the continuing occupation was frequently justified as necessary to protect Iraqis from each other, or to "achieve stability."

Many Americans, of course, rejected both the distortions of the truth, and the invasion, from the outset. Many as well, especially in more conservative regions of the country, felt terribly isolated in their views (which were widely branded as unpatriotic). Indeed, this sense of isolation led to the creation and rapid growth of political blogs and a radical expansion of the use of the Internet for political communication (and the corresponding decline of television's dominance).[45] This shift may be one of the most important political effects of the war.

Other Americans, however, just preferred to imagine noble purposes for the war and chose to accept as plausible the government's assertions regarding a threat of mushroom clouds of Iraqi origin. Some, not necessarily including all of those who had injected these tales into the media stream, actually believed them.[46] The result was several years of conduct unbecoming of a hegemonic power with a long democratic history.

Thus two small groups of people—led respectively by a murderous madman hiding in an undisclosed central Asian location and an American vice president, also often in undisclosed locations—thrust the world into a twenty-first-century variation on the Crusades. In both cases, the medieval and the postmodern, the killing was wholesale and the objectives were muddled. Could anyone have imagined that new religious wars would reemerge in a world of computers, laser surgery, and global economic integration, a world armed to the teeth with nuclear weapons?

In fairness to the Bush government, George W. Bush himself frequently reminded Americans that most Muslims including American Muslims were peaceful, decent people. In 2010, however, much of the Republican Party would put aside such delicate niceties and attack the right to build a mosque or even an Islamic community and spiritual center in New York, Tennessee, and California.[47]

Thus in the first decade of the twenty-first century humankind was at the mercy of two groups of extremists. Their collective legacy significantly undermined global cooperation, wasted vast sums of money, and cost many thousands of lives. This was not an outcome that was, or could have been, foreseen following the fall of the Berlin Wall. At times, modernity itself seemed to have come undone. America, the original postcolonial nation, found itself mired in a colonial relapse deep into the postcolonial age.

September 11 enhanced the power of three groups within the Bush administration: those that imagined that the Middle East could be remade through military occupation, those that wanted to gain access to oil by military means, and those eager to get or grant war-related contracts. All three groups believed that America was an indispensable nation led by indispensable men, a worldview not unlike the silly ideals of a bad Ayn Rand novel. Through the misbegotten notion of a global *war* on terror, this set of events elevated a ragtag al Qaeda organization to the level of global threat and in so doing increased its prestige, power, and recruitment potential.[48]

Crucially, the architects of the occupation of Iraq, and even many of the war's critics, assumed that there were few if any limits to hegemonic power. The architects dismissed with scathing disdain anyone that suggested otherwise. Whatever ideological beacon it was that led to the bombing and occupation of Baghdad, it was not anything that could reasonably be called conservatism. Genuine conservatives understand in their very bones that societies are not easily remade according to grand blueprints.[49] In the conservative mind change is organic and evolutionary and arises from local historic specificities.[50]

The neoconservative architects of the Iraq war seemed to actually believe that they could insert a Western army of occupation into the center of the Middle East and be welcomed for having done so. They quickly built military bases and a massive, built-for-eternity, embassy and either did not imagine that such edifices would incite opposition or did not care if they did. They had little if any sense of the perspective of virtually everyone living in former colonies the world over. They also knew *next to nothing* of Iraqi society and history. They either imagined that Iraq was Granada with oil or did not care what price was paid to transform it.

Iraq was not understood as a complex nation and its location was not considered beyond its convenient location in relation to Iran and the Gulf states. As it turns out, colonialism could not be reestablished in the Middle East either easily or cheaply.[51] Cheney, Rumsfeld, and the others who launched the Iraq invasion somehow had not heard about that possibility, did not believe it, did not care about the long-term fiscal viability of the US government, or imagined that they were so clever that they could undo any part of history they chose to undo.

They had Ahmad Chalabi, an exile who had lived in the West for decades, waiting in the wings for installation as a latter-day Iraqi Shah. He was ambitious, fond of kleptocratic capitalism, and a secular Shiite. He also was very bright and knew just what they wanted to hear. What other qualifications did he need?

Ayatollah Ali al-Sistani, the revered leader of the majority Shiite community in Iraq, had other ideas. He broke from his self-imposed political quietism to insist on an elected rather than the interim government "with elections to follow" put forward by occupation authorities. The earlier-than-intended elections entrenched religious Shiites, Kurdish nationalists, and a few Sunni remnants. The secular nationalists failed miserably, obtaining only a small percent of the vote. Chalabi, widely known as America's choice, received almost no votes despite a massive campaign fund. The result was that the government that American troops ushered into power preferred to see American troops gone.

That might have led to a positive, if unintended, outcome. However, the now legendarily inept administrator of the Coalition Provisional Authority, Paul Bremer, sacked the entire Iraqi Army and the Baathist bureaucracy. This instantly created a large, militarily capable resistance. The dissolved government and army were replaced by US troops, an embassy full of ambitious and generally uninformed young American neoconservatives, and an array of corporations under contract. The expected cakewalk turned into a burden that eventually turned the American public against the war. It also pushed the greatest military power in world history into a massive deficit to finance the occupation.

It is unclear whether the Bush administration believed that the occupation would be accepted by Iraqis or that American military might would deal with the objectors without suffering the extensive casualties that could undermine support at home.[52] Regardless, within a matter of months, guns, bombs, and militias, not elections, became the preferred route to a role in the political life of Iraq. Relentless violence was the norm for nearly five years.

One need only read some of the many books on the invasion and aftermath to appreciate that the administration's indifference to the existence of a functioning Iraqi government was comprehensive.[53] In contrast, *genuine* conservatives would have assumed that societal stability is easily disturbed, that volatile human nature requires stable institutions to keep it in check, and that once chaos is unleashed, order is not easily reestablished. Classical conservatives might well have spun in their graves on hearing what ensued in the name of conservatism.

Real conservatives are wary of unduly concentrated power and prefer to keep government spending within reasonable bounds, both of which tenets were utterly ignored. Real conservatives also would not have dismissed the rule of law with regard to the use of torture out of hand. Nor would they have countenanced spending trillions of public dollars on wars that changed very little.

In contrast, neoconservatives, mercifully a relatively unique breed on the global stage, seem to occupy a mental space somewhere beyond contradiction. In principle, they want to shrink government, but at the same time were *eager* to incur crippling expenditures to create a massive bureaucracy to govern a nation on the other side of the planet wherein they were almost universally loathed.

Balancing this set of beliefs requires a mix of arrogance and xenophobia. In the neoconservative mind, governing America is almost unnecessary because, being nonforeign, it is superior. Governing Iraq would be easy, hardly requiring a detailed plan, because it is an inferior place and merely requires the addition of perfecting institutions like a free market.

Thus the invasion and occupation flew in the face of conservative principles. It also paid no heed to simple human empathy—empathy regarding Iraqis, empathy for citizens of the many small countries that previously had imagined that the United Nations provided them an opportunity to be heard, empathy regarding the governments and citizens of historic allies that had trusted in the United States and in international law. All of that was cast into the desert winds.

Obama and Secretary of State Hillary Clinton did much to restore America's reputation, but enduring confidence will take time. Many outside America still worry that America will lapse back into unilateralism. America's approach to more recent crises in the Middle East helped to make a return to unilateralism seem a less likely future.[54] There have even been doubts expressed by some Republicans regarding unbridled combative neoconservatism. Broadly, however, the right in America is not stable in its foreign policy views and many neoconservatives were open, if not eager, to send US troops to both Libya and Syria.

Nonetheless the course of events in Syria seemed the opposite of the approach to Iraq. In just a few years the Bush administration alienated almost every nation and most thoughtful people on the planet, none more thoroughly than many who had previously respected the United States. So firm was the faith of those that launched the march into Baghdad that they never imagined that the antipathy of a global majority would ever be a matter of concern. Antipathy goes with the territory (of hegemonic power), they frequently said. *Hubris* does not begin to capture their view of the world.

Annually, the polling firm Environics asks Canadians this question: "In general what is your opinion of the United States?" From 1981 until 2002 those with a favorable opinion held at about 80 percent and unfavorable at about 20 percent. In 2002 the ratio abruptly shifted to 50–50.[55] It did not improve until Obama was elected. Canadians have since also been amazed by media and public opposition within the United States to each and every initiative of the Obama administration including hostility to Obama's Nobel Peace Prize and even Michelle Obama's White House garden.

The negative reaction to the Bush administration was global.[56] Much of the world instinctively distrusted American and British motives in Iraq. The invasion and occupation violated international law and moral principle. Many understood that the war was unprovoked and patently illegal even if American conservatives never did.[57] And contrary to the claims of the Bush administration, smart bombs are not very smart, white phosphorus *is* a chemical weapon, and torture is torture.

Hegemonic powers may be prone to paranoia, but the Bush administration never considered the obvious parallel reality that it is also easy for others to be paranoid about a hegemon. Military power may render fear and loathing seemingly trivial, but as the Romans and dominant powers since might attest—sooner or later fear and loathing may become an insurmountable obstacle. The world, not just Muslim nations or poor nations or sworn enemies of America, cannot help but be wary about the intentions of a hegemonic power. While it is a long way from wariness to active disapproval, during the Bush years wariness in time turned into widespread anger.

It is only reasonable that unilateral aggression by, or internal instability in, a militarily unstoppable power is going to be of wide concern. Ordinary people around the world, especially perhaps within America's traditional allies, were alarmed by the Bush administration. They continue to be concerned about future American domestic politics.[58]

Generally the world knows America better than many Americans know the world, and some non-Americans know America as well as America knows itself. The sighs of relief and the shouts of joy at the election of Obama were global, but the Republican disinclination to move toward the political center in response to electoral losses remains an ongoing concern. A continuing move of the Republican Party further to the right was visible in both the 2010 and 2012 campaigns (and since) especially with regard to social programs and taxation.

Indeed, many in Western democracies have for some time seen America as at times a bit off the deep end, especially on issues like gun ownership and rising inequality. But until the Bush years, those that held this view were more bemused and smug about it than alarmed or angry. That smug bemusement changed with the invasion of Iraq and wise Americans, including many moderate conservatives, knew that it had and knew that it mattered. Those moderate conservatives have in many cases left the Republican Party.

When Obama spoke in Berlin during the 2008 campaign, the McCain campaign could only attempt to undermine voter reaction to the stunning welcome by decrying Obama as a "celebrity"—implying that popularity with non-Americans is something to be worried about. By 2010 this attitude had somehow morphed into a belief on the part of many Americans that Obama was a Muslim and/or a socialist or not even an American citizen at all, or was intent on undermining the nation and seizing people's guns.

Prior to this ugly turn in American political culture, the world viewed overconfidence and assertiveness as part of America's rough charm and dogged competitiveness. It was not how one would want people to be at home, but it was for most a *c'est la vie* sort of thing and a chance to feel superior and more sophisticated than those living in the world's wealthy superpower.

In the bellicose verbal lead-up to the invasion of Iraq, in the visible torture at Abu Ghraib, in the rising power of religious-based American political extremism, and in utterances by both sides in the election campaign of 2004, alarm bells rang globally. They stopped ringing so loudly on November 4, 2008, but that concern, as will be discussed in later chapters, should not be put entirely aside. There are indeed ways to resolve it.

To retrigger the alarm bells one need only listen to public remarks by Dick Cheney or others since Obama was elected. For example, in December 2009, Cheney spoke for many Republicans when he in effect accused Obama of treason. Speaking with Sean Hannity on FOX News, Cheney stated that the Obama administration's decision to try accused terrorists held in Guantanamo in American courts in New York City "will give aid and comfort to the enemy." That phrase is the definition of treason in Article III, Section 3 of the Constitution.

Others continue to deny that Obama is eligible to serve as president and a significant proportion of Republican voters believe this assertion. Conservative commentators play to those inclined to racist-tinged paranoia by commenting on Obama's "anti-white" or "anticolonial" African roots, as if he had had such roots.[59] Perhaps in their minds political views are genetic.

On climate change, in the same spirit of American exceptionalism that led to Baghdad, Republican Congressman Dana Rohrabacher said of the 2010 Copenhagen climate conference: "this is about centralizing power into the hands of global government, that's what Kyoto and Copenhagen are all about, that's what the globalist alliance is all about... We must fight the globalist clique that is trying to shackle generations of Americans."[60] Sarah Palin, in commenting on the same event, suggested that the president boycott Copenhagen.

Republicans in 2009 and since have become even more hostile to climate action. Of the candidates for the Republican presidential nomination in 2012, only Jon Huntsman would acknowledge the reality of climate change and he received less than 2 percent of the votes. However, tellingly, Mitt Romney when faced with the large audience of the third presidential debate (on foreign policy) sharply softened the unilateralist belligerence he had favored on the stump. What this signaled, aside from the fact that Romney had few beliefs that he would not put aside for political advantage, is that a majority of Americans had had more than enough of aggressive foreign policies and wars in the Middle East. In 2003, few people would have imagined such a shift was possible.

During the invasion of Iraq, the tone of administration assertions did concern many people outside of the United States and some within. The vilification of the United Nations and the repeated scapegoating of France and other nations by leading American political figures created widespread, but guarded, alarm. Within America's media this global reaction to America's belligerence was hardly noticed, but what went on within the United States was visible globally. Too few Americans appreciate the significance of this everyday asymmetry.

To the outside world the practice of American politics during the 2004 presidential election campaign, like the later nomination of John Bolton as ambassador to the United Nations, was at once almost comical and darkly threatening. These were portents of possible madness at the governing center of the world's most powerful nation. The Republican convention was a globally visible display of frothing rage. The Democratic convention, while at times more tempered in tone, also frequently lapsed into a parody of jingoistic patriotism.

The Democrats tried to match the patriotic fervor of the Republican convention by exuding enthusiasm for military might. Democrats made an explicit commitment to *never* listen to other nations or international institutions when "it came to the defense of the United States." This unwillingness to challenge the prowar mindset of the day reflected the mood of American politics at the time. The assertions played very badly outside the United States. In the end candidate John Kerry was considerably less jingoistic than Bush, but the electoral outcome suggested to the world that few Americans were prepared at the time to see themselves as citizens of one nation among many.

Four years later, President Obama knew that America needed to undo the widespread perception that America had morphed into a national embodiment of Machiavelli's advice that it is better to be feared than loved. Outside America's 2004 bubble most people preferred to imagine that the world had advanced from a fifteenth-century world view. This view after all came to us from a man who rather admired the idea of inviting people to dinner and poisoning them to set an useful example to others.

Following the 2004 election, political elites in other nations labored to make nice with the Bush government, but global public perceptions were not easily dispelled. These feelings lingered even after the 2006 midterm defeat of Republicans and the dramatic shift of 2008. Lingering doubts remain because extremism could yet again come to power in Washington (and during the Obama years only rarely did conservative Republicans not hold veto power on significant changes in American domestic policy).

There has, however, been a shift within American opinion on the issue of military intervention. Political discourse had shifted by 2008 and 2012 and, more important, President Obama ended combat involvement in Iraq without significant political opposition. Moreover, Osama bin Laden is dead and Obama has consistently acted with great restraint compared to his predecessor. Most Americans understand that they simply cannot afford another war at this time. Romney courted defense contractors by emphasizing expanded military procurement, but did not raise such matters when large numbers of people were paying attention (especially after he was quickly silenced by perhaps Obama's most telling debate rebuttal).[61]

However, regarding the other two considerations this chapter addresses, the rhetorical silences of the 2012 campaign were also telling. There was almost no mention of climate change in any of the four debates. This is a clear sign that neither side saw political benefit in raising the issue. While there may be Americans that care about the issue, there are many that feel threatened by government taking climate change action.

On inequality, the issue addressed shortly below, the silence was even more stunning. Within American campaign discourse mentions of social inequality may provoke denunciations of the speaker as engaging in class warfare. President Obama was called a socialist (not by Romney) for suggesting that taxes on wealthy individuals should return to 1990s levels in the face of challenging deficits. So skewed is political discourse on this subject that the Obama administration does not mention the poor and only speaks of "helping the middle class." It is as if there *were* no poor people.[62]

Hegemonic dominance is more likely to be accommodated if the hegemon is seen to advance or exemplify a desirable direction for the world. The diminution of that acceptance during the Bush years may well have a continuing impact on the global political future. That is why the recent history of the issues addressed in this chapter is so critical. Many, in effect, felt ignored and disrespected by America's disdain regarding climate change, international law, and the very idea of multilateralism, as well as the illegal and unwarranted use of force. As well, the growing constraints on social mobility within America and the world undermines the ideal that America had previously embodied. Hegemonic power is less threatening when life within the hegemonic nation is seen as highly prized the world over. That is simply not the case when the benefits of wealth redound to a small and shrinking proportion of Americans.

These shifting impressions of America and the risks of hegemony itself for the world might not be easily dispelled without structural changes in the international system to provide some means of giving a greater global voice to citizens. Change could begin, however, if America assumed a leadership role on matters like the global environment and global social equity.

Doubts about any dominant power, especially one that so visibly celebrates the role, come easily. As noted in chapter 1 there are really only three ways to undo global hegemonic domination once that pattern is firmly established. One is the economic decline of the hegemonic power. Another is an arms race that wastes unacceptable amounts of money, especially within a hegemonic power determined to hold on to its status. The third alternative is the emergence of some system of cooperative global governance. Most American conservatives oppose the latter possibility and Democrats are often afraid to speak its name. If there is any other possibility (other than eternal global dominance by one nation) I do not know what it is.

This book seeks an alternative that includes global citizens in solutions to global problems. This search is motivated less by hostility to the status quo than by a realization that the status quo is not permanent and that shifting away from hegemonic dominance is fraught with risks. Now, in the waning shadow of the Bush years, it is important to identify the costs of the diametrical *opposite* of global governance, unilateralism. Unilateralism based on military power is inherently problematic for at least four reasons. All were transparent in the tragedy that unfolded in Baghdad. We can identify three of those reasons readily.

First, the occupation of any substantial nation by another has become far more difficult and costly because of the near-ubiquitous availability of military grade weapons. The demise of colonialism is permanent and the millennial dreams of neoconservatives have been comprehensively dashed. Second, dominant powers are nonetheless perpetually faced with a continuous need to demonstrate not just that they have power but that they are willing to use it (lest the world including their own citizens suspect that they have wasted all that money). Third, possession of seemingly overwhelming military power will almost inevitably provoke counter-assertive risky behavior, as in Iran, North Korea, and, drone attacks notwithstanding, in the back alleys and caves of the Islamist underworld. Concentrated power is inherently provocative to some.

Each of these possibilities is worrisome, but the fourth—a vulnerability within hegemonic power to internal interests—is by far the most threatening. It explains why the invasion of Iraq was so alarming. Dependence on military power can be self-perpetuating and self-advancing within the domestic politics of any nation. America is not immune to that possibility even if it has reconsidered the aggressive use of power.

In the internal politics of nations the greater the scale of military expenditures the greater the political power of those dependent on those expenditures (even when, as in the United States, the professional military is generally circumspect and quite diverse in its political views). The political effects of military spending has existed both before and since President Dwight Eisenhower uttered the phrase "military-industrial complex." However, prior to the Bush administration America usually acted within a dense network of strategic alliances. President Obama has sought to restore such networks.

The war in Iraq was a watershed event precisely because of America's new willingness to aggressively advance its interests through the surreal concept of "preventative" war and essentially unilateral military action.[63] It was all along patently obvious that Iraq had nothing to do with the terrorist attack on the United States and had no WMDs.[64] Not only did the world and international observers know, but so did the Bush administration. How else might one explain why US troops left unsearched weapons depots unprotected and available to looters as they took control of Iraq?

At the heart of the Baghdad tale is the fact that the tragic events of September 11, combined with the unwillingness of American traditional media to challenge the administration, resulted in strong initial public support for a relentlessly aggressive posture toward the world.[65] The Bush administration abandoned many restraints on the use of (nonnuclear) military power while also asserting the possibility that it would begin new nuclear weapons development.[66] A majority of Americans, even after coming to see the Iraq war as a tragic error, seem nonetheless at least grudgingly willing to continue a seemingly perpetual arms race with themselves.

This is not to say that the threat of terrorism is not real. It is all too real, but it cannot be defeated by military means alone. On the contrary, war produces the social instability that is a natural climate for creating new terrorists. And, as noted, the act of declaring a *war* on terror creates a mood in which terrorism can thrive by exalting indiscriminant murderers as worthy military opponents. As well, Iraq's killing fields might well have bred terrorist masterminds for another day.

But Iraqis were not alone in having borne the costs of the hubris to which hegemonic powers are sometimes prone. The opportunity costs of the war, what might have otherwise been done with the resources that were used, became apparent to Americans shortly after the 2004 election. The 2005 hurricane season was about to blow away illusions about American wealth, American power, American equality of opportunity, and American competence in a localized prelude to global economic troubles that would begin in 2008.

Some conservative theocrats, many of the same figures who had celebrated the invasion of Iraq, decreed that Hurricane Katrina was sent by God because New Orleans was a city of sin—a place where partying and sexuality and homosexuality and all manner of offense to what is proper were rampant. In contrast, the rest of the world was stunned to see massive incompetence and third-world levels of poverty in America, as well as overt racism that ultimately resulted in the indictments of police officers for murder. Most Americans knew that these things were possible, but had forgotten—much of the rest of the world had no idea.

Like America's theocrats, some in the wider world also saw the hand of God or just old fashioned karma coming home. Some Louisiana National Guard units that might have aided with the emergency had been assigned to Iraq. And the strength of the storm may have been enhanced by record-high water temperatures throughout the Caribbean. Katrina was, at least in part, influenced by climate change. This time the victims were not polar bears, domesticated animals in Sudan, or coral reefs, but the residents of a great and deeply historic American city.

New Orleans: Hegemony's Cost

New Orleans following Hurricane Katrina is like a ghost story—with the howling ghosts of Kyoto and Baghdad seeking revenge. The desperation in New Orleans during Katrina rendered visible the costs of misused wealth and power. They illustrated as well, to those prepared to see it, the need for effective, caring government everywhere—even within a hegemonic power.[67] Even superpowers are not exempt from the laws of nature and even hegemons have people who need help. Hegemony, however, makes it very hard for government to provide that help, especially in combination with the need to remain globally competitive in terms of tax rates. Canada's tax rates are comparable to America's, but it spends what it does not spend on its military on universal health care and public higher education. Katrina then revealed for all to see that metaphorically drowning government in the bathtub can lead to *actually* drowning Americans in their homes.[68]

The tragedy in New Orleans exposed the administration's ineptitude and indifference and was a political turning point leading into the 2006 and 2008 elections. Yet the real lesson runs even deeper and lays bare facts that Americans tend to resist: One, massive military expenditures *preclude* other possible uses of public money. America's military strength has been in part achieved rather than social justice and basic infrastructure (including the levees of New Orleans). Two, indifference to extreme social inequality carries a heavy price and not just for the poor.[69] And three, wealth and power can be utterly overwhelmed by nature and both are vulnerable to climate gone wrong.

The failures in New Orleans at the state, local, and national level were visible globally and aspects of the disaster originated at the global level. As we have seen, climate disruption will not be easily mitigated without unprecedented levels of global cooperation. The fact that some see the very possibility of global cooperation as a threat to the American way of life notwithstanding, the real threat is imagining that climate change does not exist and is a nefarious plot of "globalist" forces, as if such forces were so organized.

As noted, many governments have been happy to have America and China as an excuse for their own lack of effort on climate change.

Until very recently it has been easy to look good by comparison. Other nations, even many European nations, are still well short of effective action. Thus on this issue the dreaded forces of globalism barely exist. Many nations, like Canada, continue to shrug off the pressure. This widespread unwillingness to assume a national share of responsibility on climate change is succinctly illustrated in a set of statistics and an editorial in the leading French newspaper, *Le Monde*.

The statistical evidence is this: the worldwide increase in the output of GHGs between 2000 and 2005 was greater *by a factor of four* than in was in the *whole decade* 1990–1999. While the United States was rejecting climate action, other nations were following suit. Not only was the world not reducing GHG emissions, but those emissions *rose at a quickening pace despite the Kyoto agreement.*

Le Monde is moderately progressive. France has strongly supported internationalism, global governance, and the Kyoto agreement specifically. France was notably generous, for example, with aid to stricken New Orleans. Yet, in late 2006 *Le Monde* opined: "France causes only 1.5% of global carbon emissions. Even if it elected a nicely green President...started riding bikes, and cutting off power, it would change nothing (in terms of) the climate."[70] It is as if everyone's obligation to change is an argument that no one could or should change.

The possible connection of climate change to events in New Orleans or to severe droughts in Texas or many other weather events was generally ignored by media until Hurricane Sandy in 2012. So were, and are, the possibilities of massive species loss and the costs associated with threats to agriculture (as became increasingly visible with the failure of the 2010 Russian wheat crop and the spike in global wheat prices that followed). Human-induced climate change is still seen by many as a minor inconvenience of interest only to naïve environmentalists or a matter that can be put aside because severe effects may not be felt on the watch of today's political incumbents.

The vulnerability, sheer incompetence, and lack of public capacity visible in New Orleans was but a year before the above quoted *Le Monde* editorial. Media amnesia is not exclusive to the United States. In the days after Katrina, just to refresh memories, the anger and amazement within the United States was so palpable that America's cable news networks, *even Fox News*, the relentlessly conservative Republican advocacy channel, went off-script.

Americans and the world were stunned that four years after September 11, 2001, there was seemingly *no* capacity at the local, state, or national level to quickly respond to a catastrophic emergency in a major American city. The United States, it appeared, was less able to respond to a hurricane than Cuba had been not long before Katrina struck.

It seemed incredible. America was glaringly unable to meet the most basic needs of its citizens. It could not deliver fresh water and emergency medicine, let alone food, to thousands of survivors and was unable to quickly evacuate incapacitated hospitals. It could not put out fires in the stricken, flooded city. People who had escaped to their roofs by literally kicking their way to an air supply were left there injured for days. Some government officials appeared hysterical, others (including those purportedly in charge of the nation's emergency services) seemed utterly and completely oblivious.

Even conservative commentator George Will observed: "Americans tend to believe in God and to disbelieve in government. Time will tell how many are moved to rethink one or both of those tendencies in the aftermath of Katrina. It is, however, likely that the storm's lingering reverberations will alter the nation's mind far more than 9/11 did."[71]

Many observers later concluded that there was a causal link between the failed response to Katrina and the electoral shift in the 2006 midterm elections. This political momentum continued into 2008 when the economic collapse rooted in financial deregulation at least suggested, contrary to a central tenet of American conservatism, that effective government action is crucial to human well-being. As Maureen Dowd noted in 2006, "The good news is that this election finished what Katrina started."[72] The destruction of New Orleans made plain, at least for a time, the price of neoconservative policies.

The response to Katrina also demonstrated incontrovertibly that the Bush administration had failed to attend to homeland security needs despite the fact that that was its signature issue. It was clear that the Department of Homeland Security, on which the Bush government had lavished billions, had no clue how to deal with a catastrophe, whether of natural or human origin.

Watching what happened, television viewers might have sensed that the Federal Emergency Measures Administration (FEMA), the Red Cross, and even the US military should have been "reverse embedded" with television news organizations. CNN relocated cameras and staff from Atlanta and New York in a timely fashion. Regrettably the TV crews had little capacity to do anything for the thousands who remained in desperate need day after day.[73] The networks did continuously convey gripping live pictures. No words from the administration or their media supporters could undo the *images* on everyone's screens.

Not only were emergency organizations derelict to the point of putting lives at risk unnecessarily, but the agencies that did function seemed primarily concerned with stopping "looters." The concern of local officials that were earliest on the scene, it seemed, was to stop desperate people from taking matters into their own hands to save their families and neighbors from dying of thirst in the oppressive heat and humidity.[74] Later it became apparent that things were even worse than they had appeared at the time—both vigilantes and police had engaged in racially based violence.[75]

Decades of Hollywood disaster movies, and just plain good sense, made it obvious to people in New Orleans that they should do just what they did. People found whatever would float and hauled neighbors off roofs. They somehow got the sick and old through miles of foul water to the Superdome. One young man found an abandoned bus and drove around for hours picking up people slogging in the water and took them to safety out of the flooded parts of the city. He might have been celebrated as a hero like Will Smith would have been in the movies, and he might well have imagined he himself would be. He was instead, however, arrested for stealing the bus.

The illusions that were shattered in New Orleans were illusions about America that had long been accepted by the world. The image of an all-powerful America was undermined severely. These were not, of course, illusions created from thin air.

Americans created many of the wonders and icons of modern industrial society. They invented the light bulb, the telephone, the automobile, the skyscraper, television, computers, and the Internet. Many of the breakthroughs that Americans did not invent they showed the world how to mass produce. Challenged by Sputnik, the United States put humans on the moon with astounding dispatch. Time and again the United States has sent massive, fully equipped fighting forces to the opposite side of the Earth, but inexplicably the military that had recently traversed the road to Baghdad in the face of armed resistance was unable to travel (or rather was not promptly *ordered* to travel) the wet roads into New Orleans.[76]

The administration that had only recently asserted that *it*, rather than the United Nations or any other multilateral body, should manage the strategic and military affairs of the planet looked like a deer in the headlights in the face of a natural disaster no worse than the recent disasters handled far more effectively by Indonesia, Sri Lanka,

Thailand, and other nations with vastly fewer resources and less warning. These things are noted not to denigrate the United States, nor to revisit the singular incompetence of almost everyone responsible at every level.[77]

The reason to reflect on New Orleans is to appreciate that *every* nation has limited capacities and that *every* nation is capable of overreaching. Around the world, many, of course, understood that, but Katrina caused many Americans to also see it. In combination, climate inaction, the unfolding debacle in Iraq, and ineptitude in New Orleans gave pause to the nation's recently expanded sense of special status—it gave pause in the all-party catechism about America being the greatest nation on earth.[78]

Andrew Jackson's political career emerged in New Orleans, and George W. Bush's place in history, along with Republican prospects, were submerged there. It seemed at the time that they would not rise again anytime soon. Amazingly, less than a decade later Republican Governor Christie of New Jersey was excoriated within his party *for merely appearing with President Obama* following Hurricane Sandy devastation and was later criticized by other Republicans for even taking federal money.[79] Elephants do, apparently, forget and the lessons of New Orleans were clearly not learned universally.

The 2008 economic crisis rooted in financial deregulation seemed to assure that Republican prospects would not be easily reversed. However, by 2010 conservative media's power and the solid support of Republicans from evangelicals, Southerners, and rural dwellers produced a rapid restoration. The catechism of American greatness reemerged as memories of New Orleans faded. The Bush administration's claims of national superiority had not been worthy of a great nation, but that did not prevent Republicans from regaining considerable power in Washington.

Nonetheless, Baghdad and New Orleans in combination had provided Americans with a glimpse of just how expensive global hegemony could be, especially in the face of the deep budgetary challenges that followed the 2008 financial meltdown. With Katrina on their screens, Americans realized that America was ill-prepared in part because occupying Iraq had come at the expense of domestic needs. Discourse of *that* sort faded and the tragedy of New Orleans was seen as incompetence, rather than as a fundamentally flawed approach to both international politics and budgetary priorities.

The largely unlearned lesson of New Orleans is that no single nation can dominate in perpetuity. The world is just too big and complicated. And some things, including climate change, inequality and terrorism require that *all* nations, and citizens, participate in and contribute to solutions. Events in Kyoto, Baghdad and New Orleans suggest that any nation that purports to lead the world is obliged to lead the world where the world needs to go, rather than merely where that nation might prefer to take it. The majority of people globally were clear that invading Iraq was wrong, both morally and strategically. As New Orleans drowned, many Americans seemed to see, once the opportunity costs of war and even hegemonic power itself were clear, that this judgment might just be right.

If I were a devout apocalyptic Christian (yet still maintained my leftish green inclinations), I might be tempted to see New Orleans as a punishment for the rejection of the Kyoto Accord. I might also imagine that a just God would have picked a different city to drown. A just God would not condemn those taught for centuries that they were better off clinging to what little they had than venturing into places where minorities without American Express platinum cards, or at least a middle-class appearance and demeanor, were still not welcome. Many citizens of New Orleans did not have the resources to flee the city and most were too smart to just wander into suburban or rural Louisiana.

America's conservative media did not, of course, see things that way. Rush Limbaugh castigated those trapped in New Orleans and offered exactly no empathy regarding their plight. Glenn Beck, who at that point had not yet reached media stardom let alone his later eclipse, said the following on his radio program during the height of the suffering: "We're not hearing anything about Mississippi. We're not hearing anything about Alabama. We're hearing about the victims in New Orleans. This is a 90,000-square-mile disaster site, New Orleans is 181 square miles...0.2 percent of the disaster area is New Orleans. And that's all we're hearing about, are the people in New Orleans. Those are the only ones we're seeing on television are the scumbags—and again, it's not all the people in New Orleans. Most of the people in New Orleans got out!"[80]

The scumbags noted by Beck were those without fully fueled SUVs and high-limit credit cards at the ready. The allegedly unmentioned citizens of Mississippi and Alabama were, in the dog whistle racist code of right-wing media, ignored by the "liberal" media because they were white.

Nonetheless, in the immediate wake of Katrina, most Americans still knew unfairness and incompetence when they saw it. A thoroughly

American sense of fair play was what worried Beck and Limbaugh and what they were so eager to counter. For many Americans the sense of unspecified national greatness was adjusted a notch or two in Katrina's wake and that attitude became less of a driver of political attitudes. This shift was good preparation for the coming (luckily temporary) demise of both iconic Wall Street firms and iconic Detroit automakers.

The meaning of presumptions regarding American leadership indeed cries out for *global* debate. Americans and non-Americans alike buy into the view that America can and should fix everything. The presumption even existed within the profound sense of hope the world imposed on Barack Obama on his election as president. He, however, might be the first to reply that change is a "we" thing not an "I" thing. We *all* need to ask if global leadership (or national greatness) is primarily a measure of military power, economic might, historic achievement or something else.

Global citizens, American or otherwise, might argue that a dedication to fairness, justice, decency, creativity, civility, competence, generosity, and, yes, freedom is the better measure of national greatness.[81] Many Americans would lay claim to *all* of the possible measures (power- or virtue-oriented). At this point the world can only hope that America's better nature will prevail so long as it continues to hold hegemonic power. In the longer run, however, global leadership will hopefully involve broad citizen acceptance. Global leadership on this basis is likely to be much less expensive than hegemonic military power.

Katrina revealed some of the costs of hegemonic power. Military might had been presumed by most Americans to produce economic benefits, but those benefits look better if analysis ignores opportunity costs. Weapons production pays well and military bases create economic benefits for communities, and for nations around the world. But the opportunity costs—*all* of the things that might have been done with the same money—are at least as important.

The City of New Orleans and the Army Corps of Engineers had requested additional funds to improve the area's levees for years prior to Katrina. Most such funds and equipment were in use in Iraq and elsewhere. More generally, money spent on military procurement could not be spent on public transportation, on health capabilities, or social services capacities, or emergency preparedness, or infrastructure, or schools, not just in New Orleans but in cities throughout America.

Katrina starkly reminded those who had forgotten, or who had somehow managed not to know or not to care, that American wealth is increasingly mal-distributed. Amidst vast wealth, grinding poverty is relentless and altogether normal.[82] Astonishingly, this reality is almost never questioned or challenged, even by those who experience the worst of it. Poverty continues to grow even as the richest nation the world has ever known becomes richer still.

Katrina was, then, a very ill wind that did blow *some* good. The last time American poverty was as visible was in the 1960s when for a time the best-selling book was Michael Harrington's *The Other America*. President Lyndon Johnson's "war on poverty" followed that attention.[83] Such books are now relegated to sociology classrooms and, as noted, poverty is rarely mentioned.

Katrina, however, for a brief moment laid poverty in America bare for all to see.[84] Many in New Orleans did not own an automobile. They had no financial capability to rent a car, take an intercity bus, or even, for that matter, to buy enough gas to get out of town and back again. Yet there was *no viable contingency plan* for these people other than opening the doors of the Superdome. This incapacity existed in a hurricane-prone region, in a city that was, owing to topography and other factors, known to be unable to withstand a direct hit by a major storm.

Nor was there a clear plan for those who were too sick to be easily moved or were responsible for a family member who was too sick or were simply afraid to leave their own community. While the world knows that New Orleans has made great contributions to the cultural richness of the planet, many in neighboring Louisiana suburbs were not clear on that point and thought little of their urban neighbors.[85] For more than a century, when the poor in New Orleans were every bit as poor as they were when Katrina stuck, their neighborhoods gave spectacular gifts to the world. When the emergency struck, however, those gifts counted for little.

New Orleans produced many of the musical innovations of the twentieth century. Ragtime, blues, and jazz all have deep roots in New Orleans. Jazz has been called *the* quintessentially American music: spirited, spontaneous, individualistic, dynamic, and rhythmic. The rhythms of jazz are the rhythms of modernity and industrialism itself.

Jazz and mass production arose and evolved at the same time. Mass production began in the spinning mills of England and the steel mills of Pittsburgh, but the creative genius of jazz emerged in the African American community of New Orleans. It was played in bars and brothels and at funerals. It was invented on the streets and roofs and in the rooming houses of this cosmopolitan port city, a city whose poorer communities also gave the world an incredible array of culinary delights created out of the low cost foods locally available to those with limited funds.

Jazz influenced modern classical composers from Debussy and Ravel to Stravinsky. Jazz and blues evolved into rock and, through Gershwin and others, contributed to the evolution of American musical theater and to the development of film, cartoons, broadcast radio, and the recording industry.

Swing era jazz saw *the world* through the Great Depression and World War II and jazz remains a force in musical expression today. Whether that latter judgment is true for everyone or not, there is no denying that a predominantly African American New Orleans, gave the world gifts that may well be with humankind for as long as much of whatever else resulted from the industrial age to which they gave expression.

The causes of the damage in New Orleans were multifaceted. Many of the deaths could have been avoided had there been an orderly evacuation plan for the city and a great deal of misery could have been avoided had military rescue units been assigned in a timely manner. If the levees had been improved to the levels that had been recommended, much of the flooding might have been avoided. Though little could have been done about the storm surge in some parts of the wider region, other parts might have suffered less damage if wetlands and beaches had not been developed in the ways that they were developed during the decades leading up to Katrina.

These mistakes were compounded into a horrendous event, but there is also no mistaking the possibility that climate change was a contributing element. In the autumn of 2005 the waters of the Gulf of Mexico were as warm as they had ever been on that date. The hurricane went from a category 1 storm to a category 5 storm (the maximum on the scale) *overnight*.

The devastating impacts were *anticipated* once the trajectory was known and the likely effect of the water temperatures on that path were taken into account, but they were nonetheless unprecedented. That is, there was time to have evacuated more of the city, much as Havana had been evacuated on several occasions, but climate change had altered the odds of a category 5 hurricane hitting levees built to withstand a category 3.[86]

Events in New Orleans thus lead back to Kyoto as well as Baghdad. The outcomes are one example of what climate change is all about—disruption of patterns taken to be normal. All of nature, including humans, have adapted to the climate that we have had for millennia. We can continue to adapt as that climate shifts, but adaptation is slow and unfortunately a process that may prove fatal to some. Just as the cost of the damage exceeded the avoided cost of improving the levees, in general terms, the cost of climate change impacts will almost always be more than the cost of *not* mitigating climate change.

One reason that reducing GHG emissions is difficult *politically* is that many of the early impacts are borne by polar bears and small island nations in the Pacific. However, the largest prevention costs must be borne by the rich and powerful nations. Climate change is also politically difficult because the avoidance costs must be paid now and are certain, while the damage costs would be paid later and are less certain as to timing and location. A single digit increase in average global temperature over many decades just does not seem as threatening as having to rely on public transit to get to work while facing tax or energy price increases.

Three other conclusions can be drawn regarding this conundrum. One is global, a second is about America, and the third is about New Orleans.

Globally, allowing climate change to proceed nearly unchecked is collective madness that places a significant proportion of the human species at risk. As well, much of nature, on which human life depends, would also be threatened. Even if we were to avoid war over forced migration or food emergencies, regions on every continent will likely be rendered uninhabitable by excessive heat or rising seas. Drought-induced agricultural losses, like those in Russia in 2010 and in Texas in 2011, will become commonplace and many species of animals and plants will go extinct in the wild. Dry places will become arid and millions that depend on glacier-fed water will have few options. Others will experience unprecedented flooding as did New Orleans in 2005, Pakistan in 2010, New York and New Jersey in 2012 and Calgary, the Philippines, and elsewhere in 2013.

Rejecting decisive action *only* makes sense from a hyper-individualistic and short-term perspective. The carbon output of any single firm or nation will not in and of itself produce a dead planet, but inactions promote inaction by others. The carbon output of one person hardly makes a measurable difference, but if anyone is exempt from responsibility why would everyone not be exempt?

Climate action is only truly effective if undertaken on a global scale. A sense of obligation as global citizens is no longer a nice idea for fuzzy-minded idealists, it is essential to the collective well-being of all species, including our own. The realists, it seems, are the dreamers and the dreamers are the realists, *Le Monde* editorial writers and American conservatives notwithstanding.

The second point, regarding America, is that insufficient action on climate change is yet one more opportunity cost of the unrestrained exercise of global hegemony. Money spent on military bases in Kyrgyzstan, Diego Garcia, and other places most Americans could not find on a map is money that cannot be spent on energy alternatives to slow climate change or on ameliorating its worst consequences.

Adaptation is in fact important.[87] If the best we can hope to do is to slow climate change, we had best learn how to adapt crops and wooded areas, defend coastlines, fund the capacity to fight multiple simultaneous grass and forest fires, and learn how to minimize the effects of drought, storms, changing disease vectors, and flooding. These are very expensive undertakings and are every bit as much about *security* as is the struggle against terrorism. And, they will affect many more people. Adaptation costs are additional to the costs of reducing emissions and can only be lessened by accelerating emissions reductions.

The third point concerns New Orleans and conservative political ideas. Intelligent conservatives from Edmund Burke onward have understood that societies and communities are living entities embedded in traditions and established institutions. Communities are organic not mechanical. The greatness of New Orleans and the musical and other gifts that it gave to the world emerge from a community and a culture. Restoring New Orleans as a city and as a community is about bringing back most of the people that were there and allowing *them* to remake their lives and their culture.

Some noble efforts in this regard have been undertaken by volunteers and charitable and public programs, for example, those specifically designed to aid musicians. However, it is also true that some of the public funds devoted to restoration ended up in the hands of the rich and powerful. One of the largest recovery initiatives was a program permitting the issuing of tax-free bonds and other tax advantages. As it turned out, most of this largess went to the restoration of luxury beachfront homes, to oil companies ($1.7 billion), and to other major area industries. Too little of that money went to nonprofit or low-cost housing.[88]

Restoring New Orleans should *not* have been about high-end real estate deals. It should have been about nurturing a living, creative, diverse community and bringing back the spectacular array of small businesses and artistic creativity that came out of that diversity. Without that, a restored New Orleans could only ever be what Eugene Robinson so eloquently called a "sad little 'sin and decadence' theme park for liquored up conventioneers."[89]

Global citizens appreciate the cultural contribution that New Orleans has given the world. Real conservatives would understand that future contributions from that city require rebuilding of a culture rooted in a sense of community. The world must do everything possible to facilitate the restoration of that living human community. The physical city is coming back, but many of the city's former residents still remain scattered. Yet, if we are all very lucky, something even half as wondrous as what existed before Katrina might yet emerge again.

* * *

What can these fading memories of a past decade teach us? Will war remain an easier sell than the transformation of the energy system that underlies the global economy? Will America see the wisdom of adopting an approach to defense that is actually defense oriented? Will today's rise of inequality within most economies ever again be encountered and reversed?

It was frequently observed that the destruction of New Orleans was a blow to America's "image in the world." It might also be the case, however, that people around the world felt better about the United States having learned that so many Americans are far from rich and that America is, after all, *not* all-powerful. If America is but one nation amongst many and many Americans are needful and can die tragically just like the rest of us, perhaps we can learn to live reasonably harmoniously in one world. This perspective grew following a 2008 election outcome open to change, interconnectedness, and doubts about both the hubris of the Bush years and excessive dependence on military "solutions."

Interestingly regarding the realization that America is not all-powerful after all, many Iraqis apparently assumed that America's occupational forces *deliberately* "avoided" supplying water and electricity for several years because America wished to keep them in misery. The Iraqis were unable to imagine that so powerful a nation was unable to restore basic services. Events in New Orleans undermined this view. Indeed, people around the world imagine ordinary Americans and Europeans to be far wealthier than they really are. They especially do not appreciate that American families earning two thousand American dollars per month might not be far from hunger and may be a serious illness away from homelessness.

It is important for the world to escape the illusion that America's wealth and power is all-determining. Wealth and military might guarantees neither greatness, nor great arrogance and greed. No one should imagine that any single nation can resolve all the world's ills or resolve every dispute. A more democratic approach to international affairs depends on shedding such illusions.

Wealth and military might cannot grant *security* in any meaningful sense of the word. The events recounted in this chapter suggest that real security is a complicated matter and military spending can produce the exact opposite. In an age of global economic integration, this is especially true of foreign occupations, with regard to both the occupied and the occupier.

Have we learned this lesson? Has an American majority come to a new perspective? Since we cannot be sure, of course, other nations or a proportion of global civil society should be capable of moving forward independently should America return to unilateralism at some point in the future. Dealing with climate change will require truly global action in any case. So will the protection and expansion of the rule of law within the international arena, addressing global social equity and restraint in the use of military force. These things cannot be left to one nation, especially one whose politics are as fraught and unpredictable as America's have recently been. More than that, addressing any or all of these things effectively, I will argue, will require the active participation of citizens around the world.

Globally oriented citizens might wisely use the historic moments when America's better angels prevail to create opportunities for greater citizen input into global affairs. A global citizens' movement might offset the turbulence of possible futures where American dominance wanes and/or goes off the rails. The decade set out in this chapter suggests that a hegemonic system of global governance is an inherently unstable and undemocratic system. This tale of three cities suggests that the potential for American leadership on climate change, on limits to unilateralism, and on the rule of law in the international arena is fragile. It cannot just be assumed to be permanent, at least not without additional pressure from somewhere. It is difficult to see where such pressure on any and all governments might emerge other than from citizens worldwide.

Both citizens and national leaders must see that simply waiting for *American* leadership is an excuse to avoid responsibilities that we all share. Assuming that America will always lead the world, or worse assuming that it is "a global Satan," are sure ways to weaken the sometimes fragile hold of rational, reasonable, and fair-minded global action within American political life. Without tangible, but critical, global and citizen support, no American leader can take on the strong internal resistance to positive action regarding inequality, climate change, or excessive military spending.

A widely shared, participatory global citizenship is essential and it will not emerge out of either national arrogance or national envy. It will not develop from within a presumption that the world should perpetually defer to one or a small number of nations. Meaningful global citizenship will not fully emerge so long as most people imagine that only one or a few nations are all-powerful. The easy assumption that the richest, most technologically advanced nation in the world will or can fix anything and everything is now entombed in ashes of Baghdad and the mud of New Orleans, and drifts about with the ghosts of Kyoto's inadequacy.

America has squeezed its treasury and wounded the global economy by trying to manage the world from Washington and Wall Street. Hegemonic power is still celebrated by ordinary Americans, and even wise presidents in ritual incantations about the greatest nation in the world. That view is a point of pride, but the price of hegemony for both America and the world is too infrequently considered in a serious way.

It is rarely imagined that the felt need for hegemonic power is in large measure a function of paranoia. So is the presumption that other nations can only defer to, or defy, power. Nor is it often enough doubted that competing national military power is worth the enormous cost. That cost is widely seen in America as a price that must be paid to maintain hard-earned comforts and basic security in a hostile and dysfunctional world. In other governing circles, vast power is greeted with either envy or some eagerness to curry favor.

Nonetheless, it is hegemonic power and its single-minded and narrow application to national interests that may have begun the undoing of what was taken to be America's century before that century's first decade was over. Now that other possibilities are becoming visible, there is a unique opportunity to come to terms with the complexity of hegemonic limits and the possibility of cooperative global governance. Given the challenges ahead, if we do not act, we may never get a better chance to see this transformation through to practical reality.

3

The Evolution of Citizenship: From Athens to Earth

A poll conducted a few years ago for the King Baudouin Foundation found that: "[F]or the first time in history, one citizen in five across the world strongly identifies with being a citizen of the world ahead of being a citizen of a home country."[1] It also found that a majority of university-educated citizens from a diverse group of nations believed that there is a need for increased global rule-making and for global enforcement of those rules. The striking level of interest (and implicit solidarity) among people around the world regarding the 2008 and 2012 American elections reinforce this finding.

Could this nascent sense of global citizenship evolve into a movement capable of actually impacting global policies? Could it someday affect power relations within or between states or open up the closed conduct of global affairs? Just asking such questions requires something of a leap of faith, but what else could provide the political counter weight necessary to generate action on rising inequality or climate change? Without *some* shift in global politics there may also be a greater risk of an unchallenged hegemonic attitudes of the sort that prevailed during the Bush years.

To alter the world's present trajectory, a global citizen's movement need not evolve into anything like a membership organization. It need not even have powerful and permanent leaders. Much like the American civil rights movement, a multiplicity of organizations could emerge and evolve, a pattern all the more likely in a *global* movement. Indeed myriad citizen-based global organizations already exist, focused on a diversity of concerns: human rights, economic development, social equity, health, peace, and the environment. Many people already think of themselves as having citizenly obligations and responsibilities regarding global, as well as national and local concerns.

Citizenship is about the capacity to aspire, to imagine ways out of the eternal sameness of endless yesterdays, and to act cooperatively and democratically on those aspirations.[2] Today's challenge is to see and act on *global* needs and aspirations, much as national aspirations were added to local in the early days of the industrial revolution.

The Evolution of Citizenship[3]

Citizenship was once oriented to villages, city-states, tribes, or principalities. With the industrial revolution the nation-state emerged as citizenship's principal locus. Global citizenship would seem but a logical extension of this historic evolution, a possibility rooted in advances in communications, transportation, trade, and the now-global scale of trade, and economic integration.

We cannot yet know what global citizenship might actually mean to everyday lives and how the actions, organizations, or institutions of global citizenship might develop. We do know that over centuries the international system has seen the methodical development of law regarding individuals.[4] However, relatively few individuals are actually impacted personally by that system and the nation-state remains firmly entrenched in the human psyche as the basis of law.[5] As well, in some nations including the United States even glimmers of global governance trigger a visceral response in some.

These realities, however, do not preclude the emergence of an expanding focus for citizenship. That focus would not necessarily, or perhaps even likely, lead to global government, a possibility that is fraught with challenges. Global government is at most a remote possibility for the distant future and may not be desirable in any case. The challenge is to establish opportunities and organizations through which citizens throughout the world can communicate, interact, and influence the outcome of local, national, and global policy and political outcomes.

Today's global citizenship opportunities lie primarily within global civil society organizations. Each of these organizations focuses on a single issue or set of issues, though the array of organizations is increasingly diverse and important. Globally oriented citizens are active within (or financially support) international nongovernmental organizations (also called INGOs) like Amnesty International, Doctors without Borders, Oxfam, or the World Wildlife Fund. There are also many organizations linked to the United Nations or other world bodies.[6] There are also more comprehensive, multi-issue organizations including the World Social Forum (WSF). WSF has attracted many thousands to events in Southern Hemisphere locations including Brazil and India.[7] There are also many other organizations that promote fair trade, development, environmental protection, and human rights globally.

As well, some national delegations to international bodies like the conferences of the parties (COPs) of various treaties include representatives of nationally based NGOs.[8] Increasingly as well, universities and media outlets are providing important services to global audiences.[9] There are also new opportunities for direct participation in global affairs and explicit efforts to establish a global citizen's movement (see chapters 5 and 6). That said, those who consider themselves global citizens lack opportunities to participate directly in global decision-making. There is really no democratic global governing process or citizen-based, multi-issue movement acting at multiple levels to influence decision making regarding global concerns.

Interestingly, one of the more surprising results of the King Baudouin Foundation survey was the finding that leaders of NGOs worldwide, asked to identify the ideal form of global governance for 2020, were as likely to choose "the emergence of directly-elected world government" as "a reformed and strengthened United Nations."[10] The extent to which this is a negative judgment about the prospects for UN reform is unclear, but it does suggest that some global opinion leaders want global governance to go further than most national governments would presently countenance.

The many who see themselves as global citizens could grow in number and mobilize to become more active, organized, and self-conscious. They need to create ways to communicate, to assert their views, and to act collectively. Any such efforts will emerge within civil society because few national leaders are inclined, without citizen pressure, to boldly advance a global rather than a national agenda. Nor are they likely to consider, without citizen provocation, creating a system of global governance that includes direct citizen input. Active global citizens might countervail the comprehensive power of political and economic elites that presently dominate the global sphere of political life.

The Bush administration, as noted, resisted multilateralism, as well as global governance and any intimation of citizen input in international relations. Even today any government in Washington would be strongly challenged if it made global governance a priority. That resistance is in part a function of hegemonic power. Many also reject global initiatives on principle for fear that those efforts might grant a modicum of influence or an inch of gained ground to smaller, poorer, and less powerful nations.

A new approach to global governance might also meet resistance from other nations because *leaders* of nations might lose influence in a system that included citizen participation. Many would see citizen activism on a global scale as a threat to their prerogatives and power. At present global politics is their sphere shared only with corporate and military leaders. Political leaders of relatively powerful nations would lose doubly and might therefore resist with greater determination since their global influence in the absence of citizen and smaller nation voices is disproportionate.

A governance system that the leaders of NGOs in the King Baudouin Foundation survey might prefer to a "reformed and strengthened" United Nations will accordingly be seen in official circles as "unrealistic." Such changes are not likely to be initiated from the top.[11] Nor are corporate leaders likely to promote global governance that includes direct citizen participation. The influence of the economically powerful is maximized in a closed international system with a limited number of actors.

However, as will be argued, institutionalized forms of global governance are not necessary to the practice of global citizenship. Indeed, what is interesting regarding global political change possibilities is that it would not necessarily require wide agreement among nations to begin a change process. Change and even the creation of new global governance processes need not even begin at the global level, or be initiated by national governments.

Just for example, a *single nation*, any nation, could enhance the importance of the United Nations by making the position of United Nations Delegate an *elected* position. The European parliament is already an elected body; why not, at least in some nations, have a more open and participatory process to choose UN representatives or some or all members of the delegations to other international bodies or gatherings?

Since trade processes in particular are widely distrusted and notoriously unrepresentative of democratic opinion, why not elect representatives to trade bodies or global trade negotiation processes? Alternatively, there could be national public participation processes that truly involve citizens and citizen organizations in trade matters rather than just corporate, government, and labor representatives meeting in private (with the latter as junior partners).

Such things will not happen readily or soon. Global citizenship, and its mobilization, would need to broaden and deepen considerably before such initiatives could gain traction. Before that occurs, those that appreciate the need for active global citizenship need to mobilize undertakings independent of government. The notion that we should rethink citizenship would need to build deeper roots. This exercise could lead to a wider interest in the meaning of, and possibilities for, global citizenship. Such considerations begin with how citizenship has evolved historically.

The Concept of Citizenship

Citizenship today is a nationally based array of legal and political rights and duties. In democratic states the fundamental legal rights of citizenship include: the due process of law, freedom of speech, press and assembly, and freedom from discrimination based on, at the least, race, religion, gender, and national origin. Democracy without such protections is almost certain to be unworthy of the name.

Democratic political rights include the right to vote in a secret ballot and the right to organize political parties and other political organizations. Other fundamental rights include economic rights such as the right to enter into legally enforceable contracts, to join trade unions that are independent of government and employer control, and to own private property. Duties include obligations to participate in the political process and to support the enforcement of the law and the protection of the rights of others.

These rights and duties have evolved over the course of many centuries and are still evolving and expanding. They often cost many lives to establish and are continuously vulnerable to changing circumstances and new technologies. For example, the development of powerful new media such as film (and many since then) have altered the meaning of the right to a free press. It is also reasonable to consider whether freedom of speech is violated by the systematic monitoring of private communications by governments.[12]

Few would argue that even the most fundamental of citizenship's rights and duties is absolute. Freedom of speech, for example, is limited by considerations regarding libel, slander, pornography (especially child pornography), and public safety (as in the disallowance of hate literature, the planning of insurrectionary acts, or simply yelling fire in a crowded theater). Recent challenges to the protection of rights include terrorism, the rise of censorious religious fundamentalism within both Islam and Christianity, and a propensity within some media outlets to promote racism and violence.

In ancient Athens being a citizen meant being a man (not a woman or child) and not being a slave. One had *political* as well as legal citizenship; you could actively participate in governing the *polis*, as could all citizens, probably for the first time anywhere. But, citizens were a distinct minority (slaves, foreigners, and women were together a large majority) and Athenian democracy did not spread to other jurisdictions of the time, nor did it last indefinitely. It was a limited and fleeting, but glorious moment in the history of democratic citizenship.

It was not until after the invention of the printing press that democratic citizenship and new rights were widely established. Citizens in several nations gained an explicitly stated right to assemble—to hold meetings, or to own property, or to choose their own religion rather than it being presumed that they shared the religion of their monarch (even when the monarch decided to change religions). Many died for those rights.

The right to a fair trial, or even access to a consistent judicial system based in precedent, was also slow to emerge. The change was a very large advance from a norm of being submerged under water or set on fire to see if God would intervene sufficiently to keep you alive and thereby prove your innocence. These things are the *civic* rights of citizens. Needless to say, they have been systematically violated recently by both terrorists that target civilians and by counterterrorist actions in the Bush years.

Civic rights were advanced by the French Revolution, albeit temporarily, and took hold more permanently following the American Revolution. They evolved more slowly elsewhere, but are now citizenship rights in democratic nations throughout the world. Effective democracy cannot exist without civic rights, especially freedom of assembly, the independence of the judiciary as a check on political authority, and above all freedom of speech and press. The latter two are very fragile, subtle, and complex rights some think are potentially threatened, for example, by the highly dominant position of hyperconservative radio and television.[13]

The *political* rights of democratic citizenship include the right to run for office, to form organizations for the purpose of seeking

The Evolution of Citizenship 93

governmental offices, and the right to vote. It is hard to imagine a system that claimed to be democratic where there were not multiple candidates for office and universal adult suffrage. The attempt by religious authorities to exclude candidates for political office in Iran during 2003–2004 was an affront to anyone who believes in democracy, even those who accept in principle the dualistic (religious-secular) approach to government that Iran has put in place. But, even universal adult suffrage is a political right obtained very recently.

In France women only gained the vote in the 1940s and elsewhere in most cases it was gained earlier in the twentieth century. Not long before that only citizens who owned property could vote. The Reconstruction period in the United States saw duly elected African Americans purged from state legislatures and African American voting discouraged by many methods including poll taxes.[14] Restrictions still exist in some US states in the form of bars to voting for anyone convicted of a felony (such convictions are disproportionately racial minorities).

As well, in 2008 and 2012, African American voters (most notably in Ohio and Florida where President Obama won narrowly) waited in line up to *eight hours* to vote. Also, in Great Britain, for example, it took most of the nineteenth century for the vote to reach more than a very minor proportion of male voters, excluding a decreasing majority (and eventually a minority) that did not own sufficient property to qualify. While voting in some jurisdictions is not as assured as it might be, at least formal legal exclusion based on race, gender or property is gone in most places.[15]

Citizenship has also always carried duties. Sometimes duties are more implicit than are rights, but they are clearly no less important because without them few rights would exist. There is a duty to pay the taxes that fund public institutions and initiatives. There is also a duty to obey the law. There is as well at least an implicit duty to serve in war should that be necessary, though exemptions are granted to conscientious objectors in many jurisdictions (a moot point where there is a professional military).

There are also implicit duties to be a productive member of society, to add to the collective well-being, and to respect and promote the rights of others. Nonetheless, citizenship is usually thought to be about what the state and society within which one is situated can do for its citizens.

Recently in North American political discourse it has become commonplace to speak of *taxpayers* rather than citizens. This usage emphasizes one dimension of citizenship, while ignoring all other duties and rights. It deliberately diminishes the complex, multidimensional interaction between citizens and governments. The emphasis on the term taxpayer is part of a relentless political- and media-driven effort to remind citizens of their economic self-interest in reducing public expenditures, and to diminish the importance of the public services. Contrary to this oft-repeated mythology, many services are often both cheaper and more widely available when provided by the public sector.[16]

Identifying citizens as taxpayers also diminishes the importance of opportunities for *all* citizens to help shape the character of public actions and services. This view arises out of and feeds political cynicism. It turns states and communities into alien entities that unfairly impose upon us, and makes each of us into wholly economic beings, exclusively private consumers who are somehow diminished every time we are *imposed upon* by taxation. Taxation, however, would better be thought of as an accepted "even welcomed" responsibility of citizens, each of whom pays the necessary taxes they are able to pay and each of whom is eligible to a share in the benefits that public goods provide all citizens both individually and collectively.

Before the twentieth century the rights of citizenship were understood to encompass these civil and political rights, as well as the right to protection from foreign invasions, and economic rights such as the right to sign contracts or own property. Some see basic economic rights as civil rights on the grounds that without the possibility of owning property "especially in an agricultural society" one has little chance for the autonomy necessary to become full and independent members of society. But, it was not until the twentieth century that anyone spoke of the *social* rights of citizenship (to which we will now turn) or of environmental rights for citizens which many argue should be added to more constitutions.[17]

Further, while some rights were spoken of as universal (or referred to as the *rights of man*, at least sometimes meaning both men and women), in practice they were only available or defensible for citizens within and/or through nations. An expanding sense of rights and duties at the global scale would change the geography of citizen consciousness. It may also be a way to broaden the range of rights and duties to include widely accepted and legally and ethically stable social and environmental rights in addition to existing legal, political, civil, and economic rights and duties.

From Legal and Political to Social: the Evolution of Citizenship

Following the democratic citizenship breakthroughs of the American and French Revolutions, nineteenth century liberals gradually advanced civic and political inclusiveness and the opportunities for wider democratic participation by reducing and removing property requirements and eventually removing race and gender restrictions.

However, conservatives (especially Edmund Burke) can be credited with appreciating the extent to which citizen duties and rights are rooted in historic traditions and social habits. Neoconservatives, especially when planning wars allegedly in the name of democracy, forget that part of the conservative legacy. Socialists, social democrats, and liberals with the creation of the modern welfare state enhanced the meaning of citizenship dramatically. T. H. Marshall called this shift *social citizenship* to describe the possibility that citizenship had come to incorporate minimum standards of social and economic well-being.[18]

Marshall, writing in 1950, argued that the basic rights of citizenship (within the United Kingdom) had evolved over several centuries.[19] Assured citizen access to civil rights (freedom of speech, assembly, press, religion, as well as the right to own property, conclude contracts and have access to justice) were expanded to include political rights (voting and related rights and duties) primarily over the course of the nineteenth century via the reform acts of 1832, the 1860s, and 1880s that gradually lowered property requirements for male suffrage.

The civil and political rights of citizens of the United Kingdom (and later elsewhere) were then expanded to include basic *social* rights through the effective use of the other two sets of rights when industrialization, mass production, and citizen political action advanced and broadened prosperity. As Marshall put it: "The modern drive toward social equality is, I believe, the latest phase in the evolution of citizenship which has been in continuous progress for 250 years" (p. 78).

Marshall saw these three aspects of citizen rights (civic, political, and social) as mutually reinforcing. The franchise protects civil rights essential to the effective voting and the functioning of parliament. But, social and economic minimums are also essential to both and had, in his view, come to be an essential aspect of citizenship itself by the early twentieth century. Social citizenship, he said, provided a right to a modicum of economic welfare and security and a right to live a life of a civilized being within the standards that prevail in a society at the time.

In short, successful industrialized nations had gone beyond the 80-hour week where young children worked in mines and a majority of families lived in relentless squalor. Such commonplace nineteenth-century living and working conditions had rendered the civil and political rights all but meaningless for some. All citizens were equally free, as Anatole France observed, to sleep under bridges, but few could effectively utilize civil and political rights in the absence of at least "a modicum of economic welfare and security."

Despite the fact that social equity is now moving backwards in many places, conditions for a majority in wealthy nations remain a long way from the conditions of the nineteenth century. Nonetheless, sometime late in the twentieth century many nations lost that sense of progress regarding an expansion of citizenship into the social realm that Marshall had observed only a few decades previously.[20]

Marshall's words seem to describe a more buoyant, optimistic, and prosperous time, yet when he wrote income and assets per capita were far below what they are today. Advocates of social and political progress today rarely aspire to do more than slow the rate of decline in social equity. As well, both political citizenship and civil rights are threatened by the decline in social capital that American political scientist Robert Putnam has so eloquently observed.[21] Also contributing to the decline of all three forms of citizenship in recent years is the increased concentration of wealth linked to global economic integration and reinforced by the concentration of political power associated with concentrated wealth.

A reconceptualization of citizenship will not in and of itself reverse such fundamental shifts. However, if widely accepted, it could help to restore the ethical optimism of that earlier era and focus citizenship at the level where many of the declines of the social, the political, and the civil aspects of citizenship are rooted: the global scale.

Global economic integration, as I argued in an earlier work, threatens the efficacy of democratic citizenship in both rich and poor nations.[22] Whole industries depart communities or nations based on decisions reached in closed international trade and investment discussions. Ordinary citizens feel increasingly powerless, except perhaps when they identify with the might of their respective nations or with large ethnic and religious communities. As well, social citizenship is in decline as guarantees of well-being have been reduced as risks are downloaded from governments and corporations to individuals.[23]

This transfer of risk has been especially visible in America where social citizenship has always been less developed than in other wealthy nations. Americans love freedom and in the minds of many this includes the freedom to fail. The United States is the only wealthy nation where the treatment of illness frequently leads to bankruptcy. Taxes on high earners have been uncommonly low and in the Bush years were reduced further compared to middle-income earners.

This all-or-nothing approach to economic and social life, it is argued, makes for a dynamic society. It also likely contributes to higher crime rates and lower life expectancy than America's national wealth might predict. This approach puts pressure on America's wealthier (and typically more social citizenship oriented) trading partners to follow suit. On the other hand, America is a social policy model that most Canadians and Europeans strive hard to avoid.[24] In many nations social citizenship still has meaning: most Canadians consider their public health care system to be the very essence of being Canadian.

American conservatives strongly resist any suggestion of global political or social policy integration and resent the United Nations in principle. Curiously, few, if any, commentators have made a connection between American enthusiasm for checks and balances, and limited government, *within* the United States and rejections of global governance initiatives during the Bush administration. A system of checks and balances at the global level are anathema despite the fact that checks and balances regarding the concentration of power are one of America's signature contributions to citizenship and democratic governance.

America's Signature Contributions to Citizenship

The United States as an early adopter of liberal democratic citizen rights affirmed and deepened the world's appreciation of democratic rights and freedoms. In time the American experience changed the understanding of citizenship by limiting the power of government through a complex system of checks and balances. The relationship between government and citizens in America has come to be seen as a balance between the freedom to govern and freedom from government.

The US Constitution includes an extensive itemization of individual rights, the separation of powers with offsetting capacities among three distinct branches of government, and an exclusion of established religion. These legal and institutional limits on national power are embedded within a federal system that itself further limits concentrated power. Historically, this elaborate set of checks and balances was a response to tyrannical monarchies across Europe and British colonial rule.

As James Madison wrote in *The Federalist Papers* "The accumulation of all powers, legislative, executive and judiciary, in the same hands, whether one, a few, or many and whether hereditary, self-appointed, or elective, may justly be pronounced as the very definition of tyranny."[25] Whether dividing powers between the branches of government or between the national government and the states, or in limiting the power of political leaders through frequent elections or autonomies that were by constitutional right in the hands of individual citizens, the objective was to diffuse power and prevent domination by any individual or group.

Another singular American contribution to the evolution of citizenship is the protection of religious freedom through a clear constitutional separation of church and state. Historically, this was an important limit on the power of government—it was not just that individuals could choose to practice or not practice any religion, it was specified that government would set no religion above others through official sanction. Church and state were rendered distinct and separate spheres of society.

Citizens of any nation, all citizens, can only be truly free in their religious choices if states avoid favoring one religion, or one set of religious views, over another. Many of those that fled Europe in the seventeenth and eighteenth centuries for what was to become the United States did so to escape state-established religions. Many had risked their freedom and even their lives in Europe to practice religions that in hindsight were only modestly different from those approved exclusively by their governments. Persecution at the time was commonplace.

The newly formed United States was not hostile to religion but rather was, as a government, essentially secular; religious freedom through church-state separation was an important goal of the new nation. American governments have, for the most part, carefully avoided favoring any religion, even if one religion was freely accepted by an overwhelming majority.[26] Avoiding the establishment of religion is about minority rights and a self-conscious limitation on the power of the majority—a limitation that was welcomed by virtually all citizens at the time of America's founding. This choice is thus fundamentally *constitutional*.

Liberal constitutionalism is the essence of liberal democracy. Majority rule and minority rights are in constant tension, but both are essential to democratic citizenship. The nonestablishment of religion parallels the constitutional agreement that majorities will not undermine the liberties of minorities to speak, to assemble, to publish, to actively seek public office, and to have equal rights before the law in relation to property and all other matters. All of these are *dynamic* rights whose meaning is continuously interpreted by the courts.

For example, as communications technology changes, the right of free speech evolves—a film is a form of communication that is different from a pamphlet or novel. Television is different from both the written word and film in a number of ways. The separation of church and state is altered subtly as people from non-Christian backgrounds have entered societies that were once more disproportionately Christian. Globalization has served to diversify most societies in many ways and human rights and the separation of religion and the state are thus all the more important today. Also important as more and more societies become multicultural are collective, especially linguistic, rights as well as individual rights.[27]

It is beyond ironic that at precisely the time the United States' singular contributions to citizenship, separation of church and state, and individual rights, are so clearly needed globally, many Americans resist global governance. And, as we will see below and in the next chapter, America has allowed some of the strongest aspects of its own practice of citizenship to be weakened.

During the 2012 presidential campaign, at the Democratic National Convention, President Obama eloquently invoked citizenship as a core value of the Democratic Party. As he put it: "we...believe in something called citizenship—a word at the very heart of our founding, at the very essence of our democracy; the idea that this country only works when we accept certain obligations to one another, and to future generations.... We, the People, recognize that we have responsibilities as well as rights, that our destinies are bound together."[28] In contrast, conservatives are more inclined to emphasize the rights rather than the obligations of citizens and to even see as inevitable the horrific Hobbesian world that so repelled Hobbes.

The evolution of citizenship could expand the humane take on citizenship expressed by President Obama to a global scale. The destinies of all peoples are now bound together. If so, do we *all* not have "certain obligations to one another" and a need for the democratic participation of all citizens acting together globally regarding our mutually shared challenges, opportunities, and obligations? The world of the twenty-first century only works when the obligations to one another are accepted as global as well as national and local.

The Need for Global Checks and Balances

Nearly two and a half centuries after America's founding, today's challenge is to imagine a practice of global citizenship that incorporates many of America's innovations regarding the concept. Ironically, convincing America in particular to accept such a possibility may be a large part of the challenge. A set of checks and balances on the exercise of power in international affairs would create greater openness and place limits on domination. Eventually it might create a space for some form of democratic participation in global decisions, what Boutros Boutros-Ghali, a former UN Secretary General, called the democratization of international relations.[29]

America's own history and ethos should help Americans to understand the desirability of limits on the concentration of global power. The Bush years, as discussed above, revealed the extent to which *global* power can be held by a small number of *individuals* within one nation. Vice President Cheney and a few entrenched neoconservatives manipulated a hegemonic power and launched a pointless war. One possible way to prevent this from happening again is to establish and entrench real multilateralism and to increase citizen influence within the conduct of global affairs.

What is missing at the global scale can be best understood as an analog of a constitutional system of checks and balances. Hegemonic power creates a need to at least modestly limit the unfettered freedom of action of those that govern the United States. Needless to say America's founders did not consider that form of excessive concentration of power, nor would today's America be open to such limitations. It remains the case that a narrow American corporate-media-government elite, in some circumstances, could someday again threaten global stability *despite* America's internal system of checks and balances.

For five years (2001–2006) there was *no* effective internal or external check on the power of the few dozen people that dominated American foreign policy and commanded its military might. Without change in many matters global hegemonic power rests with a small elite of one nation while the remainder of the world's citizens taken together have no voice that can be heard.

The Evolution of Citizenship 101

There are few checks on the amoral realism of such power, yet little willingness to recognize global citizenship and global governance as ideas whose time has come.[30] The Bush administration violated most of the modest set of previously established principles of global governance, principles designed to limit the power of larger nations to ride roughshod over the rights of smaller nations and the citizens of those nations. They violated limits, including the UN Charter prohibition on initiating wars without provocation, the Geneva Conventions, the UN Charter of Human Rights, and the potential jurisdiction of the International Criminal Court.[31]

These limited legal checks on absolute power are the beginning of a system of rights in law that can reach across borders. They are modest checks on the exercise of power by governments, attempts acceptable to almost every nation save America under Bush to establish this most American of principles globally. Taken as a piece, these efforts are essentially an attempt to protect individuals, groups, and nations from excessive and arbitrary power. American neoconservatives, however, have consistently sought to undermine any such effort and see *any* check on American power as a threat to the United States itself. These limits need to be reentrenched and ways found to protect and strengthen them.

The absence of effective checks on concentrated global power is not limited to strategic and military matters. Indeed, military and strategic matters will not likely change until many other things have. As noted, there is no open system of global governance regarding international trade, trade law, and trade negotiations. Corporate and national interests are represented, but citizen interests are largely absent. Unfair practices are widespread, particularly in dealings between poorer nations and corporations based in wealthy nations.[32]

Hearing processes regarding trade practices and treaty negotiations are for the most part closed to citizen involvement even though the lives of individuals, communities, and nations are often profoundly affected. Moreover, there is no effective process for incorporating social and environmental effects of global economic integration into the design of economic integration.[33] American neoconservatives who are appalled at any hint of global governance seem (or pretend to be) blithely unaware that global governance is already firmly entrenched within the realm of "free" (managed) trade.

Again, a good way to look at democratic global governance is to see it as the application of American constitutional principles at a global scale. The weakening and decline of global governance during the Bush years followed from a widely held assumption, both within and outside the United States, that international relations are, and always will be, a different order of human affairs from domestic politics. Globally, economic and military might determine outcomes without significant regard to other considerations and without ongoing opportunities for nonelite input.

In international affairs there is at present almost no role for citizens that they do not create for themselves through civil society organizations. The only actors of consequence are corporations, nation-states, and those international organizations that corporations and nation-states deem to be of consequence. Military forces, national leaders and diplomats, economic interests, media organizations, and a small number of international humanitarian groups are taken to be the only legitimate actors. Individual citizens are there at the sufferance of these actors and power within the international sphere is presumed to be unchecked, both utterly and forever.

There are at least four reasons that democratic checks and balances are needed in global politics. First, hegemonic power can override the limited checks and balances that exist in today's international system. Second, global market integration can countervail national policies and undermine democratic decisions. Third, the dominance of global and strategic affairs by a single nation can limit democracy in less powerful nations. Fourth, emerging flaws in American governance have increased distrust within global politics. I will elaborate the latter three of these reasons; the first was already considered.

Regarding the second item, the more integrated the global economy the more democracy *within* each nation is potentially constrained. The range of domestic policy latitude is constricted by the global market and each nation's place within it. In poorer nations the International Monetary Fund (IMF) may have more power than an elected government. Even in wealthier nations social programs are determined less by the willingness of citizens to pay for them than by the willingness of foreign and domestic investors (or the EU) to tolerate them. These investors are not evil; they just know that they must compete with firms in nations with less comprehensive social programs. In my own nation, Canada, investors can move operations but a few miles to jurisdictions that serve the same markets, but where social spending may be significantly lower.

Regarding item three, militarily and economically powerful states can induce less powerful nations to behave in ways that a majority of their own citizens might oppose. How else might one explain the participation of some European nations in the invasion of Iraq? Only if an issue comes to be of central and lasting importance to a majority *and* to the political leadership of a country is domestic democracy likely to prevail against the will of a hegemonic power.

Typically national leaders have considerable latitude in foreign policy matters because many citizens do not hold strong opinions regarding these issues or are not fully informed. In everyday language, they either don't know or don't care what happens on the other side of the world. Thus in many situations national leaders around the world are able to ignore citizen opinion and accede to American preferences and, for example, join the so-called coalition of the willing in Iraq as discussed in the last chapter.

Regarding the fourth item, America's system of checks and balances was undermined during the Bush years: power was concentrated in the hands of the president through the extensive use of signing statements, the secret authorization of surveillance without warrants, increased government secrecy, and public funding of conservative religious organizations.[34] Not only were matters related to the conduct of war not closely scrutinized by the legislative branch, they were not *known* to the legislative branch. The terrorist attack on the United States greatly intensified a concentration of power that had already increased over time. The extent to which these accretions of power will be restored in future administrations is unknown.

The period between 2001 and 2006 saw perhaps the greatest concentration of global political and military power in modern history. Again, one nation stood above all others and *within* that nation, power was held closely. Thus the nation that had come into being, seeking above all to decentralize and check political power, came to hold and to champion a global hyper-concentration of power.

The hope is that this period of concentration of power, and the ongoing possibility of the return of darker motives to its helm, can be among the influences that ultimately helps establish an emerging sense of global citizenship. The worldwide enthusiasm regarding Obama's election and reelection suggests that much of the world appreciates just how out of step with both world opinion and its own history the United States had become.

The question is: will the return to more typical patterns within American governance result in a return to indifference regarding the conduct of international affairs? Or will more than a few people around the world realize that what went wrong within the United

States could go wrong again and that for any number of other reasons *citizens* should have a voice in global affairs? Is it possible for such concerns, and an emerging global citizen's movement, to coexist with a generally positive view of the role of the United States in world affairs?

The Emergence of Global Citizenship

A starting point regarding global citizenship is an assumption that global citizens remain citizens of nations. Legal and political rights and duties would continue to be predominantly tied to national citizenship, but as we have seen the concept of citizenship is already morphing for many people. Global citizenship is becoming a psychic reality even in the face of, and indeed in part because of, a global reentrenching of subcultural loyalties, an increase in religious tribalism and, especially in America, a, now perhaps abating, hyper-patriotism.[35] Many also see these narrow loyalties as outmoded and a clear threat to global security, progress, and prosperity.

When one's job can suddenly relocate to the other side of the planet and contagious human diseases can travel the earth in hours, it is increasingly difficult *not* to see things in global terms. We live in a world where small groups of terrorists can threaten cities on any continent and at one point might even have influenced an American election by releasing a video to the media on the eve of a presidential election.[36] When ice shelves in Greenland and Antarctica melt as a result of the everyday human activities and European and North American 1–800 phone numbers are seamlessly answered in India, like it or not, we are all citizens of Earth.

Global interest in American domestic politics is strong because people understand the extent to which our collective fates are now intertwined. Bush's 2004 reelection was of global concern because it was so out-of-step with the positive possibilities inherent in this emerging global reality. Much of the world saw Bush as a hyper-nationalist throwback undermining decades of slow steps toward multilateralism and civility in the affairs of nations.

A single nation, however powerful, cannot prevent a global perspective from emerging especially when aggressive unilateralism destabilizes nations and thereby facilitates terrorist blowbacks.[37] The Obama administration has increased the use of drones but has otherwise eschewed unilateralist action and has withdrawn most US troops from Iraq and Afghanistan. Until 2014 it was involved in the

Arab Spring only judiciously and multilaterally. But a more permanent shift away from the circle of violence lies in the emergence of global citizenship as a political force that responds to worldwide poverty, financial malfeasance and instability, as well as climate change. Such a movement would make citizens feel part of a more hopeful, less divided world.

This is, of course, a grand agenda for what is now only a wisp of possibility, considerably less than an amorphous social movement. But what else, what *other* actor on the global stage, actual or potential, might help to restrain future cycles of violence? An enduring change in Washington would help, but administrations that openly contemplate global governance will almost certainly rouse powerful opposition. They would need all the domestic and global support they could get to move forward. Indeed, even though the Obama administration has not acted decisively on climate change or global inequality, it nonetheless has been faced with a right-wing political ascendancy and narrowly maintained power in 2012 against an inept Republican alternative.

In the heady days of Bush's first term, neoconservatives spoke openly of empire even as Americans began to recoil from unilateralism. American dissenters understood that arrogance and the illegal exercise of power undermined much that their nation had stood for, but from 2000 until 2006, dissent was overwhelmed by internal political forces led by funding from corporations, wealthy conservatives, and politicized evangelists.

During that period, as noted, continuing fossil energy dependence cost the world dearly. Similarly, not strengthening multilateralism today may in the long term undermine America's role in the world. Those that so loudly pronounce this to be America's century would again have helped to create a world that is anything but. It makes more sense to find ways to balance American power with multilateral institutions that create a role for global citizens.

The nascent potential for global citizenship as a partial counterbalance to hegemony and for democratizing global affairs is rooted in new communications, in expanded travel, immigration and trade, and in the multiplication of centers of economic power. Global citizenship cannot overcome hegemonic military power, but, in combination with nations that base their strength primarily on nonmilitary forms of power, a large and active citizen's movement could change the global future and perhaps ultimately make military power less central to national security.

This latter step would require that those nations that spend disproportionately on defense to more fully appreciate the opportunity costs of those expenditures. In this, needless to say, we have a very long way to go.

Global Citizenship and the Environment

We are, however, all citizens of Earth for other reasons. All life depends on the air, water, climate, and the living systems of the planet. Each and every nation can now harm, or benefit, people everywhere and can do widespread harm quite unintentionally.

Persistent organic pollutants from Texas contaminate northern Canadian lakes and such pollutants find their way to the breast milk of Inuit mothers thousands of miles from where they were produced or used. Clouds of pollution from China drift across the Pacific Ocean and Indonesian forest clearing fires contaminate the atmosphere of much of Southeast Asia and even Australia. Island and low-lying nations may soon be submerged as glaciers and polar ice caps retreat in the face of climate change.

Equally crucially, the world's ocean fisheries are approaching collapse from overfishing and other threats including acidification. We catch fish at levels well beyond sustainability and seem unable to effectively limit catches in any region of the world.[38] And, many other nonhuman species that humans the world over have related to as children for millennia may soon disappear from the wild.[39] Again, humans *and all other species the world over* increasingly share a common fate.

Since hard-nosed foreign policy "realists" might find such matters trivial, one might also note that in today's reality, economic collapse in any region or large nation could readily threaten the global economy. Regional economic collapse *could* arise as a result of climate change. Clearly it is past time for citizenship to encompass environmental rights and obligations much as it expanded from the legal and political to the social in an earlier age. To be effective, this expanded citizenship would need to influence political and economic decisions globally.

An expansion of citizenship into new dimensions of concern thus parallels the shift from national to global. The old expression that the solution to pollution is dilution is well and truly outmoded. Carbon dioxide emissions that alter the climate are also acidifying the oceans. High smokestacks that cleared the urban air rain down as acid depositions or mercury deposits in other cities and other nations. Pollutants emitted around the world accumulate in the Arctic. Industrial nations emit GHGs and poor nations are especially prone to the impacts of desertification or flooding.

While some might still imagine that military action can resolve energy shortfalls, excessive dependence on fossil fuels is a challenge that can only be resolved by global, cooperative human action. Future neo-imperial occupations would only spawn new generations of diffuse enemies. Just as the 1953 overthrow of the elected secular government of Iran and the installation of a Hollywood-oriented Shah produced fundamentalist Mullahs and the Soviet occupation of Afghanistan begat the Taliban and al Qaeda, future such adventures will also be counterproductive.

Global economic integration has created a more vulnerable world. There is no going back. The best hope for peace and prosperity in a global age is through the continuous, gradual reduction of entrenched injustice. Global citizenship and the understanding that everyone's life will be better if we act collectively across cultural and national divides is an essential underpinning for this change. The reduction of injustice must be accompanied by raising the price of violence for both terrorists and states. Wars of occupation only enhance the prospects of terrorists by increasing the sense of grievance on which they feed.[40] Only when every region and nation and citizens everywhere have a real stake and a real voice in a collective human future will political violence decline.

Large majorities everywhere, including the Middle East, already oppose terrorism. A commitment to actively resist will emerge only if and when people feel that they are less under attack by other nations than by terrorists. A willingness to resist terrorism might also be enhanced by what a global citizens' movement might achieve. Having a stake in the well-being of the world requires that most people benefit from improving global prosperity. This hope is indeed what the Arab Spring has been about—having seen prosperity dramatically emerging in once poor nations in Asia and Latin America, those in North Africa and the Middle East asked: why should we be left out of a changing world?

In sum, we are global citizens whether we choose to embrace that status or not. All humans now share a common fate. Many now see their citizenship evolving to encompass globally oriented obligations and duties and to include rights as both planetary and national citizens simultaneously.

Some rights increasingly only make sense as *global* rights. Environmental rights are not "just" to do with protecting nature; they are human-centered and everyday. They are part of economic rights and elementary fairness, an opportunity for material comfort, security, and a fair share of the world's energy, as well as climate stability, access to clean water, and protection of the capacity to produce food. Global rights include some minimum of economic equity, human rights, environmental rights, and freedom from terrorism and war and might be best understood as preconditions of national citizenship rights.

Hegemony and Global Citizenship

Needless to say global citizenship is far from universally felt and the rights that advocates of global citizenship, including myself, might imagine are not yet widely appreciated, let alone defended. Nonetheless, an emerging sense of global citizen *duties* are beginning to lead in very surprising directions. Environmental, human rights, and social-justice-oriented global citizens now participate internationally where once only nation-states acted (or chose not to).

Individuals are also increasingly participating in the marketplace locally and globally as citizens, thereby creating new forms of citizen behavior. Fair trade concerns regarding wages and working conditions, an expanding market for local and organic food have resulted in pressure to establish organic food standards in many nations and within global markets. Attention to sustainability is altering, in many places globally, the meaning of what is economic and what is political. These nongovernmental initiatives are an important part of global citizenship and will be discussed in our concluding chapters.

Such initiatives are examples of an important possibility: global governance without global government. Most have been initiated by citizen organizations. Some American-based, citizen-led, globally motivated initiatives may have been in part a response to political setbacks like the 2004 election and the American rejection of Kyoto.

As well, many American cities significantly reduced their carbon emissions and many American landowners altered the deeds on their properties to restrict nonsustainable land use options in the future; and in many nations hundreds of billions of investment dollars are managed with values other than profit maximization also in mind.[41] Behavior reflecting global citizenship values has thus emerged even when governments have opposed those values.

The Evolution of Citizenship 109

At the same time, outside the United States during the Bush years, rhetorical support for multilateralism advanced as national leaders avoided being overly identified with American unilateralism lest they irretrievably alienate their own electorates. Here one might again note that the departure of troops from many nations from Iraq preceded the US commitment to step back on combat operations. Early-departing nations included Spain, Ukraine, Poland, and Italy followed by the virtual departure of Australia and Britain. Additionally, the government of Canada, following the 2004 American elections, felt it politically necessary to reverse itself and to reject participation in the development of anti-ballistic missiles (ABMs) for use in North American defense.[42]

Similarly before Britain began its exit, even Tony Blair, the Bush administration's most reliable Iraq war ally, felt compelled to intensify and continuously assert his support of Kyoto and other multilateral initiatives opposed by the Bush administration. Looking backward from the future, the Bush administration, irony of ironies, could yet prove to have been an unintentional stimulus for both intensified multilateralism and a more widely felt sense of global citizenship. If that is not the case, surely a return to power of a government in that spirit would push these things forward.

A substantial global citizen's movement will not emerge abruptly, but loudly trumpeted and aggressively asserted hegemonic power is likely to generate its own opposition. A unilateral approach to international affairs deepened the desire for multilateralism—almost everywhere that it did not provoke a desire for revenge. Many American liberal and conservative realists understand this, but most neoconservatives seem incapable of grasping the point.[43]

The Iraq war, launched in defiance of the views of a global majority, cost America dearly in terms of reputation and support. Unilateralism failed to block the desire for wider and deeper multilateral cooperation. The global financial collapse of 2008 intensified this desire. The world is quite broadly united in rejecting the spirit of those years.

Rather than fill many pages with examples of the attitude that provoked global disdain, I offer the words of John Bolton, Bush's ambassador to the United Nations. In an interview with National Public Radio in 2000, well before September 11, 2001, regarding the body where he was later to represent the United States, Bolton stated: "If I were redoing the Security Council today, I'd have one permanent member because that's the real reflection of the distribution of power in the world." That single permanent member, holding a lone veto, would of course be the United States.[44] He, perhaps barely, avoided suggesting that the organization be renamed the United Nation. Needless to say, Bolton's wish regarding the UN did not come to pass.

Unilateral attitudes were also revealed in the trial and execution of Saddam Hussein. Saddam might have been tried in The Hague before an international tribunal for war crimes including his unprovoked attack on Iran in the 1990s. Such an approach was, however, deemed either too open or too multilateral or both.[45] Saddam was instead tried and executed for events prior to receiving American support during his war with Iran, support followed by American antipathy for and opposition to his attack on Kuwait. As well, the Bush administration, as with the torture of alleged terrorists as "enemy combatants," avoided the opportunity to build the system of international criminal law by using it to deal with Saddam's crimes.

The very idea of global governance remains anathema to neoconservatives and is unimportant to many other Americans. Citizenship implies some minimum of political equality and global citizenship implies both genuine multilateralism and potentially some limitations on the power of nations. Bolton on one level simply expressed realist sentiments—realists presume that the structure of international institutions should reflect power positions. But what he did not see, and many Americans often still do not fully appreciate, is that if collective rules do not apply to dominant nations, then other nations have little reason to be involved in rule-making and rule-enforcing processes led by the self-exempting nation.

Unlike self-exempting national leaders, global citizens might argue that today's world *demands* a significant expansion of global rule-making. Only global rules can stabilize a global financial system, only global policies can effectively enhance certain aspects of environmental protection, and minimum global social and health policy standards will lessen pressures on nations to sacrifice their own less wealthy citizens to be globally competitive. Global cooperation is also necessary to protect human rights and to create new forms of collective defense that could in time restrain military expenditures in favor of more pressing needs.

Global citizens and some nations emerged from the Bush years frustrated with having one nation exercise a veto over the conduct of international affairs. It also became widely apparent that a Blair-like game of follow the unilateralist (in the hope of gaining incremental influence) only encouraged unilateralism and undermined the possibility of other voices being heard.

Most nations want something other than a stark choice between unequivocally acceding to or resisting hegemonic power. Most want meaningful multilateralism to be the normal way to conduct global affairs. The Obama administration has moved in that direction. The rest of the world could not be clearer in its agreement with that change even if America's media have not assessed this shift as extensively as they might have.

Finally it is clear that in a thoroughly integrated world it is unacceptable that *any* nation imagine that vast power comes without duties and obligations. Frank Sinatra, a quintessential American, may have proudly *done it his way*, but while brave little nations can be assertive about that sort of thing, it is unbecoming in great powers. A "you-are-with-us-or-against-us" nuclear superpower is truly terrifying. But it is now less likely that other nations or their citizens will again so readily acquiesce to such an approach for long. There is much that could be done about such a state of affairs without arming every nation to the teeth and challenging military power with countervailing military power.

Building a Sense of Global Citizenship

A nascent sense of global citizenship advanced in part in response to the attitudes and actions of the Bush administration. Many Americans, including business leaders, were acutely aware of how unpopular America had become. Tony Blair also experienced a globally oriented response on the part of Britons from the moment he committed troops to Iraq. More recently Canadian Prime Minister Stephen Harper has managed to become something of a global villain by ignoring, then rejecting Canada's Kyoto commitments.

These, however, may be exceptional outcomes in uncommon circumstances. Global citizenship is not yet a self-conscious perspective for large numbers of people and is very far from being a transnational political movement that can effect change. There is no certainty that it will ever be. However, the emergence of a politically important global citizen's movement is for the first time a real possibility. Global consciousness regarding inequality, social justice, climate change and sustainability generally, and the intense opposition to the unilateralism of the Bush years, suggests that the potential is there.

Nonetheless it remains a normal human reaction to lapse into a sense of powerlessness when considering global challenges, to simply let "them" handle it if someone broadly acceptable is "at the helm."

It is just too easy to presume that larger-than-life figures will improve things that seem beyond the capacities of most of us. We go back to our everyday lives grateful that we need no longer actually do anything. Indeed most citizens feel overwhelmed if faced with a need to influence local change.

Acting at the local and personal scale is a not unreasonable response. Indeed, people do seem increasingly willing to address global concerns at those levels, for example through purchasing fair trade products or involvement with global NGOs. These are things we *can* accomplish without the intimidating need to mobilize countless others in multiple languages in countries besides our own. However, these smaller actions may for some be steps toward acting on a larger stage.

Many conclude *as global citizens concerned about the global collective future* that they will insulate their homes and if feeling more audacious try to convince their city government to improve the bus service. But there remains a tendency to throw up one's arms and ask what else can I do? How could *I* stop military invasions or cause China to build fewer coal-fired power plants? And, if one is not a North American (or even if one is), one cannot imagine convincing America or Canada to act on climate change. Yet now the global organization 350.org is attempting to do these things and more.

The spread of active global citizenship is inevitably halting and hesitant, but its outlines are becoming visible. Millions still drive large cars because that enhances their sense of self or because they convince themselves that their children or their pets are safer or more comfortable in a spacious mobile setting. When such behaviors are the norm it is a moral challenge for even the most committed to stand in the rain waiting for a bus out of a vague sense of global citizenship. In this context it is beyond difficult to act politically on a global scale, let alone imagine how one might lessen the likelihood of wars when powerful nations are determined to fight them.

One thing that is lacking is a means to locate and communicate directly with like-minded others the world over and together to reflect about and act upon our collective frustration. New actors on the global stage need to be visible and need to be able to welcome ordinary citizens. The world stage needs to be open to those lacking power. Citizens need to have a role on that large stage and to no longer be seen as naïve and well-meaning do-gooders for daring to imagine that they should have a voice regarding the future of the planet on which they reside.

Changing today's closed global governance system requires new opportunities for transnational citizen-to-citizen communication. Informal opportunities *have* increased as travel and immigration has expanded. There are also increasing interactions within business and science and in professional and religious organizations and within global civil society, including global fora such as the World Social Forum and the Slow Food Movement.[46] But the most promising venue for making global citizenship a self-conscious reality is the Internet.

Even economically comfortable people cannot afford more than occasional international travel.[47] The Internet, however, is widely available and still expanding and developing. More than that, it allows people to purposefully locate each other regarding specific subjects or initiatives. Internet use is part of the ordinary rhythm of billions of daily lives and it eliminates both borders and distance. Barriers like language and censorship (and the cost of access) of course remain, but increasingly they too can be overcome.

More effective global initiatives regarding social justice, climate change, military spending, or other global concerns are unlikely until citizens in many nations, acting directly or through governments, seek action in a coordinated way. Only when that begins to happen will a global citizen's movement be politically consequential. I cannot imagine how that could come about without using Internet tools to create transnational citizen organizations. These organizations will only gain influence if and when they can initiate coordinated campaigns and initiatives.

The literature of international relations has extensively discussed what are called epistemic communities, transnational networks of scientists and scientific organizations. Such groups have reached a consensus position with regard to ozone depletion and climate change. A classic example of an epistemic community is the International Panel on Climate Change (IPCC), the vast network of climate scientists that documents global warming and offers broad policy guidelines and suggestions.

Epistemic communities address technical matters. A network of global citizens might be more grassroots, more political, and more value-oriented. In some circumstances, with great effort and great care for credibility on the part of those citizen-based networks, governments might listen. Such groups would operate within civil society and seek to influence public discourse. Their distinctiveness would lie in their transnational, multicultural character and their global, rather than sectarian, regional or national, perspective.

Such organizations could develop expertise and seek to influence policy on global issues across many nations. Such groups could also bridge existing gaps between peoples that governments are unwilling or unable to broach. They might in some situations, with considerable courage, even work to offset mutual fears that governments might seek to build and build support for solutions that governments fear to put forward in the face of strong domestic opposition.

I would not presume to anticipate the potential agenda of such organizations except to say that the concept of global citizenship itself implies lofty goals—perhaps pushing governments to address environmental challenges and global poverty simultaneously, addressing both militarism and terrorism, and working toward ultimately reducing recourse to war as a normal part of human affairs. Above all they would encourage greater protection of human rights and increased democratic participation in global governance.

To be effective in any, let alone all, of these undertakings global citizens would need to be sufficiently organized to have a capacity to make strategic choices and to find ways to influence international affairs in several nations or regions at a time. I will identify some ways that this might become possible over time in chapters 5 and 6. For now I will suggest how a movement might begin to emerge in a world characterized by hegemonic power and lingering wariness concerning the nation that dominates the world stage.

Actualizing Global Citizenship

Following the widely disconcerting presidential elections in 2004, a fleeting global online community arose at www.sorryeverybody.com. This website, initiated by disconsolate young Californians, began with the words: "Some of us—hopefully most of us—are trying to understand and appreciate the effect our recent election will have on the citizens of the rest of the world. As our so-called leaders redouble their efforts to screw you over, please remember that some of us—hopefully most of us—are truly, truly sorry. And we'll say we're sorry, even on behalf of the ones who aren't." The apology was elaborated in photographic messages from Americans and graciously accepted in kind by people around the world.[48]

I had a resonant response to the genuine expression of regret by so many, but I was particularly struck by the use of the phrase: *citizens of the rest of the world* by those that initiated this effort. The electoral outcome was not necessarily, of course, an expression of the will of a fixed majority, but it was a severe lunge away from a historic American commitment to multilateralism. The heartfelt and widespread reaction to the election *within* the United States suggested to me that the *idea* of global citizenship was perhaps something more than an idle hope for the future.

More than that, the attitude that dominated American media and governing circles in the lead-up to the 2004 election, labeled so tellingly by cultural commentator Frank Rich as "a triumphalist daydream," might advance a greater sense of common cause in the rest of the world.[49] Events that have followed since have encouraged the view that something positive might ultimately emerge in response to that otherwise distressing electoral outcome. A sense of global common purpose did begin to emerge and grow, even and especially perhaps in America.

Everything possible should be done to continue that growth and we cannot just assume that a global perspective and multilateral sensibility will permanently triumph within American politics. There and everywhere it will be a long struggle that may or may not succeed. As the next chapter will show, the American political system has great strengths, but also daunting flaws. Multilaterally oriented governments will be challenged every step of the way. The long-term American approach to global concerns is far from certain.

The world needs to see the United States in a clear-eyed way, neither demonizing it, nor assuming that reason and generosity will prevail. Globally oriented citizens must assume a need to mobilize to influence policy and outcomes and even, if necessary, to continue to act politically without the support of all or any governments. For leaders of other nations acting without presuming that America will always lead the world where the world needs to go is not easy. For leaders of Western nations it can be an especially delicate balancing act. Decisive assertions and actions may be easier for a global citizen's movement, even one that includes many individual Americans.

The reelection of George W. Bush that triggered "Sorry World" should not be forgotten. For many it was one of the more unsettling moments of the twenty-first century. Whatever the majority of voting Americans thought they were doing in 2004, they reelected a government that had been consistently and aggressively unilateral.[50] That alone made the election a singular event, one that suggests that both global institutional change and future prudence are warranted.

Global citizens especially need to understand the need to advance cooperative political, economic, social, and technological innovation globally. The best reaction to dark unilateralism is not smug or hostile anti-Americanism, nor is it a return to indifference when America's best face is forward. Rather, the answer lies in a movement oriented to today's global challenges and substantial progress toward citizen-influenced, multilateral global governance.

4

From New American Century to Global Age America?

America's leading position among nations has been accepted as fact for a century, especially since the demise of the Soviet Union. A global majority did not vote for disproportionate American power, but that majority might well have been less comfortable. Rich and powerful nations are rarely loved, but America was for decades admired or warily accommodated by most nations. This widespread comfort ceased abruptly during the presidency of George W. Bush. The global empathy following September 11, 2001 quickly turned to widespread distrust.[1] There were many reasons for this abrupt shift, but one was central.

Early on in its dominance, America wielded power cautiously and often seemed a reluctant hegemon. It eschewed long occupations and, for decades following the Spanish–American war, was hesitant to go to war. It was slow to enter European wars and engaged militarily primarily in response to state-to-state aggression as in Korea and Kuwait. Vietnam was different—a gross miscalculation that occurred well into America's hegemonic dominance, perhaps a sign of an emerging excess of comfort in the role.

The Bush administration, however, made a dramatic break with even a pretense of reluctance regarding hegemonic power. America became a rogue hegemon. The Bush Doctrine of preemptive war shocked friendly nations and considerable proportion of the world's attentive citizens reacted with disgust.

Many Latin Americans (or their widows and widowers) might not share this characterization of America as a reluctant hegemon, but before Bush–Cheney there was always an internal debate among

Americans advocating imperial adventure and those that preferred isolationism or restraint.[2] Twentieth-century Americans on the whole, both conservative and liberal, seemed comfortably separated by vast oceans from what they often saw as a troubled world. During the Bush years, noted older conservatives, including Brent Scowcroft, Clyde Prestowitz, and others from earlier Republican administrations, criticized Bush for replacing reluctant hegemony with unilateralism.[3]

Historically, few American governments competed for colonies and most preferred a multilateral approach. The most powerful nation in the world was even slow to enter World War II, a war that was as unavoidable as wars get. During the Bush–Cheney years, however, it was soon hard to even remember that the United States, after *both* world wars, had *initiated* complex multilateral structures in the hope of avoiding future wars. In the Bush years America turned on its own creation, the United Nations, and administration officials frequently slandered many of America's traditional allies. American hesitation to use hegemonic power vanished as the twenty-first century unfolded.

The Cold War mindset had remained alive in neoconservative circles long after the demise of the Soviet Union, even in the absence of militarily viable enemies. It became highly visible when the "New American Century" was announced in 2000 in a document that sent a chill through those who follow such things.[4] This document, signed by many who were to gain prominence in Bush's government, foreshadowed a new America that mercifully receded as the Iraq war ground on.

Through the Obama years this view was kept alive by neoconservative assertions that Obama was unwilling to defend America.[5] Astoundingly, even *after* the raid that killed Osama bin Laden, Obama was criticized by Republicans as indecisive and excessively cautious.

The Bush–Cheney years also featured torture at Abu Ghraib, the systematic violation of human rights, climate change denial, rollbacks of multilateral agreements including a refusal to ratify the Comprehensive Nuclear Test Ban Treaty, an asserted intention to develop new generation tactical nuclear weapons, the renunciation of the Anti-Ballistic Missile Treaty, resistance to environmental protection, tax cuts for the wealthy, a refusal to even speak to designated enemies, and the use of military might to advance narrowly understood national interests.[6] Yet until overwhelmed by the 2008 financial crisis, cautious opposition to these policies was central to the Democratic presidential campaign. We cannot know whether a campaign based on doubts about unilateralism would have succeeded without the economic collapse.[7] This reality requires some further assessment of American political culture and institutions.

The Obama administration altered America's approach to international affairs significantly. Despite this shift, however, it is not unreasonable to worry that America could return to unilateralism. America's disproportionate military spending remains an entrenched habit supported by powerful interests, interests likely made stronger by the decline of nonmilitary manufacturing. Americans remain divided regarding the appropriate uses of hegemonic power and hesitant regarding America playing a leading role on global challenges such as climate change and inequality. More than that America's political system seems paralyzed regarding action on its own problems including outmoded infrastructure, unaffordable higher education, rising inequality, and a slow recovery from recession.

One cannot understand this inaction or assess the prospects for a more democratic international relations without considering American domestic politics. Will future American governments support or resist new patterns in global governance? How stable is the American system of government? Is America's distinctive political system capable of the flexibility needed to accept let alone lead future global initiatives? Can American governments even accept more democratic global governance without great political difficulty? Might future American governments come to see that global governance is, at least in some matters, in America's best interest? How adaptive is America? In short, in an age of global economic integration such questions are clearly everyone's business and require an understanding of politics and government in America.

Some Distinctive Aspects of America's Political System

Hegemonic powers would seem to have much to lose if global governance were more democratic. Many Americans, as noted, feel that their lives are enhanced by America's power. In contrast, small nations and their citizens cannot help but prefer multilateral and more democratic global decision making; they have very little power within the present order.

Most European nations favor action on a global agenda for a wide range of reasons and many European economies have already adapted to policies that globally oriented governance might prefer, especially regarding climate change. As well, having experienced two world wars fought on their soil, Europeans limit military spending and spend a higher proportion of GNP on benefits for children, students, and seniors. Inequality, as a result, is significantly less extreme than almost anywhere else in the world. Finally here Europeans typically have views on global issues that are different from those of Americans. They champion multilateralism and the International Criminal Court (ICC), contribute more generously to development aid, and support strong sustainability initiatives.

American government and politics differ from other Western democracies in other ways as well, in terms of both political institutions and political culture. The cost of hegemony is a factor and America's uncommonly large gap between rich and poor also has important political effects. American voter turnout is low, particularly among the poor, and institutions like the Electoral College and partisan-drawn electoral districts concentrate power and discourage political participation.

On the surface, the Electoral College seems benign enough, if idiosyncratic. In most states (except Maine and Nebraska) presidential candidates that win a state's popular vote get all of the Electoral College votes for that state. These electoral votes are allocated by population, thus seemingly a relatively benign historical artifact. However, modern polling combined with this state-based winner-take-all system results in many states barely seeing a presidential campaign other than through news from other locations. In California, New York, and Illinois, where Democratic candidates win by wide margins, there are courtesy and fund-raising visits but few campaign stops or ads. A similar pattern holds in some southern, midwestern and mountain states where Republicans are likely to win by a wide margin. In the end, up to three-fourths of the nation gets limited attention from presidential campaigns.

However, the so-called swing states, Ohio, Florida, Missouri, and Iowa and perhaps Pennsylvania, Colorado, and Nevada, are inundated with television ads, calls, mailings, door-to-door canvassers. and more attention than any but the loneliest voters might wish for. Both the quiet indifference and the over-the-top attention may discourage voter turnout. More than that, the Electoral College can result in America's most important election being resolved by happenstance. The 2000 outcome was resolved by a Supreme Court decision regarding a few Florida ballots despite Al Gore having won the national popular vote decisively.

American elections, and policy, are also affected by an allocation of Senate seats that greatly advantages small and sparsely settled states, states that are generally more conservative and have smaller minority populations. Over and above that, informal Senate rules have allowed single senators to block presidential appointments and 40 of the 100 members of the Senate can prevent legislation from coming to a vote. These rules further enhance the power of small-state senators elected by a small minority of Americans (and these same senators often have extensive seniority and the additional advantage of choice committee assignments).

The division of seats in the House is also problematic because district boundaries are frequently determined by state legislatures (with some court oversight), not by federal agencies or nonpartisan electoral commissions. One result is that House incumbents rarely lose. Partisan district boundaries and the capacity to raise money from lobbyists insulate incumbents in all circumstances other than massive electoral shifts (as in 1994, 2006, and 2010). Again, the political rules of the game discourage voter turnout and low turnout primaries where extreme views have an advantage become crucial.

Some of these rules are constitutional limits, but gerrymandering is extraconstitutional if not unconstitutional.[8] In the 2012 House election, Democrats won the national popular vote by 1.3 million votes, but Republicans won a 34 seat majority. This result had a very large effect on policy outcomes during Obama's second term—the outcome was political gridlock.

Constitutional provisions including federalism and the separation of powers are designed to avoid excessive concentration of governmental power, reflecting the founders' fear of both excessive authority and mass democracy. These rules were, however, established before today's intense concentration of private wealth, the existence of share corporations, a globally integrated economy, and America's role as hegemonic power. America's Constitution is now spectacularly successful at limiting citizen-based political power. Limiting democratic curbs on nongovernmental power has worked perhaps too well.

The Obama administration did change America's health insurance system, but that effort took years and carried a heavy opportunity cost in terms of other policy initiatives, including legislative action on energy and climate change. Nor has Obama been able to do much regarding rising inequality, declining infrastructure, improving tax fairness, or the role of money in American political life (assuming he would have chosen to act in at least some of these areas). The role of concentrated wealth in American political life has in fact intensified. Indeed the institutional factors discussed above may be less significant to policy outcomes than concentrated wealth and campaign finance law, especially when these things play on and through American political culture.

Some Aspects of American Political Culture

Since 1980, conservatives have consistently conveyed a point of view within the rural and southern heartland of America from Georgia to Idaho, away from most of the nation's cosmopolitan centers. What is communicated, among other things, is a belief in a need for national assertiveness in a world filled with evil, combined with a race-based distrust of the social equity functions of government. Only during Obama's second term has there been any sign of conservative division on the first aspect of this perspective.[9]

Another relevant aspect of American political culture is a historic inclination to see the world in terms of good and evil. Citizens everywhere believe that their nation is right and good, but few so consistently see the world with so few shades of grey as do many in the United States. From the red scares of the 1920s through McCarthyism in the 1950s to the "war on terrorism," the focus on actual or potential enemies is prone to obsession. Such attitudes helped the "sale" of the foolishly aggressive posture of the Bush years and continues to support the scale of military spending.

Race has been at the core of politics in America for centuries. America's only Civil War was fought over slavery and the largest political realignment in the nation's history (with most Southern whites becoming Republicans) resulted when Southern schools were integrated and a Democratic president (Lyndon Johnson) signed Civil Rights legislation. A majority of Southerners shifted their support to the Republican Party.

Nonetheless America has come a very long way on race, especially since World War II. The beginnings of change were led by African Americans from returning war veterans. Also notable were artists of all kinds: authors like Ralph Ellison and James Baldwin, musicians including Billie Holiday (especially her brilliant and incredibly brave performance of the song *Strange Fruit*), Marion Anderson (and Eleanor Roosevelt), and Louis Armstrong and composers, perhaps most notably Oscar Hammerstein II.

Race, however, has remained an issue. For decades the Republican Party cultivated race-based politics to political advantage. Racial assertions came to be communicated in a highly coded manner—coded because a majority of Americans would reject racist campaigning if it was apparent. Subtlety is essential. Ronald Reagan famously launched his first presidential campaign in the obscure town of Philadelphia, Mississippi. Not coincidentally, this town had been the site of brutal civil rights murders two decades earlier. Racists heard an unspoken message of implicit solidarity, but most Americans missed the implication of his choice of venue. On other occasions Reagan spoke disparagingly of "welfare queens driving Cadillacs"—a phrase heard in racist circles as code for African American women.

In 1988 George H. W. Bush was less subtle. Key to his election was the notorious Willie Horton television commercial. Willie Horton was an African American criminal who had been pardoned by Michael Dukakis, Bush's opponent, during Dukakis' tenure as governor of Massachusetts. The ads featuring Mr. Horton suggested (to those who felt threatened by African Americans) that African American crime would run rampant were Michael Dukakis elected president. Bush himself didn't mention Horton's race, but his photo was featured prominently in the ads. Bush, Sr. was generally more politically moderate than his eldest son, but this particular ad was far more racist than anything George W. Bush did when campaigning or in office.[10] Indeed, neither Bush was racist in terms of policy actions or appointments, but "dog whistle" campaigning has been an important component in Republican electoral politics.

Lee Atwater, a noted Republican operative and chairman of the Republican National Committee, created the Willie Horton ads. As he later put it in a noted interview: "You start in 1954 by saying 'Nigger, nigger, nigger.' By 1968 you can't say 'nigger'—that stuff hurts you. Backfires. So you say stuff like forced busing, states' rights and all that stuff. You are getting so abstract now (that) you're talking about totally economic things and a byproduct of them is (that) blacks get hurt worse than whites."[11] Atwater was one of the inventors of the push poll, using fake polls to launch false rumors about opponents. Atwater died at the age of 40 of a brain tumor and in the end regretted many of the actions that were his life's work.

The electoral appeal of veiled racism regarding African Americans began to decline somewhat in post-2000 America, and failed utterly against Obama, especially in 2012 when the dog whistle attacks on his "otherness" were best heard by *all* American minorities (not just African Americans). Every visible minority in America voted Democratic in unprecedented numbers.[12] However, a sizeable minority of white Americans, especially older white Americans, remain hostile to racial minorities, foreigners, and non-Christians.[13] At the same time a *majority* of Americans reject racism, indeed Americans are likely less racist than those in many other nations, but even many who are not racist are hostile to suggestions that racist motivations are any longer in play politically. This latter view, in effect, helps to maintain an opening for subtle dog whistles and veiled foreign policy xenophobia.

Fortunately for Republican prospects, the real power of American neoconservatism and the Republican Party rests less on xenophobic appeals than on conservative dominance of the media, especially radio and television. This, of course, flies in the face of the widespread belief that America's media are liberal in their views.

Republicans were successful from the late 1990s until 2006 primarily because they and their ideas dominated radio and television. The Republican media advantage was especially apparent leading up to Clinton's impeachment and throughout George W. Bush's first term. It also persisted in the comparative treatment of candidates Gore and Bush in 2000 and in the demise of the 2004 candidacy of progressive Democrat Howard Dean.[14] Gore was decried by commentators as wooden and boring and George W. Bush was continuously lauded as the sort of person with whom Americans would like to have a beer (a curious characterization given that he is a teetotaler). Moreover, commercial network television all but ignores climate change, especially the science of climate change.[15]

Endless repetition of a consistent message requires coordination across multiple institutions and discipline on the part of the party apparatus, office holders, conservative media, and, importantly, fundamentalist religious leaders. One key means of accomplishing that coordination is conservative broadcast media. Despite the popular mythology about liberal media bias and in part perhaps because of it (since most nonconservative media bend over backwards to accommodate Republicans), conservatives dominate radio and television.[16] Conservative networks like FOX and media personalities like Rush Limbaugh, Sean Hannity, Bill O'Reilly, Larry Kudlow, Anne Coulter, Michelle Malkin, and endless others push talking points over and over again, often in tandem.

This produces an echo chamber effect that is so pervasive in some regions that few there hear any other way of thinking, other than perhaps brief and bland headlines and weather forecasts on network television. Gaining exposure to another viewpoint (again in some regions) requires that citizens actively seek it out on the Internet, in print media, or in bookstores or libraries. Conservative views are reiterated on radio and television and in faith-based classrooms and from church pulpits, especially in the all-embracing exurban mega-churches that provide entertainment, social and community services, and even onsite shopping seven days a week.

American broadcast media *have* adapted somewhat since the time when they so unabashedly supported the invasion of Iraq and down-played torture. Still missing, however, astoundingly for a nation that has interests everywhere in the world, is extensive coverage of the perspectives of other nations. Public television (PBS) and Fareed Zakaria on CNN provide detailed foreign news coverage, but otherwise for the most part (on television) only changes in major foreign governments and global disasters are reported. For example, the 2012 194-nation Doha Conference on climate change was all but invisible in America other than in print media and via the Internet.

As media critics Robert W. McChesney and John Nichols put it, speaking of the Telecommunications Act of 1996: "Citizens stopped hearing local news, as thousands of broadcast journalists were replaced by right-wing ranters from New York and Los Angeles. What diversity existed on the airwaves rapidly disappeared, as Clear Channel Communications bought up more than 1,200 radio stations nationwide...and American ears were assaulted by the heavily formatted...and ideologically narrow sound of radio produced under a regimen of concentrated media ownership."[17] The details, subtleties and complexities of both international and local political news are largely absent from America's airwaves.

These concerns, however, pale compared to the anti-democratic effects of money in American political life. The numbers are stunning. During the era of our tales from three cities, campaigns for the House of Representatives for 2006 raised $861.4 million dollars and spent $826.2 million.[18] That is nearly $2 million per seat; the highest amount raised by a single Congressman was $8.1 million—by Vernon Buchanan (R-FL) who may have won only because of a voting machine malfunction.[19] The amounts spent are particularly impressive given that most seats are not competitive. Republicans running for the House outspent Democrats, but not by much. Senatorial candidates raised and spent an additional $554 million and $547 million respectively in that year. In the presidential election of 2004, George W. Bush raised $367 million and John Kerry $328 million. Obama and both of his opponents spent well in excess of a *billion* dollars.

In addition, the amounts spent on lobbying between elections are even larger. Who spends this money? Over the time figures have been collected (through 2008): the financial, insurance, and real estate sector spent $2.157 billion; the health sector (ranked second) spent $1.921 billion; energy and natural resources (ranked 5th) spent $1.412 billion; and defense (ranked 10th) spent $533 million. In 2013 alone the health sector was highest at $360 million, the financial sector next at $359 million, energy still 5th at $261 million, and defense still 10th at just a bit under $100 million.[20] Lobbying government is in itself a major industry, and a major employer. Employees are frequently former politicians or former Congressional staffers. Lobbyists do more than just offer advice and opinion; they may actually write (and/or edit) draft legislation.

Sometimes, of course, lobbying can serve useful public purposes, providing lawmakers with necessary technical information. This is especially true when legislators get competing and offsetting information from a variety of businesses, local governments, unions, and environmental organizations and take all views into account. However, all those *not* represented by a lobby are prone to being ignored. Needless to say, few ordinary citizens are even indirectly represented by a lobbyist in Washington—especially those who are ill or poor, or employees who are neither professionals, nor unionized (an overwhelming majority),[21] nor are struggling and unaffiliated small businesses.

Lobbyists and the interests they represent are the major source of campaign funds to incumbents. This greatly enhances the power of incumbency beyond the advantages imparted by partisan districting. Campaign funds do not, of course, guarantee reelection. Former Senator Rick Santorum of Pennsylvania was defeated as an incumbent senator in 2006 despite having raised an astounding $24.6 million dollars. Ordinarily, campaign cash and electoral victory correlate very well.

A significant proportion of campaign money is spent on television advertising. Preparing and placing political advertising is a very big business. Overwhelmingly, television ads are negative—only a few tell voters what the candidate placing the ads hopes to do or what policies they favor. Most assert something threatening or worrisome about the advertiser's opponent. This pattern does not improve the reputation of politicians and does not encourage Americans to be enthusiastic about *anyone* seeking or holding public office, or to consider running themselves. This reality is also a central part of American political culture.

The role of campaign money, especially large contributions, was sharply accelerated by the Supreme Court in the ground-breaking Citizens United decision of 2010.[22] Citizens United, the organization bringing the case, is a heavily funded nonprofit that aired ads for a negative film about Hillary Clinton, at the time a candidate for the Senate. The ads were shown within 60 days prior to the election in violation of the 2002 Campaign Reform Act (also known as the McCain-Feingold law), which prohibited outside expenditures within that time frame, while setting some limits on campaign donations. The ruling has increased opportunities for very large additional political expenditures *without the source of the expenditures being visible to voters*. The ruling was supported 5–4 with Bush's court appointees voting to allow the donations. *One single donor* in 2012 was reported to have contributed $150 million to Republicans through this loophole and, according to the Center for Public Integrity, the Koch-brothers-financed Americans for Prosperity spent $122 million helping Republican candidates (compared to only $7 million in 2008).[23]

The money that flows into American politics resists taxing the wealthy, regulating carbon emissions, reducing military spending, and establishing prudent rules for financial institutions. It also aids the creation of a staggering array of special interest tax loopholes. As well, it discourages political participation and breeds cynicism. High campaign spending serves entrenched power and helps to assure almost unassailable incumbency. Even though large political contributions are sometimes unsuccessful, on balance, given the role of money in politics an American Constitution designed to avoid concentrated power lately fails to achieve that end.

This reality has important global implications. Countervailing political power working on behalf of global policies such as rising inequality or global environmental protection concerns is consistently outmatched within American political life. There are signs that American politics may be beginning to adapt, but the capacity to resist change built into America's political and policy system remains formidable. In a landmark study, Gilens and Page examined decisions on 1,779 policy issues over several decades (1981–2002).[24] They concluded that policy outcomes were better explained by theories of Economic Elite Domination and biased Pluralism (favoring business-oriented interest groups) than by Majoritarian Electoral Democracy or Majoritarian Pluralism.

The elite bias within American politics and policy will only be strengthened by a recent (2013) Supreme Court decision. *Shelby County v. Holder* overturned section 4 of the 1965 Voting Rights Act, legislation signed with great pride of Texas-born President Lyndon Johnson and celebrated by the leading conservative Republican of the day Senator Everett Dirkson of Illinois. The Voting Rights Act disallowed racial and other forms of discrimination regarding legal access to the electoral process and required states that had historically engaged in such discrimination to pre-clear changes in voting rules with the federal Department of Justice.[25] The original legislation was passed in response to the 1963 March in Washington and the brutal murder of civil rights workers who fought desegregation and aided voter registration in the South.

The Court decision held (5–4) that such procedures were no longer necessary, that, in effect, everywhere in America was now beyond such behavior and it was unfair to imagine that any state was not. As Chief Justice Roberts' rendering of the decision put it: "things have changed dramatically" in the ensuing years. The Court was almost immediately proven wrong in their assertions regarding fully established nationwide democratic virtue. Several states, including historic discriminators North Carolina and Texas, quickly moved to restrict voting hours and complicate registration procedures in ways that would disproportionately affect minority and Democratic voters including students, the poor and urban voters (who are less likely to have driver's licenses to use as government-issued photo ID and more likely to work unpredictable shifts and irregular hours and therefore needing extended voting hours).

After the decision, Justice Ruth Bader Ginsburg called out the Court majority on both the voting rights and campaign finance decisions, noting that "today's court may be the most activist court in American history." Conservatives, including those on the court, have long railed against "liberal judicial activism" and imagined themselves to be followers of noninterventionist interpretations of the Constitution of the late Mr. Justice Felix Frankfurter regarding the need for judicial restraint. The attack on liberal judicial activism, it seems now, is something of an exercise in "working the referees"—an exercise that provides a cloak for conservative judicial activism much like the myth of "the liberal media" cloaks the reality of a thoroughly conservative media establishment.

Obama and American Electoral Politics

Thus, Supreme Court decisions and other factors could weaken recent momentum in American politics toward the Democratic Party. Obama's successful 2008 campaign resulted in part from the policy failures of the Bush presidency, especially Katrina, Iraq, and the 2008 financial collapse. During that campaign, it also became clear that John McCain was temperamentally and intellectually ill-equipped to deal with a complex economic downturn and astonishingly, given his advanced age, selected a running mate with no capacity to deal with either foreign or economic policy. It is a measure of the power of conservative cultural attitudes and Republican media power that Obama did not win more decisively.

Obama also won in 2008 because his campaign transformed the American electoral process in several important ways. First and foremost, his campaign mobilized young voters, minority voters, and the traditional Democratic base, increasing voter turnout and turning ordinary voters into activists and contributors. Literally, there were millions of small contributors and the totals raised were unprecedented—with a significant proportion coming in amounts under $100, sometimes repeatedly from the same donors who did not have much money to spare at any one time.

In both 2008 and 2012, a massive army of Democratic volunteer canvassers were transported from state to state and billeted by yet more volunteers. New Yorkers (in whose state the outcome was certain) went to Pennsylvania where it was not. Californians went to Nevada and those in Illinois to Wisconsin, or in 2008 to Indiana and Missouri. Both campaigns utilized the Internet and social media to great effect. In 2008 massive rallies, taking advantage of Obama's rhetorical ability, were organized—more of them and far larger than had been seen in any previous election. The rallies were used to recruit additional volunteers.

The campaigners, stunningly young and diverse in appearance, broke through old barriers. They embodied a new more inclusive America. History was being made and those involved felt empowered by that fact. The campaigns also frightened those who were not comfortable with such a future. Entrenched forces were mobilized to respond but could not stop what was clearly coming. Most dramatically in 2012 the change was about the political power of minorities including Hispanics, Asian Americans, and Native Americans, as well as gays, the young, and women.

The stickiness of the American political system (as described above), however, prevented action on many of the policies that Obama supporters had sought, especially on climate change, rising inequality, and controls on gun sales. The term stickiness is mild but accurate descriptive term for what is a constitutionally and culturally constrained democracy. America arguably has a governmental system ill-suited for a key nation in an age where urgent problems require innovative global action. But there are factors that could over time at least partially offset these shortcomings.

One factor is American federalism. Even if Washington is paralyzed state and local governments can innovate and those innovations can spread. During the Bush years the mayors of most American cities agreed to, in effect, subnational, unofficial participation in the Kyoto Accord. Many state governments, including some that at the time had Republican governors (including Massachusetts, New York, and California), also took significant climate change action.[26] As previously noted, even arch-conservative Texas has established innovative policies with regard to wind energy and initiatives at the municipal level have been even more striking.[27] Two other key factors are America's evolving political culture and rapidly shifting demographics.

Some aspects of American political culture, of course, constrain innovation. Since 1980, neoconservative ideas have had a broad appeal in rural and the southern heartland and within areas of industrial decline, places generally distant from America's cosmopolitan coastal and midwestern cities. A belief that national assertiveness, combined with a radical diminution of the social equity functions of government, is needed to protect the American way of life in a world full of evil is popular. Conservatives have also played on culturally rooted attitudes regarding gays, abortion, and guns (as well as race). All of this was wrapped in rural imagery by a series of presidential candidates (Reagan, George W. Bush, and John McCain) who, in effect, played cowboys with plain-folks American values for the television cameras.

Another reason conservative ideas ring true for many is profoundly American, Puritanism—religion-based morality that fervently eschews personal behaviors of various sorts, but is prone to indifference regarding social injustice. One classic fictional portrayal of this attitude is captured in the slave boat captain in the novel *Roots*.[28] The captain is a sternly moral man who will not abide even a drop of alcohol on his lips, but sees slavery as a normal part of doing business.

The abstemious slave ship captain is a fictional embodiment of today's sometimes tension-filled Republican coalition of Puritanical theocrats and wealthy plutocrats, the latter seeking tax cuts in lieu of help for widows, orphans, the poor, and pensioners. Many in both groups join in angry solidarity with the unilateralist neoconservatives. Sometimes these strands exist in the same people, but many evangelicals and elderly neoconservatives carry excessive personal debt and have inadequate health insurance. Yet their vote can be determined by "values" questions—gays, abortion, xenophobia, or the right to bear arms. The distribution of wealth is not, for many of these people, an ethical matter, nor is the environment. Within such a view the economy is a cutthroat world and there is little that can be done about it. Morality is about sex. The economy is immutable—and best managed by powerful people.

That said, America's political culture is highly dynamic and also celebrates fairness, innovation, and change. In 2004 Republicans successfully placed bans on gay marriage on the ballot in key states to increase the turnout of conservative voters who would likely vote Republican. Opposition to gay marriage at the time was widespread and intensely felt. By 2013, however, a solid majority of Americans accepted gay marriage and many states have approved it. The issue is no longer useful as an appeal capable of causing voters to put aside their own economic interests; it is now a net vote loser, along with racist dog-whistles.

Also crucial to the future of American politics is an ongoing demographic shift wherein a *majority* of Americans will soon be members of some visible minority. Recent events including hostility to and disrespect of President Obama, as well as Republican intransigence on immigration policy and on social programs generally, have turned an overwhelming majority of people in these groups to the Democratic Party and to a greater openness to policy initiatives on inequality and other global concerns.

America in a Global Age

Despite a political system designed to avoid "excessive" change, America *as a society* is highly adaptive. There are many reasons for this: an open frontier, immigration, vast natural resources, economic dynamism, social mobility, few wars within its territory, an enthusiasm for technology and education, and an historic (if sometimes selective) belief in equality of opportunity. In many ways global economic integration is the greatest adaptation challenge America has yet faced. A global system dominated by a single hegemonic power is not well-suited to a planet with a single economy. Nor is America's political system, whereby a determined minority within that one nation can now block adaptive action even in the face of the desires and needs of both Americans and most people on the planet.

In many ways humankind now shares a common fate. Environmental damage, mobile disease, terrorism, increasingly concentrated wealth, and multidimensional deregulation can affect global majorities. Some believe that resolving such challenges will cost them disproportionately. Great power domination of global policy and law might be diminished were global decisions more citizen-centric. However, it is arguable that *virtually everyone* would gain more than they would lose from progress on these issues. Clearly this is true of effective action on climate change and financial sector stability, but even a shift from hegemonic dominance to global governance might well benefit most Americans. Perhaps the greatest challenge of a global citizens' movement, however, would be to convince Americans of that possibility.

One can, however, try. To begin with the most obvious observations: climate change increases sociopolitical instability, clearly something not in America's best interest. Melting Arctic ice will impact America's east coast, especially Florida, soon after it impacts distant Pacific Island nations. Rising inequality in America is very costly to retail and other businesses, government, and less-than-wealthy Americans. As has been widely noted recently, a low minimum wage directly adds to public deficits through the need to supplement the income of working families earning too little to survive. As well, rising global inequality is politically destabilizing and the poor who are desperately poor cannot purchase the products that advanced economies produce.

Moreover, hegemonic power is staggeringly expensive. America's economy is growing more slowly than its purported future rivals, and thus the cost of staying far ahead will continue to rise. Military spending also means that America has not updated infrastructure, including bridges, the electrical grid, and its rail system. Like most nations, America faces huge costs to adapt to climate change and already has a structural public debt problem. Finally here, poverty is increasing in America and its middle class is losing ground. Small steps have been taken during the Obama administration, but deficits and the political impossibility of raising taxes have prevented strong action.[29] Many of these problems would be manageable if defense spending were reduced. Such a possibility is bound with new more globally balanced approaches to security including fewer American overseas bases and reductions in spending on new weapons systems.

Stepping back from the view that America must resolve every conflict would shrink the target on America's back. President Obama has encouraged multilateralism and resisted most neoconservative calls for direct intervention in Libya, Egypt, and elsewhere. In time such an approach may open qualitatively new possibilities. Outside of the Middle East the possibilities for sharing or globalizing security are even better.

Even regarding terrorism modest steps away from continuous dependence on hegemonic power might be possible. For example, the 2013 capture of a terrorist like Abu Anas al Libi might, in the future, be handled differently even assuming it is only American forces that could make such a capture. Al Libi was criminally tried in the United States (an option more compliant with international law than indefinite incarceration in Guantanamo or a US military tribunal). But other options include trial in the ICC. This approach, in the long run, might help to reduce the appeal of terrorism.

After the 2008 election, *New York Times* columnist Roger Cohen authored a plea that President Obama support the ICC. Cohen observed that "even if court membership is not quickly attainable, the United States plays a part in the court's 2010 review conference."[30] He went on to argue for active court membership, well aware, no doubt, that membership will be resisted politically. The undertaking was not at the time a priority for the Obama administration, which was far more concerned with drawing down troops in Iraq and Afghanistan and dealing with the economy. With thorny problems like al Libi and Syria, an American president might well appreciate having the ICC as an option.

Al Libi was captured in Libya, committed his alleged crimes in Kenya and elsewhere, crimes directed against the United States, but endangering citizens of many nations. Using the ICC makes clear that those guilty of such terrorist acts are committing crimes against *all* humans. They are not "just" enemies of the United States, but enemies of humanity. Most people understand this, but it is important that citizens of every nation see these crimes as potentially directed at them. Most terrorist victims are Muslim and include citizens of all religions or no religion from most nations. The broader the rejection of these acts the more likely it is that more of them can be prevented—and effectively prosecuted. It is not in America's interest to perpetuate the impression that terrorism is especially directed at America.

All nations would also broadly benefit from action on climate change. Effective climate action especially requires action within the largest emitters (the United States and China). Otherwise efforts in other nations are too easily seen as futile. Yet, one half of one of the three branches of American government can block decisive federal action. A majority in the House currently (in early 2014) represents a minority of the 50 percent of Americans that vote. As well, the Senate majority often represents a minority of voters and virtually any action on any policy realm can be prevented by as few as 41 senators. The conservative majority on the Supreme Court still dates to the Bush administration and it is rare that all three branches are in concurrence. Thus a minority within a nation with 6 percent of the world's population can stymie progress on a matter crucial to the well-being of all humanity. Given this, it will be easier to get a majority of Americans onside with global concerns than to get the United States as a nation to take effective policy action on those concerns.

Given that so many issues now require global solutions the world, especially Americans, need to think about the implications of having a single nation able to block urgent global action—especially when a majority of Americans themselves favor action. Their wishes too are stymied by a Constitutional system designed in a much slower and preglobal age to block too-rapid change. America's founders lived when the impacts of inaction were almost always local. Nor could they imagine vast fortunes applied to *preventing* the passage of public policies of global importance, policies that were favored by both American and global majorities.

Social inequality is more complicated politically but action is also in the interest of most Americans. A case can be made that the world's present economic doldrums are the result of too little economic demand[31]—in turn a result of the undue concentration of wealth (combined with public sector austerity that results from the increased power of wealth within the political processes of many countries). Too few people have the wherewithal to purchase the goods they desperately need, and governments, fearful of the wealthy, are unwilling to tax them in order to stimulate economies through spending on collective needs. In short, inequality poses a threat to financial stability and long-term growth.

In particular the emerging American "minority majority" and lately beleaguered American industrial workers would gain from inequality initiatives, not just in America but elsewhere. Higher wages in Asia might benefit some North American manufacturing (e.g., where shipping costs were especially high). In the concluding chapter I will make the case that this would not necessarily result in Asian job losses since higher wages there would support the increased purchase of locally manufactured products.

As well, American democracy has been weakened by increases in inequality and shifts in its political economy that have been policy-driven. Effective democracy *requires* some minimum of economic equity. American democracy is vulnerable to wealth distribution trends and this, given America's global position, is the world's business. Paul Krugman has noted that "Between 1972 and 2001 the wage and salary income of Americans at the 90th percent of income distribution rose only 34%, or about 1% per year... But income at the 99th percentile rose 8 percent; income at the 99.9th percentile rose 181 percent; and income at the 99.99th percentile rose 497 percent. No, that's not a misprint."[32]

Since 2001 the gap has grown with gains at the top accelerated by tax cuts and by fewer industrial job opportunities. Saez, for example, notes that from 1993 to 2012 the top 1 percent of American earners gained 86.1 percent and the bottom 99 percent only added 6.6 percent, much of it going to those within the upper echelons of that category.[33] How is such a dramatic shift in income distribution (to the disadvantage of the overwhelming majority) possible within a democracy? Globalization is a partial explanation, but another part of the explanation is low voter turnout and a political culture fixated on non-economic issues such as gun rights and abortion. In nonpresidential election years, voter turnout can be less than 50 percent of eligible voters—in part because turnout among minorities and the poor has been especially low—a trend partially reversed in presidential years and by Obama's historic candidacy.

Clearly there are limits and tradeoffs here, but wage gains in poor nations do not simply come at the expense of consumers or workers in wealthy nations.[34] Nor is dealing with global environmental issues merely a cost to economies. Climate action costs some industries, but it is an opportunity for others. Similarly, in a *global* economy, improved wages anywhere provide economic opportunities in many places.

In sum, Europe, America, China, or Brazil could all enhance their national positions as world leaders by being role models on the key global issues. Poverty is at least as much a function of policy decisions (e.g., on taxes or minimum wages) as it is on global economic integration per se. Excessive policy caution regarding poverty can be countered if governments can be pressed to act concurrently rather than waiting for overall economic growth to somehow magically help everyone.

Such policy changes in both America and elsewhere would be more likely were there a politically consequential global citizens' movement. It is incumbent on global citizens to communicate their concerns to *all* governments.

Imagining a New America for a Global Century

American conservatives rarely tire of talking about American exceptionalism. In 2012 nearly every Republican presidential candidate asserted a belief in it (without being clear about what they meant by the term). For some it means that Americans are just better than everyone else. Others believe that the rules that apply to other nations do not apply to America (for a few, this exemption from the rules exists because America has been chosen by God for some special role in the world). Such assertions are not likely to endear America to the rest of the world.

American conservatives may be prone to this view because they sense an eclipse of America and fear global governance or any distribution of international influence not based on military power. They, in effect, perceive global cooperation as a threat. At the same time, domestically these same people are part of an aging and shrinking minority. That, as we have seen, can make them or those they elect dangerous, but there is another side to the changes slowly coming to America that makes them so fearful. The other side is that *another America is possible*, a transformed America is a not completely unrealistic dream. A new America may be, among other things, capable of letting go of unilateralism and of advancing genuinely global solutions to global problems.

America is changing demographically, culturally, and politically. Americans have always been adaptive and inventive.[35] There has been considerable political learning regarding the issues raised by events in Kyoto, Baghdad, and New Orleans. There is presently a declining desire in America for military action in distant lands.[36] With Hurricane Sandy and other unprecedented storms and droughts, there is a growing understanding that climate change is real—and that there are possible solutions that do not foreclose everyday comforts.

The challenge that remains is getting past racial divisions and appreciating that America's diversity is the nation's most important asset in a global age. Most young Americans already understand that. The recent Hollywood film, *The Butler*, gives a glimpse of how far America has come regarding race. Only those cowering in fear will resist the change. While the fearful have become more visible since Obama's election, they are not necessarily more numerous. The challenge of race is crucial because the lingering remnants of racial division blind too many Americans to the key lessons of New Orleans: that inequality is real and collective public action is necessary within nations and globally and even wealthy nations and wealthy people would be better off if greater social fairness were the norm.

Many in America's wonderfully diverse younger generation can see the implications of global economic integration because this integration has profoundly affected their lives. They also understand that the world faces challenges that can only be resolved by globally accepted initiatives, policies, and institutional change. Fewer among the young are likely to resist rethinking how global decisions are made and more are likely to be open about joining with their peers in other nations to actively pursue such change. The millions of younger Americans that campaigned for Obama and that strongly advocate for gay marriage and other forms of inclusiveness are the embodiment of America's long-standing positive traditions best expressed in Abraham Lincoln's words from his 1863 Gettysburg Address and repeated by Martin Luther King, Jr. in his day: "we hold these truths to be self-evident, that all men are created equal."[37]

Such views evolve with time. Were they alive today, Lincoln and King would say *people*, rather than *men*. They might also reflect on the governance of the world as well as that in their own nation. Global efforts may well need to be initiated and led by citizens, not nations. Nations, including the United States, can be pressed by their own citizens to resolve key problems *globally* and to find ways to slowly step away from excessive dependence on national military power with grace and wisdom—and begin to redirect those resources and capabilities and to focus their attention on human needs on a planetary scale.

5

Global Citizenship without Global Government

The dilemma is apparent: with the slow economic growth typical of mature economies and a politically constrained capacity to tax concentrated wealth, America cannot indefinitely maintain disproportionate hegemonic power without imposing additional burdens on its own people.[1] This is not an American failing; hegemonic power is inherently impermanent and is increasingly outmoded as a way to organize global affairs. America and the world would be better off with another governance system, if the new system is widely accepted, stable, fair, and open to citizen input.

It is fortuitous when an impossible task, like maintaining disproportionate hegemonic power, is an unnecessary one. Indeed, with a globally integrated economy and diverse and expanding citizen-to-citizen linkages wholly nationally based armies are a foolish extravagance. There needs to be a citizen-driven way to establish policy and law globally, not in all things, but if and when such a scale is necessary.

The clear danger is that hegemonic power could give way to rivalries that carry significant risks and costs. An arms race would involve tragic opportunity costs for the nations involved and the world as a whole. It would detract from what is essential to the quality of our collective future: cooperation on global law and policy on several fronts. As noted in chapter 1, developing a multi-national security system would likely reduce costs compared to either hegemony or great power rivalry. This option is increasingly necessary and at present is relatively achievable.

In a global economy the quality of daily life may depend as much on global policy outcomes as on local or national factors. Global democratic institutions to influence those global outcomes are largely absent. Indeed, it is hard to even imagine effective democratic institutions at a global scale. It is sometimes difficult enough to believe that we can effect change in our cities or neighborhoods. It is little wonder we feel powerless. We know that the world is becoming more interdependent, but cannot influence outcomes at that scale. Few would even know who to contact to communicate an opinion regarding the global future.

This does not mean, however, that transnational systems that protect basic human rights or the environment cannot be established. So too transnational economic and political entities have been established, including the European Union. As well, David Miller argues that a system of global justice is possible using international organizations and other large human institutions including states.[2] This does not require a world state. I would argue, however, that achieving an effective system of justice may require a sense of global citizenship among individuals in most nations and a broad willingness to act politically on that perspective.

Global citizenship, in the first instance, is about locating, contacting, and communicating *with each other.* Individuals in every corner of the globe have the potential capacity to persuade each other that citizens can and should influence global political, social, and economic outcomes. Technologically, the possibilities are unique in human history. However, we need first to realize that it is *not* inevitable that inequality will always and inexorably increase and also that it is *not* inevitable that the global environment will deteriorate. It is not even inevitable that wars between nations will always be with us.

Though nothing *global* is ever easily accomplished, citizens can act at every level with global needs in mind. We can now communicate across once seemingly insurmountable barriers. Even homeless people in India, South Africa, and other nations have, with access help, linked together using new technologies. Many common needs are indeed nearly universal and have common causes and solutions. The technical means to link with others to pursue those needs are emerging.

How many people around the world are still unemployed today because some years ago American mortgage lenders made dubious loans? Those sellers then protected themselves by bundling and selling those loans, were protected by self-interested ratings agencies and giant insurance companies issued policies on those bad investments, policies that they could not possibly cover. All of this was permissible within the rules of that one nation, to the detriment of the whole planet.

How many citizens' livelihoods were then more recently threatened by large (mostly European) banks that made excessive loans to European nations and would not or could not absorb the ensuing losses? How many are hungry or homeless as a result of spreading deserts or endangered by floods or storms or wildfires or coastal erosion resulting from climate change? How many live with fear motivated by the machinations of global power struggles or ancient religious grievances and prejudices?

Such problems can, in my view, in some contexts be avoided or ameliorated without formal global government. In Dryzek's view what is needed in broad terms is transnational discursive democracy—transnational public debate led by citizens.[3] This debate need not be formally linked to binding collective decisions at the international or national level. It does need to be sufficiently widespread and intense to undermine the "logic of no alternative" of today's global economic integration based on market liberal principles.

The world is now bound together. The risks we face are shared and cannot effectively be dealt with other than globally. Yet nations seem all but powerless to act on the problems we face: rising inequality, the need to prevent concentrated financial industries from repeatedly endangering the global economy and the need for decisive action on global environmental threats. We have understood the causes of climate change for a quarter century, but still lack enforceable international agreements that significantly slow greenhouse gas (GHG) emissions. The threats are glaringly obvious, yet global collective action seems all but impossible.

Positive possibilities are also left unattended. Few nations reduce wasteful military spending even though we are all now each other's customers and each other's investors. Global economic integration leads to efficiencies and improved productivity, but intra-national inequality continues to expand almost everywhere. Increasing wealth could create well-being if even modest social policy standards were set within trade agreements or by multilateral trade organizations—or simply adopted by more nations to slow race-to-the-bottom competitiveness.

Global citizens see the importance of these things. If one thinks first in terms of *humanity's* interests many things are suddenly in-your-face obvious. The only remaining question is what political process would make global political action possible? Is there an alternative to waiting and hoping for *nations* to come together to take decisive action? Perhaps it is as plausible that citizens will come together and act together.

A Global Citizen's Movement Is Necessary

The world has changed dramatically in recent decades. The rules that guide the global economy are less about increased trade than about the instantaneous and unimpeded movement of capital. Those rules were set largely without citizen input. Employment opportunities move with capital, but labor is far less mobile. Capital is free to come and go, citizens are rooted in the nation of their birth unless they have the skills and savings to venture across the planet. Many defy the law and depart their nations anyway, moving as far as they can afford to move.

Investment capital is sought after by every nation to such an extent that investors can often write their own rules and can usually prevent or avoid policy-based burdens on concentrated wealth because capital is free to move where the costs and burdens are least. Thus when economic growth slows, few governments are able to maintain public sector employment, initiate environmental protection, or maintain elemental social justice.

Global economic integration creates other costs less intentionally. When local goods are consumed locally buyers usually know something about the working conditions under which they were produced. In the case of food, buyers know some producers personally and food producers may know their customers. People also know more about what they are consuming, consuming literally in the case of food. Even within a national economy consumers have some assurances regarding food safety requirements or workplace safety rules or child labor or minimum wages laws. Today, however, it is challenging enough just to know *where* a product was produced let alone on the ground working conditions and product safety rules.[4]

This product anonymity has spurred a partial, citizen-based solution: the fair trade movement. Products from distant lands are certified when an acceptable share of the proceeds goes to the producers, working conditions are above some minimum and/or sound environmental practices are adopted. Many European and North American consumers pay attention to such labeling, but the results are short of transformative in some locations.[5] These initiatives will be discussed further in chapter 6.

As well, the burgeoning *local* food movement can also be seen as global citizenship in action. Indeed a multi-issue global citizen's movement could add perspective and a sense of solidarity to *many* existing civil society organizations and citizen-based efforts including economic development, human rights, peace, social justice, and environmental protection. Food security is particularly important because it brings together people around a concern that is universal and which cannot help but simultaneously address environmental concerns, social justice, and the character of economic development.

Food is different from other products. It is ingested and therefore everyone arguably has a *right* to know how it was produced and what it contains. If it was not produced by someone with whom one has direct, on-going contact, people other than those who are desperate would expect and demand protection via public health agencies. Regardless, many increasingly prefer direct purchase in farmer's markets. This is a market-based solution that addresses a widely felt concern regarding globalization. Local food production also has environmental benefits and positive social effects especially within poorer nations.[6]

Food policies and politics are but one dimension of the global-local dynamics of global citizenship. The need for a global citizen's movement is rooted in fundamental changes in the global economy and the human condition. The environment can for the first time in history be impacted globally. It is not just that economic activities anywhere can damage every place they happen, but today's activities have impacts everywhere. The most obvious case is climate change. The political significance of this new reality is that all humans have a stake in the regulatory policies of *every* nation. As well, Arctic peoples in many nations need to have a voice regarding chemical releases in Texas and elsewhere.[7] As well, many endangered species (such as whales, grizzlies, tigers, and elephants) are global public goods requiring global voices in their defense.

Inequality, the other core challenge of global economic integration, has two dimensions: economic distribution between rich nations and poor nations, and distribution within nations. Within most poor nations there is in effect double maldistribution—the nation as a whole is poor and internal distribution is also highly skewed.[8] Within some rich nations, most notably America, internal income distribution has been getting steadily more unequal since the early 1980s, with a brief pause during the low unemployment Clinton years. Between nations there have been relative gains by many middle rank nations like China and Brazil, but internal distribution of those gains is grossly unequal.

The effects of global economic integration on social equity are complex, but political action in defense of equity is essential to its achievement. Without a global citizen's movement, citizens may be left to keep *their* nation competitive through reduced taxation, public sector restraint, declining wages and benefits, and reduced social spending. Those restraints, and inequality generally, despite austerity mythologies can undermine economic growth in poor nations and wealthy ones alike.[9]

Finally, a global citizen's movement could help to keep governmental power in check within nations where internal repression is the norm. A worldwide citizen's movement dedicated to democracy and citizens' rights could pressure governments to not engage in, or look the other way, regarding human rights abuses. A global citizen's movement could also raise the issue of arms spending and the export of weapons as a public policy priority.

A Global Citizen's Movement Is Possible

A global citizen's movement could make a difference *and it is possible*. It is possible because global media has been, to coin a word, "unmassed"— and mass media are in decline. Today's communications technologies can locate and link like-minded people in every corner of the world. Those intent on addressing global concerns can find each other and can locate organizations of like-minded people, or create new ones.

Search engines and other interactive media make such connections possible and they are global, instantaneous, increasingly affordable, sharable, and often highly mobile. The communication they enable is asynchronous and thereby affected only inconsequentially by time zones and international datelines. These communications are citizen-based, unedited, and participatory—and can involve large and small numbers of people. These capabilities are increasingly accessible even in remote locations. Politically, this has profound potential.

In the early days of the Arab Spring interactive media was the scourge of tyrants. They tried and failed to render it ineffective. New media could also be used to build citizen-to-citizen connections globally. Nothing like this has ever previously been possible at any time in human history. The effects may be politically as important as the printing of the Gutenberg Bible was within the Christian church.

Seymour Martin Lipset, in his 1960s reflections on the social science of political participation and the propensity for "left" politics, tried to determine why certain groups joined together to act politically and change established orders.[10] Groups like cigar rollers were politicized and politically active when other groups of similar station were not because the cigar rollers worked sitting in a circle at large tables and could readily converse while they worked. Workers in other work settings did not have this opportunity. New media make ongoing *global* conversations and the creation of *global* organizations possible.

The broadcast (mass) media remain influential, but increasingly are just one voice among many, a voice people are free to distrust. In most large markets broadcast media require vast sums of money to acquire and operate. Thus they will almost always serve wealth and power since they are controlled by those who have a considerable share of both. The grip that radio and television has held over information for decades is waning. Those media *concentrated* political power and influence in a small number of hands.

New media disperse that power and influence. Computers and hand-held communications devices make everyone a potential communication initiator and local, national, or global conversation participant. Sometimes humble communications "go viral" and are, in effect, turned into mass communications by large numbers of ordinary citizens.

The array of new technologies, websites, and software options is stunning, and millions, mostly younger than I, are adept at handling them. They include: simple listserves, Facebook, blogs, YouTube, file and photo sharing, Reddit, Twitter, Instagram, Skype, Tumblr, webcasts, podcasts, and virtual conferencing. People as citizens have only begun to tap the potential. Additional tools that open the possibility of citizen-initiated global communications will continue to be developed and to become more widely available.

The Arab Spring showed the political potential (and in some cases the limits) of these communications possibilities. This potential has global reach. Global corporations, national governments, militaries, and terrorists will not easily maintain their exclusive place on the world stage as the twenty-first century unfolds. Citizens and civil society organizations will also come together and will, one way or another, bring public participation to bear on global issues, global needs, global institutions, and global decisions. They will, to repeat a phrase, find ways to democratize international relations.

Communing with the Ghost of Jean-Jacques Rousseau

Recently in the basement of the Pantheon in Paris I had an imaginary conversation with the remains of political philosopher Jean-Jacques Rousseau. At least I thought it was imaginary. I am not sure how he took it.

I did not intend to have this conversation, but in the presence of Rousseau's casket and with this book in mind Rousseau's hesitations regarding large-scale democracy seemed present in the room and resonated strongly. In Rousseau's view democracy was only possible for communities of limited size and scope. Rousseau was wary of nationalism and national governments, the emerging political communities of his day. Trying to imagine democracy at a global scale would have been, to him, outrageous—and would have seemed more outrageous had he imagined today's world of multiple billions.

Rousseau lived in an age before motorized transport or electronic communications or for that matter much by way of indoor plumbing and medical care, but there remains a valid caution in his assessment. A single global government, comprehensive in scope may well still be beyond human capacities. Eight or ten billion people are not easily governable or easily brought to a majority view or any semblance of agreement on many issues. The very idea of world government frightens the wits out of most people for good reason. It runs the risk of being altogether too monolithic.

Even in theory government at this scale might be problematic to American democracy's founders given their views regarding the excessive concentration of power. But a global citizen's movement would not necessarily lead to global government let alone comprehensive—all issues—global government. The movement could work through existing governments at any or all levels, by simultaneously advancing initiatives locally and/or nationally or incorporating subsidiarity as a principled approach.

Alternatively, the movement could act directly by, for example, establishing development initiatives itself or raising funds or volunteers to aid victims of war or climate change. Recall as well, for example, fair trade campaigns. Additionally, global citizens might work through the United Nations or other international or through civil society organizations like Oxfam, Avaaz, Amnesty International, or the International Union for the Conservation of Nature.

It might do all of those things, but doing so would not move the world nearer to global government. Some global citizens themselves might recoil at the thought of global government even while working tirelessly toward the global resolution of global social justice concerns or other issues. They might work to democratize international relations or even build a global civilization, but not necessarily want a global government, now or even some day. Change *could* be accomplished, even collective global change, without global government.

Getting millions of individuals to work in common cause across cultural, language, and geographic boundaries and in the face of an endless array of historic animosities—to trust one another and to cooperate in the global interest—is, in itself, a more than sufficient challenge to human ingenuity and civility. It also is in keeping with building something akin to Rousseau's general will at the global level—not a sum total of national self-interests as one might find operating within traditional international organizations or international negotiations, but "what reasonable (people), leaving aside their self-interest and having the community's (in this case the world's) interests at heart, would regard as the right and proper course of action."[11]

Global citizenship is about global political communications involving large numbers of diverse people who would not ordinarily interact. Some might jointly undertake actions or urge governmental and nongovernmental institutions to act (or desist from acting). They might press for global, national, or local decisions regarding inequality or the protection of biodiversity. They might even demand altering the very logic and possibility of war. None of these great causes, the most important of our time, *necessarily* require global government. Indeed this movement would not require even the granting of formal citizen input opportunities in global forums—it is about citizens coming together and pressing their issues at all levels and varied institutional settings.

Regardless of whether a global citizen's movement emerges or does not emerge, government, as an institution of law-making and enforcement, will continue on the relatively manageable scale at which it presently exists (and would even if there *were* a global government of some sort). A large proportion of humans, however, can over and above that come to understand ourselves as simultaneously, and perhaps even first and foremost, as citizens of a global community.

The global community, and all of the sub-communities within it, however, can no longer continue to thrive without a deeper and more inclusive sense of global common purpose. That is the implication of sharing a common fate. Rousseau could not have imagined a functioning global community of citizens any more than he could imagine effective democratic government for large numbers or large areas. The latter is indeed problematic at least in the sense that one normally imagines a democratic government, but that does not exclude a widely felt sense of global common purpose given the extent to which we are now bound together economically, socially, and ecologically. To think otherwise is to abandon hope.

It took months to send messages across the globe in Rousseau's time and many locations simply could not be reached. Only a small minority was literate in even a single language. The notion that a *machine* could translate, or even that a human could provide simultaneous translation through an earpiece, was unimaginable. Travel across France, let alone an ocean, was a massive effort unaffordable to most. Now to amuse ourselves and our friends we send images taken through the window of a moving train around the world to hundreds of people the very instant that we take them. Others, in a forest or on a boat 10,000 miles away respond to the image equally instantly and *could* travel across a continent or an ocean to respond in person in a matter of hours. None of this makes democracy, large or small, easy, but it does make sustained global social, economic or political activities a genuine possibility.

Actual global governance, if it were to emerge, would not necessarily lead to vast new bureaucracies. The scope of such governance could, and probably should, be highly circumscribed or for the most part ad hoc. The foci of such governance might begin with, and be presently limited to, initiatives that advance social equity and ameliorate and/or help us adapt to climate change and threats to biodiversity. A bonus possibility, almost too unlikely to even imagine out loud, might be declining national inclinations to go to war and eventual reductions in military spending. Accomplishing any of these things will require long-term building of widespread trust through extensive participation in the citizen-based pursuit of the global interest.

Trust could be reinforced within a wide variety of undertakings. One might be the establishment of shared symbols of global interconnectedness. Related efforts exist already, for example, within the United Nations' efforts to designate World Heritage sites, but there are other possibilities. One, for example, would be a wider recognition and celebration of the site of human origin in East Africa (a point discussed in chapter 6). Other recognized world heritage sites might celebrate the early establishment of democracy in Greece or, in modern times, in France or elsewhere. A third possibility might be the sites of transformative human invention, quite a few of which would be in America (and should include the creation of the Internet).

Another possibility would be the creation of World Parks. This might aid poorer nations needing help with maintaining areas of national and global importance. The United Nations has taken steps in this direction with Biosphere Reserves and World Heritage sites. Biosphere Reserves are part of the Man and Biosphere Program run by UNESCO and there are reserves recognized in over 100 countries. UNESCO also recognizes 725 cultural, 83 natural, and 28 mixed World Heritage sites in 153. On its website it asserts: "What makes the concept of World Heritage exceptional is its universal application. World Heritage sites belong to all the peoples of the world irrespective of the territory on which they are located."[12] Wider recognition and support for these efforts might help to build a global perspective.

Some already think as *humankind*, beings living together on a beautiful and hospitable planet. This is a logical and necessary step in the evolution of our species. Everyone need not think of themselves in these terms, but if large numbers of us do we can influence—or create—outcomes and decisions at the global scale: one locale at a time, one institution at a time or through persuading or pressuring nations to act in concert through international organizations or ad hoc agreements. Global government, or even what might be called global governance, may never fully emerge. In any case some issues, including climate change or better global management of financial institutions, need resolution long before anything as systemic as global government could ever be established.

Some global concerns do not necessarily need formal global regulations so much as they need simultaneous citizen pressure in many nations leading to citizen, governmental, and/or corporate actions. Some needs would even benefit from spirited competition—not between firms for profits or governments reducing public investments in health, education, and well-being, but competition with regard to Gini coefficients or GNP generated per unit of energy consumed. Gini coefficients are a measure of the gap between rich and poor. If *these* changes undermine the capacity to attract investment (and I am not convinced that they would) then minimum global standards are necessary.

Rousseau spoke of solidarity and the general will (the collective interest of the political whole rather than a sum of the interests of individuals and factions)—but he took this to be a possibility only within a community of modest size. Today, given the new realities we face, we have a vastly larger task. A *global* social contract is needed regarding a limited set of shared priorities—some now unavoidable and others patently desirable to an overwhelming majority and unattainable without cross-border solidarity and cooperation.

Happily, the list of irretrievably global issues is mercifully a short one. Only these issues need engage the attention of global citizens. The list might include energy use and energy sources (the "reinvention of fire" as Lovins recently put it[13]), some other environmental issues that can only be resolved globally, global financial stability and those social equity issues that arise out of global economic integration. Such challenges are daunting, but seem now impossible to avoid even if few yet imagine acting on them and most national leaders seem determined to shirk responsibility even while going through the motions of grappling with these very issues.

One reason for inaction on the part of national leaders is that taking bold actions in the global interest can put one's nation at a competitive disadvantage. In an age of global economic integration disproportionate expenditures on social justice, taking the lead on anti-pollution regulations or raising corporate tax rates can, in some circumstances, weaken a nation's competitive position. For this reason one group has advocated for *simultaneous* legislation on such matters.[14] In effect such an outcome is a form of limited global governance without global government.

With or without this approach a global agenda remains vitally important and resolution of the items on it does not require lawmaking and enforcement by a global government. Regardless as well opponents of *any* limitation on the unencumbered power of capital will claim that its advocates seek global government and that that is dangerous. However, global government may not be essential and we need not even speculate about whether it might be desirable. An effective citizen-based movement may be sufficient and must in any case emerge first. I take that possibility to be the next stage in human evolution, a stage we urgently need.

The Russian venture capitalist Yuri Milner has recently asserted the emerging notional possibility of a "global brain,"—something he describes as consisting "of all the humans connected to each other and to the machine and interacting in a very unique and profound way, creating an intelligence that does not belong to any single human or computer."[15] When I mentioned this to Rousseau's remains and explained to him what the Internet, social media, blogs, computers and, when he seemed puzzled, electricity were he thought that this sounded a lot like a global general will. I thought it was also a bit like the dreaded borg of overwrought science fiction.

Nonetheless we were agreed that given that humankind in less than two decades had come from a few thousand websites to more than 100 million, it was hard to say where we might get to in another few decades. Mass global interconnectivity seems all but unavoidable—at least unless someone somewhere finds a way to pull the plug. Whether democratized media will lead to a wider proliferation of teen idols, pornography and bad music or a viable and effective global citizen's movement (or both) is difficult to predict.

As noted, local governments, businesses, and civil society can contribute significantly to resolving global scale problems even, and perhaps especially, when national governments will not participate in global initiatives or live up to what they have agreed to in multilateral agreements. National leaders' actions, or just their strutting and fretting on the global stage, get the attention of media, but regarding climate change a more effective role has been played by other levels of government, including for example, Ontario's Feed-in Tariff Program or the renewable portfolio standard of many American states.

The brief visibility of the Occupy Wall Street movement brought socio-economic inequality to global attention, as has Thomas Piketty's *Capital in the 21st Century*, discussed below. Occupy was accomplished by a civil society organization without a formal membership structure or visible leaders. As well, hundreds of other organizations, including the Quakers and Mennonites, have for decades acted to reduce global inequality.

A global citizen's movement need not lead to global government, global governance, or even additional global agreements to be effective. Successes may come through the direct actions of civil society organizations or through the courageous leadership of a small number of governments open to the goals of the movement. As Rousseau might tell us, if he could see today's world and its needs and possibilities, the important thing is that citizens from many places see and act in favor of the global interest rather than only think of political life as a way to advance their own or their particular nation's interests.

Citizen-Driven Global Decisions

National governments, when acting in the global arena regarding economic and trade matters, are chiefly influenced by business interests and, when dealing with national security, by their military and national security apparatus. Citizens and civil society organizations are not encumbered in this way. Accordingly, they see the world and these issues differently. Most would be mindful of the economic and security implications of global issues, but are also likely to take into account factors beyond the interests of the military or influential corporations and economic sectors.

Civil society organizations and citizens are largely excluded from trade negotiations and trade dispute resolution. This is in effect a form of *already existing* global governance, one without democratic input, global governance far more influential on everyday life than the United Nations which so many North American conservatives seem to fear so comprehensively. Joseph Stiglitz has argued that these agreements undermine national democracy especially in the global South.

Within trade negotiations and trade disputes civil society organizations and citizens would likely be concerned about the effects of trade rules on employment, working conditions and wages as well as returns on particular investments. Business interests would and could not be excluded from such processes, but the addition of other voices would change the dynamic and open the process to public visibility. An even more important effect of civil society involvement might involve *nondecisions*, the matters that are rarely considered and the debates that never take place.[16]

Nondecisions regarding global economic integration and trade rules include important questions that are simply not discussed. What are the effects of global economic integration on wages in both historically low wage and historically high wage nations? Would, for example, a global minimum wage for export industries affect these outcomes? Should there be enforced global minimum standards for workplace safety, child labor and basic working conditions and the length of the work day or work week? Should they be enforced by civil society organizations working with importing nations or built into trade agreements? Corporate interests may try to reject such considerations as unwarranted interference and governments might claim that they are an imposition on national sovereignty, but an effective citizen's movement might in time shift such opinions.

Constraints on drift toward a lowest common denominator might leave some additional manufacturing jobs in high wage nations and, while there might be slightly fewer new jobs in low wage nations, there would be improved lives and working conditions. The job losses in poor countries might be less than the job gains in rich ones because higher wages in the poorer nations would increase local purchasing power. Requiring (in trade agreements) the right to form unions in nations might have similar effects and would also help to preserve unions in rich nations where they are being systematically eroded. Have such possibilities ever even been broached in a trade negotiation (or is this another nondecision)?

What specific initiatives will result is impossible to predict, but new perspectives would enter global policy proceedings and global rule-making if citizens were a part of global economic and trade decision-making processes. Global trade agreements impact a far broader range of public policies than "just" trade and are created with little public input and thereafter there is little citizen scrutiny of adjudication processes. As Joseph Stiglitz recently put it regarding trade agreements: "Corporations are attempting to achieve by stealth—through secretly negotiated trade agreements—what they could not attain in an open political process."[17]

Citizen input might also usefully introduce different perspectives to debates regarding national security. National governments are steeped in exclusive consideration of national interests and national leaders are wary of doing anything that could be perceived as in any way weakening national security. Citizens are freer to see the world other than through a narrow national interest/national security lens. Citizens are at once part of a community, a nation, and the world in a way that national leaders and national security professionals can never be.

Seeing the world as a global citizen is different from seeing the world as a national citizen. From a global perspective security is the *absence* of war. When citizens of most nations have economic interests (investments, customers, employers, and suppliers), personal links, and relatives almost everywhere that is especially true. In an age of global integration war makes less and less sense through any lens but one that is narrowly and exclusively nation-centric. From a global citizen's perspective there are security priorities other than arms expenditures—poverty, disease and environmental sustainability are also security priorities from a citizen perspective.

This increasing need and inclination to think globally applies to corporations as well. Most corporations of any size today are globally integrated. They produce, sell and have employees, customers, and investments everywhere. At the same time, from a community perspective security is all about sustainability: sustainability of food supplies, energy, and socio-economic viability. David Orr and others, for example, have worked to build a sustainable community in Oberlin, Ohio and similar efforts are underway in communities around the world.[18] This is a very different meaning of security than is usually thought of when national security is considered.

Illustrative of just how much perspectives are changing in these matters, Orr's undertaking has gotten the attention of American defense analysts Mark Mykleby and Wayne Porter. Mykleby and Porter appreciate that sustainability can indeed contribute to national security. Regarding energy policy, this was an argument raised in Amory and Hunter Lovins's book *Brittle Power: Energy Strategy for National Security* in 1982. Lovins and Lovins argued that small scale renewable energy sources were more easily integrated into national security considerations than were large centralized energy supply sources especially nuclear power.

The argument presented by Mykleby and Porter is broader than the Lovins' argument. Mykleby and Porter consider sustainability, globalization, and national security suggesting that such linkages are increasingly appreciated today. Indeed the US Army Net Zero energy program already looks to radically improve energy efficiency and onsite renewable energy production and to apply a Net Zero approach to both water and waste as well.[19]

In the same spirit, Porter was quoted in May of 2011 by the *New York Times* as noting that: "Poorly fitted air-conditioners cost New York City 130 to 180 million dollars a year in extra energy consumption" and "They generate 370,535 extra tons of carbon dioxide."[20] In this, there is a potential to fundamentally rethink the meaning of vulnerability, security, national interests, and defense—a global citizen's movement could encourage such rethinking both within the United States and globally.

In a paper for the Woodrow Wilson Center Porter and Mykleby (under the pseudonym "Mr. Y") argued that: "while the dramatic acceleration of globalization over the last fifteen years has provided for the cultural, intellectual and social commingling among people on every continent, of every race, and of every ideology, it has also increased international economic interdependence and has made a narrowly domestic economic perspective an unattractive impossibility."[21] America's national interest, they asserted, requires a healthy *global* economy—and that global prosperity is in and of itself an enduring American national interest.

Security in this more comprehensive sense is seen by Porter and Mykleby as America's other enduring national interest and in that regard they say: "In our complex, interdependent, and constantly changing global environment security is not for one nation, or by one people alone; rather it must be recognized as a common interest among all peoples."[22] They went on some months later to specifically support less dependence on globally sourced energy and food as a way to enhance America's sense of security. Coupled with seeing global prosperity as an element of American security, defense and security come to be seen very differently. Rather than understanding security exclusively in terms of military threats defense and security can be understood in relation to global prosperity and community-based sustainability. These insights, held by analysts within America's military (one in the Navy, one in the Marines) suggest that a global citizen's movement could indeed potentially have a broad base.

China and Global Citizenship's Core Challenge

Global citizenship's core challenge is two-headed. Paul Collier, referencing Nicholas Stern, identified the heart of the central challenge when he wrote: "Restoring environmental order and eradicating global poverty have become the two defining challenges of our era.... if we fail in either we fail in both."[23] The challenge is, of course, complicated by the reality that economic growth has historically posed new environmental costs, as may as in some ways be the case regarding biodiversity, habitat, and climate change. As well, economic growth does not necessarily lead to poverty reduction. The challenges visible in Kyoto and New Orleans are thus bound together as these are the solutions to those problems.

Tariq Banuri and Niclas Hällström have broadly considered the links between climate and economic development policies, specifically the need for simultaneous delivery of *broader* energy access globally and *reduced* greenhouse gas emissions.[24] These authors make the case that very low energy use nations do not consume enough electricity to meet basic health and human development needs while high energy use nations beyond a threshold of total consumption do not gain positive health and human development increments from additional energy use. The authors also argue for globally funded national feed-in tariffs for renewable energy. This is an approach potentially consistent with global governance without full-blown global government.

As noted, in recent decades economic inequality has risen within most nations including the United States and China.[25] As well, the economic advance of China over the past several decades has been dramatic. This shift, a singular achievement, has helped to lift millions out of poverty. The extent of the transformation came home to me recently in a Chinese restaurant in Milan where I went for a meal when I arrived in the city on an unknown-to-me local holiday. I wanted Italian food, but most restaurants were closed for the day. The one restaurant that was open was filled with busloads of prosperous young Chinese tourists, many of whom spoke fluent English. They were touring Italy, viewing world cultural treasures and had shopped at Prada while in Milan. Twenty years ago such mass excursions, which they told me were common, would have been unimaginable.

China's economic miracle has, however, come at a very great price. Not only has China become the leading contributor to climate change, it has done enormous damage to its own air and water quality.[26] Recently China has made strides in the field of solar energy, but economic expansion has been so rapid that it also continues to increase fossil fuel use and remains the world's leading consumer of coal. When economic growth at a rate of 9 to 10 percent is seen as necessary to expand employment sufficiently to avoid social unrest it is a very great challenge to also *reduce* fossil fuel consumption.

Thus global carbon emissions continue to rise. Even if Europe and North America find ways to reduce demand, an uncertain prospect, slowing total global use will not be easy. Even in 2010, a poor year economically in most places, global carbon emissions grew by 5.9 percent—in absolute terms the highest increase in emissions on record. The tension between the goal of reducing economic inequality and the goal of protecting the environment is a staggering challenge that will require massive efforts from every nation, especially the wealthiest nations. This dual objective is an enormous challenge, but it is possible if governments, firms, and individuals accept the responsibility of taking it on.

North America: Exceptional in Reluctance?

Without a shift in global politics larger than "just" the continuing election of globally mindful administrations in Washington progress on key global issues may be insufficient. One of the crucial tasks of global citizens is convincing Americans and through them America that global governance is desirable and possible. Much of that task falls to those Americans open to a global perspective.[27] American suspicion of "globalism" arises primarily out of long-standing hegemonic power. Somehow more Americans need to see that hegemonic power is not an at-all-costs priority and that global affairs could be managed both more effectively and at a lower cost.

The best-case scenario would see more Americans realize that a *truly* exceptional hegemonic power would focus on both global and American needs and that the two sets of needs do not necessarily conflict. American political ideas at their best would support and enrich a democratization of global governance. American enrichments could arise out of centuries of everyday practice regarding federalism, subsidiarity, and democracy.

America also, albeit slowly and painfully, continues to reduce prejudice and has become comprehensively diverse in terms of race, religion, and national origin. This diversity is an insufficiently appreciated asset globally. It is a great irony that those who most vehemently celebrate America's global power often resist the increased political role of America's visible minorities.

The United States is, however, nothing if not politically complex. Historically it has moved the world toward global governance on more than one occasion. It played a central role in the creation of both the League of Nations and the United Nations. More recently, Americans led the Earth Charter initiative. North Americans inspired the modern environmental movement and created many of its leading global organizations. In the late 1960s and the 1970s the United States passed pathbreaking environmental legislation that has been imitated around the world. Support for that legislation included (hard as it is to remember now) many leading Republicans of the day.

Also, as noted, individual Americans are involved in global citizenship undertakings including the Great Transition Initiative (GTI). GTI seeks to advance "a just and sustainable society and a global consciousness."[28] Other Americans are active in the gamut of global development organizations and lead many of them. While American foreign aid contributions are low as a proportion of GNP compared to European nations, many American-based civil society organizations are creative, active, and generous in their development efforts. Many such organizations work to simultaneously advance economic development and environmental protection.[29]

In contrast, leading Republicans still recite a mantra of American exceptionalism as a doctrine of military dominance and could return to power with this ideology intact. In 2012 Republican primary candidates competed to deny climate change and to advocate abandoning spending on health, education, infrastructure, and public pensions in favor of additional spending on weapons. During Obama's second term leading Republicans favored American military action in many nations and, with some Democrats, flatly opposed diplomatic engagement with Iran regarding nuclear power and nuclear weapons.

American *citizens*, however, by choosing to act with citizens around the world, could express positive ways America actually is exceptional. They could infuse America's historic strengths into citizen-led global politics. Those historic strengths include citizen participation, technological and entrepreneurial creativity, democracy, the hard-won evolution of tolerance, and an abiding concern with the excessive concentration of power.

Recalling events in our tale of three cities those strengths remain an ongoing struggle, but they are still there—in the writings of America's founders and in the nation's history, including its recent history. America could still assume technological and even policy leadership regarding a post-carbon future. It could gradually reduce military spending thereby encouraging others to do the same. It might even reduce poverty both internally and globally, support the coordinated global regulation of financial industries and return to global leadership regarding environmental protection and human rights. Even if unlikely in the short term, all of these things are possible.

These things are consistent with the positive side of American history and with the desires of many of its citizens, even though the political opposition to such initiatives would be intense. One can hear the shouts: "betraying America's greatness," "undermining the nation's defenses," "weakening the economy," "expanding government," "bankrupting the nation," and "destroying freedom." In his first term President Obama was wisely cautious, excessively so some would say, and yet was branded as a Kenyan Muslim Socialist on talk radio, conservative websites, and at Tea Party rallies, as if there were many such persons anywhere on earth, let alone in the White House. One can only hope that this climate will moderate in time.

Another positive side of America is found in local, deliberative democracy as in the famed New England town meetings. As noted municipal governments have done the most (at least within the United States) regarding climate change. Many other local initiatives on many issues are identified by Susan Clark and Woden Teachout in their book *Slow Democracy* (a title adapted from the highly participatory slow food movement).³⁰ For these authors and many Americans local policy settings work best.

This perspective is important to moving global citizenship and global needs forward—it is only locally, for example, that climate damaging sprawl can be changed and it is only locally that most citizens have the confidence, resources, and connections to act. The challenge is to motivate them to act *simultaneously* in many places regarding global needs that in most cases have both local outcomes and (partial) solutions.

Without citizen activism few national leaders will be assertive regarding these matters. Most national leaders are cautious regarding both entrenched wealth within their own nations and resistance from other, more powerful, nations. More than that, national leaders are predisposed to thinking through a nationalistic lens. A global perspective, for them, will be suspect unless many within their nation are visibly supportive of such a perspective. Leadership on these matters must originate with active citizens—perhaps supported, issue by issue, by national leaders of exceptional courage and foresight.

Where else in the world might policy leadership, whether citizen or official, emerge? The answer is that it can and must emerge everywhere. Global change regarding economic inequality, environmental protection, and human rights must be just that, global.

Europe, especially before the post-2010 austerity binge, provided global leadership on many issues and was the leading source of concrete steps toward global objectives. Centuries of war dampened European enthusiasm for nation-centric egotism and created popular support for limited military budgets. European nations and citizens still lead the way on resolving global-scale problems. Scandinavian nations in particular contribute heavily to development aid. Indeed Europe and some Latin American nations are where support by national governments for a global agenda is most advanced.

Regarding climate change Europe has for decades led on energy efficiency and renewable energy. The efforts of Germany, Denmark, Spain, and others on renewables have been exemplary and the community and small-owner base of these developments a model for how to overcome NIMBYism. Europeans have also championed the International Criminal Court and led on protecting human rights globally and on per capita aid to poor nations. Unlike the United States there remains in Europe a political consensus on valuing the core components of the welfare state. One might reasonably expect citizen participation in global environmental and equity initiatives from Europeans.

Though other than in Brazil support for a global agenda in rapidly industrializing nations is less reliable than in Europe, the world might benefit from the transformation in expectations in those nations. The so-called BRIIC nations (Brazil, Russia, India, Indonesia, and China) all have had rapid economic growth, but face a daunting need to continuously expand employment. Weapons procurement is money that cannot be spent on job-rich infrastructure or economically crucial health and education. Weapons production is less employment intensive and recent estimates suggest that violence and its consequences cost 11 percent of global GDP in 2012.[31] For these reasons these nations may be open to improved global governance or might be open to resisting arms races.

Japan has great potential as a contributor to global citizenship. It is highly advanced technologically but has long been mired in slow growth. Japan has steadfastly opposed militarism and resists entreaties to spend more on arms. It has a very trade-oriented economy, plays an important role in global finance, and is now committed to reducing dependence on nuclear power. Lacking fossil fuel resources it has great potential as a leader in renewable energy development. As well, as a long-standing American ally with regional and global influence it could play a large role in advancing global initiatives.

Smaller nations, especially in the global South, would gain a greater voice were global governance to advance. Addressing climate change, developing energy alternatives, protecting human rights and improving social equity will aid citizens in these nations. Many of these nations are already well ahead of the curve in terms of the proportion of energy from renewable sources and have the potential to continue on that path. Nicaragua hopes to be above 94 percent renewable electricity by 2017 and many African and Asian nations get much of their electricity from hydro alone.[32] Kenya produces solar panels domestically and plans, incredibly, to get as much as 50 percent of its electricity from solar by 2016.[33] As well, perhaps the most cost effective global strategy for rapid GHG reductions is providing efficient cookers to the poor in poor nations to reduce black carbon (soot) emissions from cooking fires.[34]

Some nations in the Middle East, North Africa, and South Asia have great potential regarding renewable energy. Some are also both highly unequal and among the worst offenders on human rights, especially the rights of women—global initiatives in these realms will have at least muted support in these nations.[35] In the realm of renewable energy Saudi Arabia and others are investing heavily in solar and wind. A gradual slowing of global oil demand would make Middle Eastern oil wealth last longer and solar energy development there would leave more oil for long-term export. Enhanced global governance would benefit all nations in the global South by creating forums wherein citizen voices might be heard. If global governance has any meaning citizen voices will be heard unrelated to the size of their nation.

Canada and Australia are highly trade oriented and both use energy inefficiently. Historically both have been open to global governance. However, Canada's Harper government has been systematically hostile to climate initiatives and has made the unlimited expansion of the tar sands the centerpiece of Canada's economic future. This government has put aside Canada's multilateral traditions that have included a deep commitment to diplomacy and peacekeeping and become the only nation to renounce its Kyoto commitments. It has pursued a policy strategy that is problematic both environmentally and economically.[36] Australia's government alternates between climate action and rejection of action despite the vulnerability of Australia to climate impacts.

Canadian citizens played a central role in the Brundtland Commission and in founding key global civil society organizations including Greenpeace and Doctors without Borders.[37] This and Canada's long-standing support for multilateralism and global environmental initiatives, most notably the treaties on ozone depletion and persistent organic pollutants (POPs), have seemingly been forgotten and the nation has instead become a global climate pariah. Australia's Howard government rejected climate action despite the fact that Australia had just benefitted disproportionately from the Montreal Protocol, the pioneering global ozone depletion initiative. Both nations are severely divided regarding global concerns, but as in America many individual citizens are actively involved.

America and Canada face significant challenges regarding their roles *as nations* in the emergence of global citizenship. *Citizens* of these nations, however, are not necessarily constrained by these circumstances. Indeed, individual citizens could be further motivated by their sometimes embarrassing national context. Citizens might be inspired to address the very issues their governments will not address. Electing governments that will act effectively is the primary challenge.

Citizens in many nations are well ahead of national leaders in understanding human needs from a global perspective. Many more would act on those needs were there more opportunities to do so. Too many political figures are self-interested above all and narrowly nationalist. Collectively, as climate change negotiations in Copenhagen, Durban, and Warsaw demonstrated, most leaders are unable to act effectively with regard to pressing global challenges. Collective action on global inequality is a consistent failure. Some new political actor, citizens, must alter the conversation and change the global political mix.

All nations are exceptional in some way. One dimension of American exceptionalism is a centuries-long capacity to invent, evolve, and adapt. Given the pressures America faces today related to the cost of hegemonic military power and the declining need for power *in traditional forms* in a world that is rapidly integrating, many Americans understand that it is time to adapt again. It is time to walk away from a perceived perpetual need for overwhelming military superiority. America's military is more than sufficient within a world where no combination of other nations can mount a serious challenge.

America *could* refocus its military on literal defense and rebuild America's economy, infrastructure and social equity on the savings. American citizens, and its government, could join in the collective resolution of global problems. That would be a genuine and exciting demonstration of American exceptionalism for the twenty-first century.

Great Power Rivalry, National Interests and Global Citizenship

Just as Occupy Wall Street briefly changed the political conversation in North America and elsewhere from deficits and austerity to rising social inequality, a global citizen's movement could shift the center of attention in global affairs from national interests and great power rivalries to an enduring emphasis on the real problems that citizens face. Just as deficits are not forgotten when issues more urgent to a majority are raised so too global citizens remain national citizens not unaware of their nations' concerns and interests.

Indeed a global conversation about everyday human needs would provide expanded opportunities for national concerns to be heard. It is, of course, crucial that national aspirations not come at the expense of other nations or peoples. There is a difference between national aspirations that seek domination internally or externally and those which seek greater equality. One cannot pretend that universal agreement within a global citizen's movement will be easily achieved.

It is, however, in the interest of *all* nations to avoid great power rivalries and arms races. Such rivalries pressure smaller nations to take sides and expend capital that cannot then be spent on other priorities, including global priorities. Smaller nations then increase their own military spending either to please great powers or to raise the cost of being attacked. They too end up spending less on their own people's everyday needs and are, at the same time, under reduced pressure to make social expenditures since rich nations engaged in an arms race are not setting the standard of broad-based prosperity they might otherwise set.

Without civil society organizations other perspectives would rarely be heard. Rivalries and arms races are just assumed to be the all-but-inevitable way of the world. Military expenditures are automatically assumed to be a high priority and inequality something that little can be done about. Other perspectives are needed within the worlds of statecraft and media-intoned urgency including those that assert that energy policy and environmental protection are at the heart of protecting our security, those who imagine that fewer foreign military bases are necessary and those who think that rising economic inequality is an urgent matter. These voices need to be heard.

Rather unexpectedly in 2014 one such voice regarding inequality was widely heard. Thomas Piketty, a French economist, produced a 700-page book that in translation suddenly became a bestseller.[38] *Capital in the 21st Century* reviews detailed data from hundreds of years of economic history in multiple Western nations to painstakingly demonstrate that in most times and places the return on capital exceeds the rate of economic growth. As a result those who hold capital gain ground relative to the larger number of citizens who do not, thus a tendency to rising inequality is inherent in the system. It is also likely, of course, self-reinforcing politically.

Piketty's policy solution to this systemic flaw is a global tax on wealth. Some argue that he does not adequately address how such policies might come to be adopted. He does, however, show that the pattern of rising inequality did not hold everywhere in the decades following World War II when among other things unemployment in Western nations was low and pent up demand and rapid growth empowered labor and citizens to press for anti-inequality wages, benefits and policies. Clearly, as Piketty argues, global policies are what is needed today. These will require global scale political action in some form.[39] Again, there appears to be no alternative to citizen action on a global scale.

Wicked Problems and Elegant Solutions

Global problems are mostly *wicked problems*, but a global citizen's movement might help to build the knowledge and will necessary to adopt *elegant solutions* at all levels of governance and within many sectors of society. To understand why citizen action on a global scale is crucial, we need to review definitions of these terms.

Wicked problems have far-reaching consequences, have no "right" answer (only better and worse options for action), offer few or no opportunities to learn through trial and error, and time is running out to take action.[40] Some are highly likely to become global problems when they are not resolved elsewhere. Climate change is a thoroughly wicked problem. Social inequality does offer some opportunities for trial and error and it is not "on the clock" in the same way as climate change, but it does have far-reaching social consequences and few obvious answers in many circumstances. Mercifully, not all issues that would face a global citizen's movement are wicked problems.

Indeed many of the global problems discussed here, including inequality, violations of human rights, military spending and war are wicked in a different way: they may be eternal. At the least they have always been with us. In this sense there is not a deadline by which they *must* be resolved. Yet they are compellingly urgent to millions of victims. Resolving these problems is so complex and challenging that humans have not yet resolved them though arguably we have slowly gained ground over the centuries.

Perhaps the greatest challenge is to imagine that solutions to these problems are possible and that, especially on a global scale, individuals can do anything meaningful about them. That is precisely why a *movement* is essential. Getting people to expend time and money on problems that are seemingly eternal and/or wicked problems, requires that ongoing action is visible and that allies, in vast numbers or with great influence, or both, exist. That is what only a social movement can do.

It is otherwise too easy to just assume that problems that have always existed always will exist or, as is too often the case with climate change, to just claim or even believe that the problem does not exist. Or, that since its worst effects are not yet in our face we can leave it to the future (when action will be too late). Initiating a movement may also require conveying a wide appreciation of the possibility of elegant solutions.

Elegant solutions are undertakings that contribute to the solution of a variety of problems *simultaneously*. The first time I came upon the term was in the early 1970s, in the comments of Amory Lovins.[41] In Lovins's view small scale, renewable energy sources and energy efficiency were an elegant solution that led to more secure sources of supply, less pollution, more jobs, a lower likelihood of nuclear proliferation and greater economic stability compared to energy from fossil fuels and/or nuclear power.

Potentially, many elegant solutions to global problems are possible. Consider, for example, that public expenditures on education produce three times as many jobs per dollar spent as spending on military procurement. Health care expenditures produce twice the jobs per dollar of military spending. Health and education improvements also have a very large effect on the quality of human lives. Educational advances reduce the incidence of crime, lead to greater optimism about the future and to voluntary restraints on family size, strengthen families and promote innovation and economic growth above and beyond the more direct employment increases. That is as elegant as solutions get, yet in many nations educational budgets are slashed while military budgets grow.

Advances in gender equality also have multiple positive effects. So too do initiatives that advance the self-production and local production of food and something as simple as the availability of clean water. In each of these cases economies gain ground, health is improved and medical costs are reduced or avoided. In combination work time available is increased and life expectancy is extended. More readily available small business loans would create additional positive social and economic effects.

The restoration and protection of forests can also be an elegant solution. Forests supply wildlife habitat, food (nuts, berries, roots, fungi, honey, meat, and other foods) as well as fuel. They protect watersheds, build soil and help to fight desertification and the resulting poverty. Forests sequester carbon and thus reduce climate change while they help humans to adapt to it by protecting soil and reducing aridity. Planting and maintaining forests supplies jobs and the resulting forests create jobs in perpetuity.

Many new technologies also have the potential to contribute to the resolution of global problems in multiple ways. Cell phones and low-cost devices that can access the Internet open the possibility of communicating more cheaply. They could make access to the libraries, art and music of the world near to universal and do so using only relatively modest amounts of energy. The potential to improve education and health care in poor nations, especially where transportation is a great challenge, is enormous. Powering these devices and providing access to clean water with renewable energy is also an exciting and increasingly affordable possibility.

We face such an array of global problems we *need* elegant solutions and are fortunate that they exist and that we have the capacity to invent new ones. We also now have the ability to globally communicate those new possibilities instantly.[42] The creation and pressure to adopt elegant solutions could be accelerated by a global citizen's movement working through civil society organizations, international organizations and all levels of government.

Global Citizenship and Policy Innovation

A viable global citizen's movement could greatly expand the opportunities for human ingenuity to create and communicate solutions to global problems. Innovative policy, market and personal and organizational initiatives at all levels and within civil society are already communicated globally, but a global citizen's movement could create new online forums and new face-to-face contacts to accelerate communication to everyday citizens who can then urge the ideas on *their* governments and organizations.

A global citizen's movement could also accelerate technological and policy innovations by making more people aware of the array of challenges facing communities all over the planet. There are individuals and organizations determined to help with the challenges that others face, but too few fully understand what those challenges are in direct and personal terms. Communication through new kinds of global interaction can only help. Other communities may have faced similar challenges previously. Distant people might also learn that their own nations have contributed to creating those challenges and that the solution lies other than with those who personally face the challenge.

In some cases problems can only be resolved by much of the world working together toward a solution. This is another reason why a global citizen's movement is essential, particularly with regard to climate change where not only policy changes are necessary but some modifications of personal behavior are as well. It would be far easier for individuals, communities and firms to change behaviors if they were confident that others were making equivalent adjustments. That vital communication is within the power of a movement.

When new rules regarding the behavior of corporations or governmental institutions is required, citizen pressure will need to be mobilized and coordinated globally. Such an effort is likely needed regarding the regulation of financial institutions so influential that governments impose austerity on entire populations rather than allow those interests to bear the costs of their own business decisions.[43] These institutions will not easily come to accept regulation. Nor will defense industries or oil companies simply accept that some of what they produce with taxpayer help is now less essential than it once was and indeed does more harm than good given the rate at which we use it. These are indeed issues where *only* a global citizen's movement with considerable political power can tip the political scales away from the status quo.

Our final chapter discusses signs that active global citizenship may be emerging.

6
Conclusion: Building Global Citizenship

Modern anthropology and archeology suggest that everyone presently living on earth may descend from a single woman who lived in East-Central Africa about 150 millennia ago. This hypothetical person has been called "Mitochondrial Eve.". Mitochondrial DNA passes from mother to child. Fossil and DNA evidence points to the possibility that she is everyone's most recent common ancestor. She was not the only living person at the time, but direct lines from the others were presumably discontinuous (life along the way not having been easy). Whether this particular common human origin is entirely correct or not, there is little doubt that today's humans are of common descent.

More importantly, we also now share a common fate that requires a widely shared policy, regulatory and legal response. Nuclear weapons, terrorism, and technologically advanced armies, climate change, global economic integration, hegemonic power, and habitat loss are all part of that shared fate.

It is in this context that global citizens embrace the collective interests of all nations and people. We who hope to see where a wider acceptance of this perspective might lead are not a majority, but we can imagine a common global interest, very open in its content, that includes the concerns that flow from events in our three cities. Presently national leaders embrace that vision comprehensively at considerable political risk.

Thus it is frustrating that those who see the potential of active global citizenship are for the most part isolated from each other. Given polling data and other clues we know that many who share these views exist, but it is hard to know who or where they are or how deep a commitment they might be prepared to accept.

This isolation can end. Emerging communications capacities open the way to new global linkages. World cities where the global array of languages, cultures, commerce, arts, and science mix daily are increasingly common. People everywhere are increasingly familiar with the music, sports, food, literature, film, economies, and recent history of world regions other than their own. As well, larger numbers than ever have resided in other nations or maintain a media-based familiarity with other cultures. These things do not guarantee a wide embrace of global citizenship, but they can help to make it a possibility.

Humankind now instantly shares events globally—starting each year with the first major New Year's celebration in the harbor in Sydney, Australia, and moving around the planet electronically. Music of all kinds, the Olympics and soccer (as well as basketball, golf, and tennis) increasingly share a world following, and top competitors from most nations. These things are arguably superficial, but science and commerce are also now globally shared endeavors. And every academic discipline and profession has global networks. English is spoken globally, as a primary or second language, especially in business and scholarship. Indeed, almost every human activity now has a global network.

Even though increasingly the risks we face and the solutions to them are global this hardly means that an influential global citizen's movement is imminent. Some global risks require citizen action at every level, including individual actions, civil society organizations, corporations, and governments, as well as global cooperation, but neither the stark reality of the problems, nor the possibility of global solutions guarantees the emergence of a global citizen's movement.

There are many reasons for this. Language and cultural differences remain and rivalries and resentments are common even among nations similarly situated. The gaps between rich nations and poor are formidable and it is not easy for citizens of either to imagine objectives in common with those in the other. Economic challenges also produce resistance to multilateral initiatives. Most of all the possibility of global cooperation seems if not impossible, surely something that is someone else's business, not something regarding which many can imagine playing a significant role.

Finally here there are intellectual objections to cosmopolitanism and global governance—objections beyond the usual xenophobic inclinations. Michael Lind, for example, makes the case that *only* nation states command a popular willingness to pay taxes, support armies, obey legislation, and tolerate redistribution on behalf of all. As he puts it: "The nation-state is the largest unit that has been able to combine effective government with a sense of solidarity among its citizens."[1] True enough, but this does not limit citizens anywhere from engaging in actions regarding global challenges or pressing for government initiatives regarding those challenges. Citizen action is especially important regarding matters that government leaders hesitate to advance lest national (or their own) power and authority be diminished.

Global Citizenship and National Democracy

When bombing Baghdad and, despite having made the largest historical contribution to climate change, refusing to acknowledge the problem or participate in a collective solution, America was a rogue hegemon. Even during Obama's first term, despite important initiatives on renewable energy and automobile fuel efficiency, in Durban the Obama administration accepted delaying extension of Kyoto, hardly a position of leadership.

Lind argues that there is an inherent reluctance in powerful nations to cede autonomous national power.[2] It is particularly a challenge for an American president to lead on many global matters—both because of the distrust within other nations regarding American motives and because of *American* expectations regarding American power. Even *appearing* to cede autonomous power is politically risky. American citizens, local and state governments, corporations and civil society are perhaps better placed to initially act on global challenges.

However, in some contexts, "even hegemonic governments may act on matters that are" pressed on them. One of those contexts may arise in the face of "budgetary restraints." Some will defend any and all military spending, but in the face of rising deficits others might remember that America need not be the world's policeman. As well, others might come on side if restraint of military spending is needed to avoid slashing social programs. Where such possibilities might lead is unknown, but they might be political opportunities for global citizens.

Lind imagines a future where the world's leading powers are America, China, India, and Brazil. Like most traditional foreign policy analysts, he contemplates rivalries and weighs relative national power and, like many conservative Americans, he dismisses Europe's prospects. Lind appreciates that smaller powers will prefer increased global governance wherein they might have a less negligible voice. Otherwise they would, as he indelicately puts it, have no more capacity to alter the course of events than the barnacles on the back of a whale.[3] The *citizens* of smaller nations might well also prefer multilateralism, but, and here Lind would likely disagree, so too might some citizens of great powers, the whales of the world. They might especially prefer multilateralism if it meant not having to move in with their children in old age.

Seeing the world from the point of view of *citizens* of the United States, China, India, and Brazil often escapes foreign policy analysts for whom the nation state is the central unit of analysis and national power, not citizen well-being, the currency of political life. In this view citizens (including American citizens) are in effect microbes on those barnacles on the side of the whales. Citizens of great powers (as noted earlier) vicariously identify with the power of their nations, but they also increasingly understand that the power comes in lieu of other needs and priorities. Events in Baghdad and New Orleans could not have rendered that more apparent.

As well, as a Canadian observer of Asian politics recently noted, "Fully half of China's billion citizens subsist on sub-Saharan incomes of less than $2 a day and they're growing increasingly impatient with the corruption, oppression and persecution that has accompanied the stuffing of Beijing's foreign-reserves treasury."[4] Spending on military hardware necessary to challenge American hegemony even regionally is money not spent on advancing China's poor. India is poorer. Millions of these nation's citizens want better housing and consumer products like refrigerators, cell phones, and motorbikes.

Are rising nations necessarily America's rivals? Is there any reason that citizens of these nations (including America) could not forge direct connections, build trust and establish a sense of common purpose that includes mutually restrained military spending and sustainable economic well-being as a shared priority? In today's world these nations are already, and increasingly, business partners, why would they become rivals locked in an arms race? If national leaders cannot see the folly of militarism in today's world, surely citizens who pay for arms races in missed opportunities can come to do so. Some foreign policy analysts may prefer the logic of earlier centuries, but citizens must live in this one. We can see the ways it is different.

Anka Lee urges Americans to see that improved labor rights for Chinese workers would be to both China and America's economic benefit.[5] Prices for Chinese goods would rise and thus more products would be manufactured in the United States. However, more Chinese workers could buy Chinese goods and the Chinese state would perhaps feel less compelled to subsidize exports. A comparable case could be made for restoring unionization and middle-class industrial wages in America as to the advantage of Chinese workers. Those workers would be able to buy more Chinese made goods. Obviously there are trade-offs to be made here and who better to make them than workers and unions from *both* countries communicating with each other. That is clearly a step well beyond rivalry, one that might be greeted with suspicion by elites in both nations.

There is another compelling reason for direct contact among citizens: climate change seems to be beyond the diplomatic capacities of national governments. The core problem is this: long-term solutions involve leaving some fossil energy in the ground—to use it more slowly than we might, even at the possible cost of slowing development that is desperately needed to lift people in rising nations out of poverty. Given historic fossil energy use patterns, this is fundamentally unfair and would be one of the great injustices of an often unjust human history.

What this great unfairness implies from the perspective of global citizenship is that economic development in China, India, and many other nations is now very much *our problem* here in the North. Climate change can only be kept in check if wealthy nations do two things: one, make it easier for poor nations to achieve low carbon economic development[6] and two, rapidly reduce our own dependence on fossil fuels—without undermining *our* economic and social stability, a stability that still anchors the global economy (making *our* economic success the business of China, India, and the others). In short, we are now unavoidably in this together.

I cannot think of any other way for the dual challenges of climate change and development than for *citizens of all nations* to better understand our common needs and each other's domestic challenges. Nussbaum's narrative imagination, the capacity to appreciate not just how we would experience the existence of others, but how *they* experience it, would aid this understanding.[7] That understanding must be sufficiently deep that nations and citizens actually take ownership not only of their own social and economic problems, but also those of other nations and their citizens. Is such mutual resolve and the global conversation it implies possible? If citizens were to lead the way national leaders and foreign policy analysts can perhaps begin to break away from a focus on great power rivalries.

A global citizen's movement would be "a new actor on the global stage" and could induce such reconsideration.[8] It might even help to make citizen well-being the highest priority and increasingly unaffordable military power, especially disproportionate power, an unnecessary luxury. Until that shift comes it is just too easy for national leaders to imagine (or pretend) that power in their hands is the best route to citizen well-being and for citizens to imagine that national military power makes their lives better than other uses of those resources might.

A global citizen's movement, with active, interlinked groups in communities in many nations would enhance democracy around the world. Citizens could learn about public initiatives in other nations directly from those that participate in them (rather than, e.g., Americans just hearing them dismissed as "European socialism" or simply ignored by their media). More as well might come to see the diversity in American opinion and experience rather than knowing America only as a nation of vast wealth with a military presence everywhere. Surely this would broaden the range of considerations that enter public discourse.

It is not that people around the world do not know each other and how government functions elsewhere better than previously, it is that they do not know these things as well as they might. Opportunities for direct citizen-to-citizen communication regarding comparative experiences and concerns would make everyone better citizens within their own nations.

As well, linking single-issue global campaigns and organizations might facilitate more communication across borders and language barriers and generate positive synergies. In particular it is crucial to know how parallel concerns have been resolved in other jurisdictions. How does child care operate in Danish communities? What do others think of the policies and actions of one's own nation? How were people mobilized elsewhere to achieve something deeply desired at home? How could citizen cooperation get governments to collectively confront common problems? Global interaction would make individuals better citizens locally and nationally.

In sum, participation in a global citizen's movement would enhance democracy by adding comparative information and increasing citizen efficacy. It would also reduce fears regarding other peoples and places. Needless to say xenophobes will not readily participate, but their children or grandchildren or neighbors might. A movement may not quickly lead to change in global governance processes. In time, however, it could influence the behavior of particular nations, alter the political priorities of individuals and change what people think might be possible regarding global problems.

Even modest changes may not come easily. Patience and long-term thinking are essential, though small victories are important. The admirable Millennium Development Goals were set and continue going forward, but too few nations have acted decisively on an agenda that benefits a global majority.[9] One can only wonder what might happen if those goals are pushed on governments by millions of citizens acting in concert.

In contrast the stability, security, and safety of the world remain at risk if most people continue to accept the conventional meanings of those terms. An active global citizen's movement might slowly shift that reality. The hope in particular is that an inclusive, participatory, democratic, citizen-oriented way of thinking about and acting upon global concerns could lead more Americans to see that even a limited expansion of global governance could lighten the burdens of hegemonic power. Many Americans would, of course, resist that, but they are not necessarily a majority. Indeed, even some very conservative Americans are more open to some global goals than might be expected.

For example, the ultraconservative Tea Party in the conservative state of Georgia has worked with the Sierra Club to advance local renewable energy initiatives through a joint campaign cleverly called the Green Tea Coalition.[10] Solar power in the sunny state of Georgia is economically efficient, advances local jobs, decentralization and small businesses—all goals to which conservatives can relate. The advancement of global goals regarding climate change is, in effect, incidental. The important thing is policy change on the ground. The Georgia Public Service Commission in a 3–2 vote incorporated 775 megawatts of solar power into its 20-year electricity capacity plan.

As noted, the idea of global agendas can cause people to instinctively retreat into distrust. It is difficult to imagine influencing governance in a medium sized city, let alone a planet. Yet global citizens *already* address each of these problems at many levels—from the personal to the local, national, and global.

First Steps

Citizenship is inherently an amateur activity in the best sense of the word. It is one of the things people do when they are not trying to earn a living (though citizenship of course comes into play within the economic realm as well). For most, however, being a citizen is an incidental matter. For others it is a consuming passion. Increasingly, citizenship may have a global dimension. Citizens open to global concerns understand that if the twenty-first century is to be better than, or even as good as, earlier centuries they, and many others, must accept global obligations as well as national and local obligations.

For many, global concern begins at a very basic level. They come to realize that within a global economy everyday activities like buying goods, working or investing have global impacts and the implications of everyday activities are unavoidable. We cannot just pretend that global impacts of our actions do not exist. Our work and our consumption habits affect how people on the other side of the planet live their lives and how our grandchildren will live theirs.

Increasingly these essentially moral arguments are compelling. The logical conclusion is that since economies are now global the obligations and rights of citizenship operate at the same level. Since the fate and the activities of every community and nation are bound up with the fate and the activities of every other community and nation, many new things are everyone's business at least in part. Even absent new global forums, global citizenship manifests itself in our behavior (or our indifference). Global citizenship can be exercised through our day-to-day decisions and through global civil society.

Citizenship, of course, first and foremost, is political, though within that arena the professionals now often overwhelm the amateurs. That could, however, change. Globally, ordinary citizens have always been largely excluded (though the World Social Forum and global civil society are changing that to some extent). Until now there have been few opportunities for citizens to influence policy regarding global concerns.[11] The initiative must begin with citizens, they will not gain opportunities to influence global proceedings without considerable political pressure. They can also build their own sense of political efficacy by pressing for policy action on global concerns locally and nationally. Initiatives might then be spread to other jurisdictions, or initiatives could be pressed concurrently in multiple jurisdictions.[12]

Citizen influence is especially and conspicuously absent within trade negotiations and trade treaty adjudication. Arguably these venues are the nearest thing that exists to global governance or even global government today. The virtual exclusion of social and environmental policy and regulation from these agreements in effects create pressures within every jurisdiction against strong policies in these areas lest nations or smaller jurisdictions place themselves at a competitive disadvantage by acting too decisively. Again, simultaneous similar policy initiatives in multiple jurisdictions might lessen that pressure.

The Internet creates communications possibilities regarding these ends. It makes interactive, self-initiated *global* political communication possible as a broad-based *amateur* activity. In an age when traditional media, especially network television, are in a few hands, these new communications technologies are crucial to the quality of democracy in a global age and can be used creatively in the service of global citizenship.

The Internet and Global Citizenship Revisited

Just as broadly available printing presses enhanced early democracy and narrowly controlled television aided Bush administration unilateralism, new media open opportunities for a citizen role in global political life.[13] It has been decades since Marshall McLuhan observed that we live in a global village, but until recently few fully appreciated the global *political* potential of the multicentered Internet. Again, because it is highly interactive, the Internet can turn citizens into media providers. New media incorporate citizen produced text, sound, photography, and video and instantly connect people directly to the lives and the ideas of others anywhere.

Those in academic, corporate, and governmental circles are familiar with the power of recent innovations and have likely webcast words, images, and ideas. They may have responded directly to follow-up questions from a diverse audience thousands of miles away—questions seamlessly blended with questions from live in-the-room participants. These systems could become more widely available. They could be deployed in public libraries, classrooms, and community centers. They radically lower the cost of global interaction and citizenship activities across borders and, potentially, language barriers. A global citizen's movement could itself broaden access to these communications opportunities.

Another media form with potential for contributing to the creation of a global citizen's movement is the interactive political blog. In America, blog development was spurred by Bush administration malfeasance. The emergence of blogs as a significant political force was one result of the unwillingness of traditional media to challenge the administration in the early days of the Iraq war. Many who opposed the war, deregulation, and tax cuts for the wealthy felt isolated and powerless. Within that political climate political blogs quickly attracted participants.

The Internet has, of course, been seen for some time to have the potential to improve democratic practice by simplifying voter registration and voting.[14] One can be skeptical about those claims, but blogs have impacted political activism in America. One characteristic worth noting is the speed of blog reporting—an item can be noted and confirmed by eye-witnesses, analyzed and compared, linked to related sources, joked about, and connected to similar personal experiences by thousands of citizens around the nation, or around the world, in minutes. Therein rests the potential for *global* citizen journalism and political activism.

Two examples illustrate the potential of this form of communication. After only a few years participation in the political blog *Daily Kos* approached the viewership of cable news stations and exceeded the readership of many major newspapers.[15] It now has over a million registered commenters and a readership larger than that. As important, political blogs *interconnect* with each other and are readily accessible to new readers through search engines and social media. Successful blog writers have moved into other media forms including television, mass circulation newspapers, and books.

Another leading blog www.talkingpointsmemo.com (TPM) from modest beginnings now has a growing staff in offices in New York and Washington. TPM continues to include open comments on most stories and features contributions from readers. In the 2007 US Department of Justice scandal TPM had *readers* sort through thousands of pages of emails released by the administration. The task was completed in a matter of hours.

The blog as a communications form could be a tool for building a global citizen's movement. Blogs and social media enable citizen activism and connect citizens with global civil society organizations. They could also link citizens attuned to global issues. Citizens could interact globally, simultaneously or selectively influence national or local governments regarding global concerns, initiate direct citizen-to-citizen diplomacy, raise funds, or work to change public policies, consumption habits or workplace practices. Some of this, as we will see, is underway.

New media can distribute creative materials as influential as the YouTube presentation by William of the narrative song Yes We Can in Barack Obama's 2008 political campaign. That stunning artistic success built around Obama's own words was viewed multiple millions of times at a crucial point in the primary campaign. It reinforced the political message and made campaign volunteers feel part of an exciting effort. New media can make initiatives visual and visuals viral and do so globally at low cost. Much more could be done were there an established global citizen's movement.

Decentralized media have been utilized particularly effectively by 350.org, the climate change citizen-based juggernaut. Interestingly Bill McKibben has observed that 350.org organizationally and in terms of events is multi-centered much like the energy system it advocates to replace fossil fuels. As he put it the organization is like a "loosely-linked well-distributed power system." They seek "a spread-out and yet thoroughly interconnected movement, a new kind of engaged citizenry." Using social media 350.org triggered simultaneous demonstrations in almost every nation through a web of local organizations and made it all visible globally through a Flickr account. McKibben added that "most of the people doing the work didn't look like environmentalists were supposed to. They were largely poor, black, brown, Asian and young, because that's what the world mostly is."[16]

More could be done to take interconnectivity global. Other examples of the potential exist. Prior to 2008 a blog by an Iraqi woman, under the pseudonym Riverbend, achieved worldwide readership and provided insights into the plight of everyday citizens in war torn Iraq. Such insights were not available in traditional media sources. The Internet is not easily censored. It leaps national borders. Indeed during the early days of the Arab Spring in Egypt and Libya many worked to help social media bypass attempts at closure by threatened dictators.

International organizations and global civil society groups have increasingly used new media effectively. Protests at the time of the 2011 Durban climate change Greenpeace International led meetings were ignored by commercial media, but covered extensively on online sites like Democracy Now. Engineers without Borders and Architects without Borders, two of many associations of sustainability and development minded professionals, recruit members and publicize their undertakings via the Internet.[17] These organizations now have chapters worldwide. But the Internet can also create unexpected global connections; for example, among the urban poor as has been accomplished by Shack/Slum Dwellers International.[18]

The Internet is readily searchable and recallable. Since print, audio, and video is readily stored everywhere, information is less ephemeral.

It is more readily retrieved and forwarded *by citizens* than has been the case with earlier media forms.[19] Those citizens can be anywhere in the world, and information can be quickly and cheaply delivered across borders. The political amnesia beloved of the powerful can be undermined by citizens anywhere using the accessible digital record of earlier words and deeds.[20]

As well, the possibility of public *conversation*, so thoroughly undermined in the television age, can be restored not only on line, but face-to-face in Internet-organized meet-ups, where virtual acquaintances turn into real ones.[21] The annual meetings of American progressive blog participants is called Netroots Nation. As well, under headings like "green drinks" and "drinking liberally" people who have not previously met come together for sociability and discourse in multiple communities. This pattern too can be taken global—if distant contacts are traveling a visit can easily become an occasion to gather like-minded global citizens.

Again, the Internet suspends distance, radically reduces production and distribution costs and is asynchronous in time. It is the first new mass communication tool widely available to ordinary citizens since the pamphlet.[22] If democracy is to thrive and grow, open, low-cost access to the Internet must be expanded and defended (especially through defending net neutrality, the protection of a minimum of access equality). Given the threat to democracy inherent in the increasing concentration of wealth, the quality of democracy depends on communication forms unmediated by wealth. With new media come new possibilities.

Venues for Global Citizen Action

The most important venue for the practice of global citizenship may be national and local politics wherein cosmopolitan citizens' in every nation press their governments to act on global needs. However, the movement may emerge elsewhere initially. Indeed much of today's global citizenship practice exists within global civil society organizations. A great deal has been written about the growing array of citizen organizations within global politics.[23]

Global civil society is comprised of thousands of international organizations, many of them citizen-driven. Organizations include human rights groups like Human Rights Watch and Amnesty International, environmental organizations like Greenpeace and the Rainforest Action Network, aid and development groups like Oxfam and Doctors without Borders and groups that promote fair trade or respond to and participate in major international meetings or negotiations.

These organizations are perhaps today's best opportunity for citizens, other than national and corporate leaders, to participate in global affairs. Citizen participation may go no further than writing a check, reading websites and signing petitions, but other than an opportunity to vote for candidates, this limited participation is not unlike most citizens' participation *within* nations. However, there is potential for more active involvement through these organizations and many global civil society organizations have grown in recent years.

There has been much academic discussion regarding global civil society, but the emergence of global civil society may be only a first step in a deeper democratization of international relations. Citizen participation through global civil society and international organizations is important, but the multitude of organizations could act more synergistically across issues and more individuals could see themselves in a new light—as *citizens* acting globally and more consistently informing their local and national citizen activities with concerns arising out of their global activism.

One step in this direction was the initiative to establish an Earth Charter.[24] This large global consultation process mobilized civic organizations, municipal governments, and other entities in many nations. Thousands of organizations endorsed a "Declaration of Interdependence" and asserted a universal responsibility for natural systems. The declaration also expressed social justice concerns, the peaceful resolution of disputes, and sustainability themes. The initiative was significant because it mobilized and connected local and national organizations everywhere in the service of global needs.

Three other initiatives are Humanwave, On the Commons and Electoral Rebellion.[25] Humanwave mainstreams humanitarianism through visibility created by musicians and others. Its slogan is: "People who are crazy enough to believe that they can change the world might just be crazy enough to do it." The group links donors and volunteers with organizations and needs worldwide. On the Commons seeks to advance a community-oriented, shared resources perspective. The organization sponsors conferences, a magazine and a website and cites the World Social Forum assertion that "Commons-based management, participation, collaborative and transparent, offers the best hope for building a world that is sustainable, fair and life-giving."

Electoral Rebellion for Global Democracy is the full name of the third organization. It began with individual Israelis offering their votes to individual Palestinians on the grounds that Palestinians were vitally affected by Israeli elections, but could not vote. The website grew, using facebook, and many votes have been transferred through it. The mission broadened to include Germans offering their votes to southern Europeans whose lives were "affected by German politics." Messages exchanged on the site suggest a need for more effective European elections as well as an elected UN parliamentary assembly. These efforts all seek to better align democracy with the political jurisdictions that most affect people's lives.

These three initiatives create new opportunities for global citizen action. Thousands of others exist. More ongoing actions including very tough-minded citizen initiatives are needed. One possibility is through greater politicization of economic behavior, in effect the creation of global *citizen-based soft power*. There are new venues within global civil society that show considerable potential. They take citizen action further into global economic realms primarily through fair trade, marketing products and even organizing production in ways that embody many things that the Global Charter identified as shared global concerns.

As noted, everyday knowledge of producers and production processes and their environmental and social impacts has been obscured by global economic integration. Consumers now often know little about what they buy beyond country of origin. Working conditions, pollution impacts and raw materials sources are unknown. Local production is visible first hand and within national markets consumers at least have some sense of what work and environmental standards were likely to be. In a global economy it is often challenging enough to locate the product's country of origin on a mental map, let alone have knowledge of its agricultural techniques, unionization, or social policies.

Fair trade reduces this information gap by informing consumers when goods are not manufactured using child labor and when employees are not mistreated or working for starvation wages. Fair trade organizations often also provide assurance regarding environmental impacts and that products, especially food products, are safe.[26] Leading fair trade products are coffee, tea, and tropical fruits (an industry where heavy pesticide use and forest clearing are commonplace) and, increasingly, clothing (where exploitative labor conditions are widespread).[27] Fair trade is expanding rapidly, encompasses a widening array of goods and is finding its way into larger distribution systems and mainstream retail outlets.

Fair trade goods may cost more, but many European and North American consumers are willing and able to pay the modest price difference. Given that labor is typically a small percentage of the retail price, incomes could increase significantly without triggering large price increases. Fair trade goods now encompass millions of production workers in nearly 60 countries. Fair traded goods are valued at billions of dollars annually and the market has grown rapidly since 2005.[28] These figures do not include increases in certified organic foods imported from *commercial* (as opposed to fair trade) growers in developing nations or clothing produced under improved conditions in response to demands directly from commercial importers.

There is considerable debate over whether voluntary fair trade arrangements that depend on consumer choice can overcome unfair trade treaties, arrangements and practices among nations.[29] The key is to avoid assuming that the voluntary choices of firms and consumers are a substitute for political action, but are rather a complement to such actions. In the long-term global regulations on child labor, working conditions, the right to form unions, global minimum wages and rules regarding environmental quality and sustainability are needed. Creating "islands" in poor nations where such practices come into being are not in themselves the solution, but are a beginning and can trigger political pressure by visibly breaking seemingly eternal patterns.

New technologies could improve fair trade process. The Internet could be used to create interactive links between distant producers and consumers and/or trusted global organizations could provide detailed information via Universal Product Code (UPC) labels readable by cell phones. As well, free trade campaigns could be hard hitting in those cases where it was warranted as in an ad by www.shopyyourvalues.org which asserted regarding one retailer (Banana Republic): "Would her clothes still make her happy if she knew the pregnant worker who made them was beaten with a stick for requesting time off?" The site www.publiceye.ch singled out another retailer (Gap) for refusing to sign an accord with Bangladesh unions on fire and building safety.

Another important opportunity to actualize global citizenship in the economic sphere is green and ethical investment. Billions of dollars are now invested with social and environmental factors in mind in tandem with profit considerations.[30] Obviously, this will never obviate the need for regulation, but it can affect corporate behavior.

As well, in January 2012 California become the seventh state to allow the creation of a new form of corporation, the benefit corporation. California law now allows firms to "consider social and environmental benefits as part of their missions. So registering prevents shareholders from filing suit against management for failing to maximize stock yields."[31] The California-based clothing manufacturer Patagonia joined 400 other American benefit corporations. Patagonia contributes significantly to environmental organizations, produces durable products in a sustainable way and treats its employees fairly. Most benefit corporations have comparable goals. Participating in and improving the social and environmental performance of corporations is one activity in which global citizens might engage.

Another possibility within the economic sphere is the expansion of micro-loans.[32] Newer variations here utilize the Internet to link individual lenders to potential loan recipients in Africa, Asia and elsewhere who need micro-loans to help build very small businesses. Lending organizations screen potential recipients and oversee loan collection. Lenders usually leave the repaid money within the system.[33]

All of these activities are expressions of global citizenship within the economic realm, but there is another economic manifestation that could in the long run be more significant. Trade, branding and telecommunications, the very core of global economic integration, could in some circumstances, especially if there were an established global citizen's movement, pose a challenge to highly negative behavior by powerful states. There was a small and unorganized glimmer of such a possibility following the invasion of Iraq when the sales of some iconic American brands spontaneously declined in Europe, Canada, and the Middle East.

This outcome has not been widely discussed, but it could become a form of citizen-based intervention in global affairs. Eighty percent of Coca-Cola's profits, for example, come from outside the United States. After the Iraq invasion foreign sales declined dramatically for several iconic American brands (such as McDonald's, Disney, Walmart, and Marlboro). Marlboro sales fell 24 percent in France and 18 percent in Germany. Brand selection is not necessarily a politically conscious act, but clearly after George W. Bush's policies became visible to the world—even without an organized campaign of any kind—cowboys were diminished as a "cool image" in the eyes of many.[34] A global citizen's movement could in extreme circumstances impose economic costs on trading nations including hegemonic powers.

Unilateralism could carry a measurable price in the global marketplace and a savvy global citizen's movement could increase that price if other options are ineffective. Global citizen undertakings might take many forms, not all of which are necessarily mild-mannered or politically bland.

A different potential venue for global citizen action flows through community life and local government—the classic *thinking globally, acting locally* approach. Instead of buying fair trade global goods, many buy locally produced goods—for many reasons some of which are consistent with, and even rooted in, global citizenship. They buy food directly from local growers and producers to know better how and where it was produced. Local food is fresher and healthier, requires fewer preservatives, and less transportation thereby contributing less to climate change and the depletion of nonrenewable energy resources. This is for many a first step in practicing global citizenship at home.

Buying locally produced products and second hand goods will almost always reduce greenhouse emissions. So will using public transportation and living in compact, well insulated, conveniently located homes. Many do these things quite self-consciously to slow climate change and other environmental impacts. Others reduce energy use to avoid adding to the risk of future wars for oil.

Global citizenship is also, of course, practiced globally. Some new global communications initiatives are explicit about global citizenship. One, started under the name Independent World Television produces global news via the Internet at www.therealnews.com. Other undertakings mobilize activism globally. Avaaz is a joint initiative cofounded by MoveOn.org, Res Publica, and Civic Action, organizations associated with www.opendemocracy.net, an initiative of George Soros. Avaaz, the word for voice or song in several languages including Hindi, Urdu, and Farsi, seeks to build an online community that urges "global citizens to take action on urgent global issues, from climate change to global poverty to the crisis in the Middle East."[35] The organization sends email alerts regarding global issues. Avaaz builds its worldwide lists though its initiating organizations are based in America and Europe.

A long-established organization, the Inter Press Service (www.ipsnews.net) has adapted to the new media age. Inter Press Service, which was created to provide news links between Latin America and Europe now looks to communicate the voices of the global South to the wider world especially concerning the impacts of globalization. It also links civil society organizations, the media, local authorities and international agencies. It has offices in Rome, Johannesburg, Bangkok, Berlin, Montevideo, and New York.

These are relatively large scale initiatives, but there are numerous small, citizen-initiated efforts. One was from a student who sought in 2006 to raise money to directly finance an African National Union military presence in Darfur in lieu of any significant commitment forthcoming from nations. Another was the citizen posting photographs of daily life in Tehran as the United States ratcheted up anti-Iranian tensions in 2007 and asserted repeatedly that "all options were on the table." The photos were striking because such scenes were so utterly absent in North American media and few Americans had ever seen what life in Tehran looked like. A global citizen's movement might provide initiatives like these greater visibility and thereby inspire many more.

Could many very modest initiatives become a global citizen's movement? Absent formal global governance, is a large transnational movement even possible? One reason to imagine that it is possible is to recall that the social democratic internationals of the twentieth century, whatever their flaws, arose long before today's communications capabilities and before so many challenges were so irretrievably global in character. More recently green parties have emerged in most democratic nations and cooperate internationally.

Global citizen groups could pressure national governments to take global initiatives. By bringing pressure to bear at carefully chosen moments a global citizen's movement could also help to spur a more effective United Nations, an anti-unilateralist alliance or fairer approaches to global economic integration. Global citizens might also ultimately convince other citizens, and governments, that the obligations of power are not primarily military in character.

From Global Citizenship to Global Governance

Believing that people with a shared sense of global citizenship, from 200 nations and myriad cultures and circumstances, can act together to influence policy outcomes may seem hopelessly idealistic. Nonetheless the political impact of a global citizen's movement could be consequential even if it takes years to focus political energy because modest steps could come sooner. For example, even a modestly coordinated campaign could push already like-minded nations into more decisive action and, for example, *any* advance on global social equity would be a stunning achievement. Inequality and climate change are issues where inaction or never-enforced "decisions" have been the norm.

Even without multilateral agreements important steps can be taken by single determined nations. In early 2012 the government of Norway pledged $300 million *per year* to providing access to energy to the poorest people in the world in ways that will *reduce* carbon emissions. *That is more than $50 per Norwegian per year.* Working with governments in Bhutan, Nepal, Tanzania, Morocco, and other countries this bold initiative simultaneously addresses social equity and climate change.[36] Denmark is using *its* North Sea oil revenues to convert its entire locomotive fleet into an energy-efficient electric rail system to sharply cut greenhouse emissions.

Initiatives of this sort could spread were these initiatives widely communicated and were there concerted pressure on governments. Global civil society organizations could campaign in more coordinated ways. Organizations could advance direct citizen action (regarding fair trade or human rights abuses, for example) while campaigning for policy action by national governments. Some governments that were reluctant to stand up to powerful interests might do so if they faced other, competing, pressures.

First steps could lead to further steps through movement-initiated local, national, and global pressure. This could actualize a perspective that is sometimes, in the international relations literature, called rooted cosmopolitanism.[37] Citizenship at its core is about shared political power and influence. Global citizenship is about finding channels at any level from the neighborhood or firm to global governance. Actions can be primarily market based or aim at building the political influence needed to alter policy outcomes, ultimately leading to democratizing international relations.

A Global Citizen's Movement: Possible Beginnings

One organization advocating a global citizen's movement sees today's situation regarding the creation of such a movement as "overripe." This group, with which I have participated, originated in Boston. It is called the Great Transition Initiative (GTI), in part an online discussion forum. An affiliated group that more explicitly seeks to advance a movement is called the Widening Circle.

In their words:

> While most of human history was dominated by scarcity and the challenge of survival, today's huge economies have created the conditions for a post-scarcity society. Attention can turn now to *quality-of-life*:

human fulfillment rather than wealth as the primary measure of success and well-being. The sense of *solidarity*—social connectedness, responsibility and loyalty—can begin to extend beyond nation and tribe to people of distant places, the unborn of distant futures, and the other creatures of the earth. *Reverence for nature*, an ecological sensibility of wonder and enjoyment in the natural world, is nourished by the growing appreciation of humanity's place in the web of life and our dependence on a bountiful earth.[38]

The Widening Circle "aims to strengthen the global citizen's movement, nurturing the idea of global citizenship and promoting integrated action."[39] Civil society organizations at the global scale are seen within this discussion as doing vital work, but not as in themselves sufficient without an integrated strategy for achieving their highly diverse objectives. Systemic change is needed, including cooperative advances in global policy and law.

This particular effort may or may not succeed. What is important is that individuals in many nations come to think as global citizens and find ways to act together. The very idea of global citizenship would, as noted, be seen as a form of leftist idealism by conservatives, especially in America. However, in truth the need to collectively address challenges that can only be effectively addressed globally is not necessarily either left or right as a political perspective. It is about creating opportunities for democratic input at the level at which many contemporary problems arise and can be resolved.

Perhaps ironically, the most exceptional aspect of American character and history has been a commitment to innovation and adaptation, both technological and socio-political. Resolving today's global challenges requires both. Bringing together diverse peoples in common purpose is quintessentially American. Matching governance to the level at which problems can be best resolved—the idea of subsidiarity—is a principal of government that has served America well and which has been greatly admired by American conservatives and their beloved American "founding fathers" (Madison and Jefferson especially). The GTI's core principles of a global citizen's movement focuses on this very concept.[40]

Some other important organizations working to build global citizenship include CIVICUS (World Alliance for Citizens), the Charles Leopold Mayer Foundation, CONCORD (the European Confederation of Development NGOs), GCAP (Global Call to Action against Poverty), Forum for a New World Governance and global citizen organizations and foundations in Switzerland, Germany, Britain and elsewhere. The first four of these organizations sponsored a major gathering in Johannesburg in 2013.[41] The fifth, in its Civil Society Politics Manifesto, argues that "the active participation of citizens is required to solve the pressing social, economic and environmental problems of our time."[42]

The World Economic Forum, the body that hosts an annual gathering of global, political, and economic elites in Davos, Switzerland is certainly not tied to the political left. Yet their 2012 Annual Report on Global Risks identifies 50 global risks "none of which respects national boundaries." The risks identified include: "severe economic disparity, water supply crises, rising greenhouse gas emissions, systemic financial failures and chronic financial imbalances."[43] The report calls for collective attention to this array of risks. They do not explicitly call for a global citizen's movement, but the ongoing inaction regarding these global risks would suggest that citizen action is needed.

The challenge is to communicate *the possibility* of effective action on problems of staggering scale. Frances Moore Lappé makes the case that sharing information about even small scale solutions that have worked somewhere is a more revolutionary act than we might suppose. It is crucial to overcoming human instincts of powerlessness and a sense of scarcity, isolation, fear, and defensiveness. That in turn is crucial to the widespread co-creation and cooperation which she calls eco-mind.[44] The challenge is to find ways to, as the Pachamama Alliance puts it, awaken the dreamer in us all.[45]

The Pachamama Alliance began as an international initiative to preserve the Amazon rainforest. Its goals broadened and evolved. As the group puts it they seek to empower "the indigenous people of the Amazon rainforest to preserve their lands and culture and, using insights gained from the work, to educate and inspire individuals everywhere to bring forth a thriving, just and sustainable world." It is very much an organization in the spirit of global citizenship.

In 2007 Nelson Mandela created an organization called the Elders, senior figures in political life and diplomacy who continue to pursue peace and a broad global agenda. Kofi Annan is currently chair of the group. They have recently worked to promote more effective action on climate change, calling it the biggest challenge of our time leading up to the 2015 UN meetings.[46] Annan and the group have taken up the concept of climate justice wherein wealthy nations that have gained the most from the use of fossil fuels to help poorer nations to adapt to a post-carbon era.

Another initiative important to the practice of global citizenship is offered by noted American educator Arlie Hochschild. Hochschild discusses the need to teach empathy to young children and notes the work of Kids for Peace and Roots of Empathy. Kids for Peace connects American school children with peers in other countries. Roots of Empathy, operating in Canada and the United States, teaches empathy through direct experiences with infants and mothers. Hochschild proposes teaching children to identify with role models like Paul Farmer who founded Partners in Health. Farmer, an American, grew up poor but ended up graduating from Harvard Medical School. Instead of pursuing a high-income career he has spent his life creating health clinics in Haiti, Rwanda and elsewhere that focus on reducing poverty as a source of disease.[47]

Other efforts have used music to inspire global co-creation. UNESCO has sponsored annual World Jazz Day concerts and made them globally available via YouTube. The 2013 concert was broadcast live from Istanbul via the Internet to 196 countries and featured American jazz stars Herbie Hancock and Wayne Shorter among others. It also included comments about globally shared cultural values and creating the possibility of common global actions from Irena Bokova, the UNESCO general director.

In another musical undertaking, noted Argentine-Israeli conductor Daniel Barenboim has created a youth orchestra from Israel, the Arab world, and Iran. The West-Eastern Divan Orchestra has played widely including a performance of all nine Beethoven symphonies at the Proms (in Britain) in 2012. As well, an organization based in Britain and Australia, the Global Poverty Project, sponsored a concert in New York City featuring Stevie Wonder, Alicia Keys and others that explicitly called on people to think of themselves as global citizens, responsible for and capable of ending global poverty. These efforts aim to break through the powerlessness that prevents people from imagining themselves as having broad citizenly obligations as potential contributors to global change.

One visual artist, Isaac Cordal of Spain, has made a breakthrough in this regard. His small plaster figures called Cement Eclipses depict urban decay and an unwillingness to accept responsibility. Most striking perhaps is a work in Berlin "electoral campaign," which depicts politicians debating climate change while rising waters leave them underwater up to their chins. Cordal then photographs his street works and posts the images on the Internet. He intends with his works to counteract collective inertia "that leads us to think that our small actions cannot change anything." His view is that many small actions can "manipulate the global inertia and turn it into something more positive."[48] Cordal's works have been placed widely in Europe and some have gone viral on the Internet.

One other creative endeavor in this spirit is *Jerusalem: A Cookbook* by Yotam Ottolenghi and Sami Tamimi. The book, by a Jew and a Palestinian (both emigrants from Jerusalem who operate five restaurants in London), is profusely illustrated with everyday life shared by the two communities in Jerusalem.[49] It is about the foods they share and have shared for centuries and thus about the city and country (or countries) that they might share peacefully. This work, like all of those depicted here are the tiny efforts (Cordal's "small actions") that together are essential to understanding what we all share and necessary to build toward a shared global culture and ultimately a sense of global citizenship and the possibility of global governance.

Global Citizenship in North America: Challenge and Promise

Many North Americans are politically resistant to global governance, America by virtue of hegemonic power and habits and Canada because it is building its economy around accelerating GHG emissions. These nations could contribute more given their wealth and technological skills.[50] Too few North Americans understand that *we* would gain from a global movement to address global challenges. A more democratic world, with citizens more active in governance, is likely to be more politically and economically stable.[51] As well, to reiterate, greater global social equity expand markets for products and services from wealthy nations—solar energy innovations, industrial and medical equipment and pharmaceuticals. Moreover, a world addressing shared concerns transnationally is simply a better and safer world.

There is also another, deeper reason for North Americans to favor citizen-led global actions, one more subtle and perhaps ironic. In an era of economic globalization, global political influence of citizens and civil society is crucial to preserving a sense of political efficacy at *any* level. Political efficacy, the belief that one can influence politics and policy, engenders citizenship and democracy at the *national*, *state or local* level. Low rates of political participation are associated with the sense that one cannot fight city hall, that politics belongs to those with money or that outcomes will not change regardless of which party is elected, the assumption that "they are all the same."

In a world where events on the other side of the planet or business decisions made in locations one cannot even determine change one's life it is hard to imagine that citizens have influence.[52] When the economy is global and largely unregulated, political fatalism becomes the norm. Jobs disappear and the media mantra is that "we" must cut government programs, wages and jobs to "remain competitive." There may be some truth to this assertion, but that is primarily because citizens have no way to influence *global* policy outcomes. People simply come to assume that they cannot influence policy in their community or nation, or change their own everyday lives.

The irony here is that many assert that global citizenship, and even international organizations, somehow threaten national sovereignty and democracy. Such arguments are commonplace among American conservatives. Yet those same people also support the process of global economic integration. For what it is worth I favor international trade and investment and global economic integration, but I believe that these things *require* a parallel expansion of democratic global governance—some means of global rule setting and rule enforcement, and therefore global political participation. Such a shift would protect democracy *within* nations and is needed to create a stable and more equitable global economy.

There are profound risks associated with the absence of global, democratic rule-making, some form of citizen-based political check on the unfettered power of global economic decision-makers. We need to embed market forces in democratic society globally, much as it was embedded nationally, at least in wealthy Western nations for a time prior to the 1980s. Without such a shift the environment will continue to deteriorate, inequality will continue to increase and democracy itself could be at risk. As the conservative, more recently moderate, political thinker Francis Fukuyama noted in *Foreign Affairs,* "Serious intellectual debate is urgently needed, since the current form of globalized capitalism is eroding the middle-class social base on which liberal democracy rests."[53]

There is considerable truth to Fukuyama's claim. In China and other rising nations there is a rapidly rising class of wealthy entrepreneurs and a large emerging class of urban professionals and middle managers. The incomes of these groups are significantly higher than those still living in rural areas or laboring in giant factories. Income gaps are growing rapidly. At the same time, in many wealthy nations wage-based incomes are stagnant or shrinking and many young people are struggling to enter the labor market. In America, the gap between the rich (the upper 1–2 percent) and everyone else has been increasing since the 1980s.[54]

Guy Standing has argued that a new class, which he calls the precariat, is emerging in Western societies. Those in the precariat are employed in even less stable positions than the old proletariat, the industrial working class. The working hours of the precariat are often less than full time, prone to seasonality, highly flexible and irregular (at an employer's discretion, often with little notice). Work, even for more than one employer, may not be adequate to establish an independent household. This new class is growing rapidly and is primarily populated by the young, former industrial workers whose previous jobs have been "off-shored" and immigrants.

Standing argues that the emergence and growth of the precariat could threaten democracy and societal stability. In his view the "precariat" is dangerous because many are "disengaged from twentieth century political discourses."[55] Given these risks he proposes policy offsets especially publicly funded income stabilization and efforts to enhance deliberative democracy. Others have called such an income policy a negative income tax or a guaranteed annual income. Standing links such policies to citizen participation in democratic political processes. "Chronically insecure people," he notes, "make poor democrats."[56]

In contrast, Fukuyama observes that income polarization undermines gains associated with globalization in terms of *global* wealth distribution. Globalization has raised the incomes of many in rising nations including Korea, China, Brazil, India, and Mexico. However, at the same time income equity *within* nations has eroded in both those nations and mature economies.[57] The wealthy of the world are rapidly gaining ground relative to everyone else.[58]

As noted earlier with regard to America, inequality undermines democracy by concentrating political power. Between 2002 and 2007, 65 percent of all American income gains went to the top 1 percent of earners and since 2000 despite significant productivity gains average annual incomes have fallen by 10 percent.[59] America is the most unequal society among wealthy democracies and as such the quality of its democracy, despite its long stability, will be challenged in the years ahead.[60] Standing sees these challenges as existing in much of Europe as well.

Concentrated wealth combined with the globalization of social and economic decisions, placing them at least seemingly beyond the reach of national governments, can make democratic citizenship seem inadequate if not moot.[61] Enhancing, or perhaps even preserving, democracy *within nations*, then, may require a growing sense of efficacy among citizens everywhere regarding the possibility of influencing *global* outcomes. Achieving a citizen role in global decisions, whether achieved through global forums or nation by nation (or even within cities and workplaces), may be the best way to protect democracy in a global age.

Seeing global citizenship as a threat to American democracy is thus the ultimate irony. Global citizenship would *bolster* democracy everywhere, including within the United States. It would advance, and benefit from, America's self-identified ideals: democracy, civil rights, and civil liberties, equality of opportunity and subsidiarity (wherein initiatives are taken at the most localized possible level, mindful that given global economic integration a few issues can only be resolved globally).

The key question is: *can Americans adapt their ideals for a global age?* America, for centuries a land of immigrants, is thoroughly cosmopolitan. Its citizens would seem to have a natural role to play in any emerging global citizen's movement. But such participation will likely be resisted within America as forcefully as anywhere. Ironically, authoritarian governments will also, probably justifiably, imagine that such citizen efforts are a form of resistance to the established power of the regime.

America's demographics are on the side of cosmopolitanism, but America still faces a time of fearful, back-to-the-wall reaction to the nation's multiracial realities especially among older voters. That reaction was at the heart of much of the conservative overreaction to Obama's Presidency.[62] America's many minorities will, taken together, soon be a majority. Today's politics in America is characterized by a deep, hang on by your fingernails, attitude among older white males against anything even vaguely cosmopolitan. Today's Republican Party is predominantly anti-immigrant, antiunion, pro-patriarchy, anti-Muslim, and xenophobic. Those holding such views will resist American participation in *any* global initiative, even one with heavy involvement by fellow Americans.

The great good news is that within a decade or two those who hold these views, if they do not manage to block the future that they are convinced they will hate, will be so small proportionately that they will just have to accept a profoundly diverse America (or just pretend it is not there). Perhaps there will also by then be American and global leadership that can hear the voice of the world's citizens. If those who resist such outcomes live to see them they might more accurately remember America's *actual* origins and early principles and appreciate the result.

Daring to Dream: Global Citizenship and a Better World

Unless one is young, building a global citizen's movement is about change beyond the span of our lifetimes. But it remains important to imagine what might be possible. A sense of where we might go is needed to make the necessary effort possible. Global citizens are not likely to celebrate dramatic or comprehensive victories anytime soon, but without imagining where we might go global citizens could not recognize small interim victories for what they were.

Recalling the twin interlinked challenges of global equity and environmental sustainability, let me close with a dream about possibilities. Ironically, some possibilities from which a global citizen's movement might gain momentum would take advantage of today's extreme inequality. One might say that many places are so far behind that they are ahead (in the sense that lives in such places could be lifted dramatically by quite modest global initiatives).

Development advocates understand well that poor nations can bypass many relatively unsustainable steps that rich societies once took. One commonly cited example is the rapid introduction of cell phones in locations that did not have massive sunk costs in ground line telephone technology. Materials, energy and labor intensive wires and poles need never be produced, installed and maintained. Such realities open up many possibilities.

From a global perspective gains anywhere are a gain for all. As was clear I hope from my reflections on Rousseau, if we think as humankind rather than some segment thereof we are no longer playing a zero sum game. We live on one planet and while that planet has many limits we can simultaneously gain ground environmentally and economically. Gains on either or both fronts in poor nations can come at a very low comparative cost. As a result the gains that redound as a result will often seem to exceed the cost of any investment citizens of wealthy nations might make.

We can appreciate this better through a few concrete cases, starting with one so simple that children will grasp it. The global common benefits from protecting the wild existence of giraffes, orangutans, rhinos, lions, elephants, and other endangered species are transparent. One does not have to actually be physically near these creatures to appreciate the fact of their wild existence. Many of the most threatened wildlife habitats—threatened by human poverty, human numbers, settlement expansion, or climate change—are in relatively poor nations. One of the greatest threats is poaching. Another is deforestation. Simply put, the cost of protecting habitat should be shared and the cost of hiring additional park wardens in, for example, East Africa is low by European or North American standards.

Parallel possibilities exist regarding the preservation of *cultural* heritage treasures located in poor nations. Tourism helps to cover maintenance costs, but more could be done. Cultural treasures are part of *humankind's* heritage. Just as money within the European Union flows to European nations especially rich in ancient heritage sites that are expensive to maintain, the same could be done globally to a greater extent than it is.

One simple possibility that might expand global perspectives would be the greater utilization of new media to enhance virtual access to such sites and to use that access as an ongoing fund-raising tool. Funds for such efforts might also come from a small surcharge on museum admissions within wealthy countries that house artistic treasures from nations challenged to protect treasures remaining at home. Again this could work because modest charges in wealthy nations can have big impacts in poor ones.

Needless to say cultural treasures within wealthy nations—from Rome to New Orleans and from the Kremlin to the Great Wall—should also be celebrated by global citizens. In these cases, however, financial help would only be necessary in emergency situations. Collectively appreciate great human achievements, as well as the natural wonders of every nation builds human solidarity. Celebration of the planet we share and the wonders we have added are very much in the spirit of the global perspective that is so urgently needed. Such efforts are easy places to begin.

Climate change is a starker challenge. The collective global possibilities are accordingly larger (and may temporarily require non-optimal allocations of resources). Such realities should not slow addressing climate change. There is no avoiding reducing emissions and mitigating impacts. Climate impacts fall heavily on poor nations which have contributed little to the problem. If emissions reductions prevent some of the worst effects, mitigation challenges may be confined to a limited number of regions: the Arctic, the dry zones of Africa, regions dependent on glaciers for water and low-lying coastal and island nations.

The cost of mitigation in these regions should be broadly shared as a matter of simple justice. The stark political challenge comes here: the global funding source for mitigation is glaringly obvious, fossil fuels. The world long since should have been building a reserve fund to deal with climate impacts on nations that have contributed negligibly to the problem. Again, the cost of mitigation—building sea walls, moving coastal villages, or piping fresh drinking water—within poor nations would be less in monetary terms than it might be in rich nations (though no less disruptive). In other nations, rich and poor, investments should be made now to propagate plants adapted to dryer or warmer conditions. In some cases, of course, the only adaptive solution may be compensation and increased opportunities for immigration.

Widely adopted policies that imposed a surcharge on fossil fuels to meet these challenges would both raise the price of fossil fuels and accelerate energy alternatives and increased energy efficiency. These alternatives are often more affordable in poor nations. The so-far-behind-they-are-ahead reality opens low-cost opportunities for emission reductions to these new funding sources. If solar devices are even partially assembled in Africa or Latin America, they can be made, delivered and installed more cheaply, as can more efficient cookers. Even retailing equipment produced elsewhere provides new jobs. As well, new lighting possibilities and cell phone recharging using solar energy are economically viable and can bring light and communications to locations beyond the electrical grid where two billion people still reside.[63]

But who would or could collect a levy on oil, who determines its scope and who would allocate funds and audit expenditures? This takes us back to Michael Lind's doubts about cosmopolitanism noted earlier—namely that few are prepared to pay taxes or abide by laws set globally. One can readily imagine the political challenges. Europeans might object that they already pay high taxes on oil and this would drive their prices up further. Many Americans are against even funding UNICEF or providing foreign aid, let alone paying higher oil prices to reduce seaside erosion in East Africa or Bangladesh. These same people do not believe that such outcomes have anything to do with their use of fossil fuels, science be damned. Global citizens will need to be very good at communicating the need for collective action.

Institutionally the monies could be required by international agreement and collected by national governments, pooled and spent according to agreements to which participating governments are party. If the levy were on fossil fuels (perhaps weighted by carbon emissions), not just exports or imports some of the most problematic economic distortions might be avoided. Kyoto having failed; only measures affecting most fossil fuel consumers are at this late date likely to suffice.

A global agency such as UNEP, advised by scientific, economic, and citizen-based organizations, could be charged with evaluating projects according to criteria that included consideration of GDP/capita relative to mitigation needs and energy transformation achieved per dollar. All this might require a modest-sized bureaucracy, but this is one challenge that cannot be met by ad hoc efforts.

Also necessary but politically challenging is additional global law and regulation. Here Lind's cautions about today's limits on cosmopolitanism must again be noted, this time regarding people's willingness to obey laws other than national laws. For example, one area where global action is particularly urgent is for rules regarding global shipping. The global economy's thousands of transport ships plying the seas burn Bunker C oil adding significantly to air pollution, to the acidification of the oceans and to climate change.

Bunker C fuel is cheap and if cleaner fuels were used cost calculations regarding production locations might well shift, especially for heavy, low-cost goods. In some cases now ships are required by *national* regulations to switch fuels when they near ports, but in the open seas pretty much anything still goes.[64] It is as if we were still living in the nineteenth century. It should not take a global citizen's movement to produce a multilateral treaty on such issues, but it probably will. Endangering the planet is somehow not seen as piracy, indeed it is for the most part not seen at all.

Effective action on global food issues might also be taken up by a global citizen's movement. For decades wealthy nations have subsidized agricultural exports undermining local agricultural production in poor nations. Poor nations cannot match the subsidies.[65] Despite decades of trade negotiations and poor nation objections subsidies continue to cost American and European taxpayers billions even in the face of deep cuts to other parts of government budgets. If the plight of farmers in poor nations were more visible within rich ones, might this not change? Food politics is another clear political opportunity for a global citizen's movement.

Humans have traded foods for millennia beginning with salt and spices and this will doubtless continue as will trade in seasonally unavailable foods. It is a concern, however, when food trade undermines local capacities to produce food for domestic markets and the global food trade is based on environmentally problematic monocultures or nonsustainable fisheries. Fair trade and the local food movement, as noted, arise from a desire to know the quality of one's food and the conditions under which it is produced. These movements are part of emerging global citizenship. A global citizen's movement would celebrate foods from every culture, but recognize the environmental advantages of local and seasonal eating and make certain that globally traded foods meet well-established global regulatory standards.

Food production, energy use and climate change are inextricably linked. Many climate advocates have made the case, for example, that reduced meat consumption would reduce greenhouse emissions as well as excessive land and water use.[66] Adequate food, shelter, and clean water are crucial to global social equity. A global citizen's movement must address these concerns and urge change in the global food system and in the environmental cost of building materials and promote innovation in low-cost building design.

Changes in food and shelter production will take decades. A greater emphasis on local production need not be universal or absolute, but humans in most locations should be able produce needed food and shelter from nearby resources. People's lives would *feel* more secure and *be* more sustainable. It makes little sense to ship food around the world that can be grown in our back yards or to transport massively heavy and widely distributed products like cement across the planet. A global citizen's movement is thus likely to advocate strengthening the core economy of every locality.

There are many limits to local capacities, but this is not to deny that we have too often abandoned local production. Deserts will not readily grow rice, nor should they. Some nations will likely always need to import some energy. However, many of today's production systems are unsustainable and if we are to reduce economic insecurity, potential conflicts and excessive concentrations of power people should be able to more often meet core needs locally.

Social equity is perhaps the greatest challenge, the most dreamlike of these dreams of a possible future. The millennium development goals were a good beginning, but just a beginning and at best partially achieved thus far. In an earlier work I suggested ways to countervail the negative equity effects of globalization, but I now understand that

I did not get to the heart of the problem. I suggested globally established minimum wages in export industries pegged to GDP/capita, but offered little regarding the politics of such possibilities.[67]

It is clearer now that any such initiatives require a movement able to overcome the unwillingness noted by Lind to generate, or at least use, revenue globally and to demand globally regulated social, environmental, and financial practices. These things sound impossible, but are not. One way might be to pressure key national governments to set new rules simultaneously. We have already had *many* nations approve regulations simultaneously with regard to ozone depletion, trade in endangered species and many other matters. Simultaneous regulation is possible. A tax used to meet global objectives might be imposed on something truly global such as the movement of investment dollars (or, as noted, on fossil fuels).

Taxing financial transactions including currency transfers, a so-called Tobin tax or, as is likely to be adopted in Europe, a Financial Transfer Tax (FTT), even at a very low, seemingly almost trivial, rate would generate significant revenue. If adopted globally, this would be a huge step forward in the conduct of human affairs because such revenue could visibly be used for the benefit of people in every nation. Funds might for example help eradicate communicable diseases especially those that have the potential for trans-border transmission. Such a tax might also provide capital to allow poorer nations to acquire advanced products from wealthy nations, including medicines, electronics, software, and renewable energy equipment (or the capacity to produce such things). Again, all would benefit.

What might contribute to overcoming resistance to global taxation and regulation within wealthy nations? Why might even conservatives come to support such initiatives? Kemal Derviş, the former Minister of economics for Turkey and former World Bank Vice President, recently noted that in the 1930s it was argued by some that "Capitalism...tends to generate chronic weakness in effective demand due to growing concentration of income, leading to a "savings glut," because the very rich save a lot. This would spur "trade wars as countries tried to find more demand abroad."[68] Derviş went on to make the case that many economies may now be unable to expand economically (even with low interest rates) because of global inequality and its by-product: falling demand.

In other words global taxation and expenditure may not only be good for poor nations, but may also be necessary to reduce seemingly perpetual economic stagnation in wealthy ones. Desperately poor people do not make good customers and capital is of no use if there is insufficient demand. Arguably only a citizen's movement capable of inspiring redistribution can keep this from being a chronic condition. Otherwise we will continue to face lower wages and capital holders continuously gaining in relative wealth. Another possible solution to this dilemma is taxation that redirects capital into public investments that help to offset climate change and slow rising inequality by creating new work in the global public interest.

As noted, expenditures at the global scale could be overseen or managed by civil society and international organizations. These organizations use funds efficiently and effectively and are widely known and trusted. Hopefully hesitations regarding modest steps forward in global governance can be overcome at least in those whose concerns are not rooted in paranoia.

Paranoid specters of global government aside, creating political will regarding such initiatives will not come easily or quickly. Even the concept of global revenue will not come readily. The political resistance to such a change in the conduct of human affairs will be well-financed. Events like New Orleans in 2005 and the countless less visible everyday examples of unnecessary and avoidable human suffering are illustrations of what might be prevented or ameliorated. Citizens everywhere can come to see such things as risks we all face and responsibilities we all share. We can learn to see global problems as challenges that, working together, we can meet.

Those of us in wealthy nations need to appreciate that problems elsewhere are not just a potential cost to those lucky enough to have avoided them by good fortune or an accident of birth. Resolving global problems is a great benefit to us as well. As Derviş's analysis made clear we benefit collectively from meeting the unmet needs of others. Successes in other corners of the world create potential customers. Improved economic well-being also supports democracy and political stability—realities that benefit everyone. In an interconnected world reducing diseases anywhere reduces disease risks everywhere. Helping to educate others anywhere makes them more capable of solving their own problems, or perhaps ours.

The essential lesson from our consideration of hegemony and the evolution of citizenship and our tale of three cities is that we must learn to think as if we were one people. Anyone's problems are at least in part everyone's problems. Humankind has far too much to deal with to have time for wars. From this vantage point we can also see that any nation, even the richest and mightiest, can be overwhelmed at least for a moment by events and in need of help from the world. Social inequalities have grown far too large. Not only are the poor too vulnerable, but also concentrated wealth is far too powerful. Concentrated wealth prevented the adequate regulation of the global financial system until it was too late and stands in the way of sufficient action regarding climate change. It is past time for citizens acting globally to provide a counterweight to excessively concentrated power and solutions to the problems we collectively face.

Notes

1 Hegemony's Comforts, Hegemony's Price

1. See, for example, www.globalsecurity.org.
2. President Obama acknowledged this disparity when he said in 2013: "Mr. Assad...has capacity relative to children (and) to an opposition that is still getting itself organized and are not professional, trained fighters. He doesn't have a credible means to threaten the United States." See www.cnn.com (September 10, 2013). This remark contrasts dramatically with Bush's preinvasion allegations of an Iraqi capacity to attack America.
3. Some Americans, of course, are willing to forgo other priorities including social spending and education. See, Editorial, "The Human Cost of Ideology," www.nytimes.com (May 10, 2012). Accessed May 13, 2012.
4. See, for example, Lawrence J. Korb, "Surging to Disaster," www.prospect.org/article/surging-disaster (December 20, 2006).
5. This is also, of course, an argument for why America should lead on climate change, the ultimate destabilizer of the global economy and the world order.
6. Democratic, or even pro-American, governments could emerge, but only in rare circumstances can they be installed by force.
7. The Project for the New American Century (PNAC) all but advocated an invasion of Iraq well before September 11, 2001. See www.newamericancentury.org.
8. Larry Kahaner, "Weapon of Mass Destruction," www.washingtonpost.com (November 26, 2006).
9. This is a complex distinction of course. Global stability will always to some extent be to the advantage of the rich and powerful nations. Resisting self-interested national advantage achieved by military means is about avoiding nondefensive actions solely to gain economic, political, or strategic opportunities. Military means should only be used rarely, with the support of broad-based international organizations, serving global objectives. The occupation of Iraq clearly failed on most counts.
10. The reaction to the 2013 debt default threat in countries like Mexico and Russia was telling regarding global interest in, and attitudes regarding, the United States. See Damien Cave, "Viewing US in Fear and Dismay," www.nytimes.com (October 15, 2013).

11. The cost of protecting cities and coastlines against sea level rises is estimated to be in the trillions of dollars. Hurricane Sandy's impacts on the New York City area showed that this is already necessary. See, Robert Kuttner, "Fix the Debt or Save the Coasts?" *The American Prospect* (November 2, 2012), www.prospect.org.
12. George Monbiot, *Heat: How to Stop the Planet from Burning* (Toronto: Doubleday Canada, 2006).
13. Peak oil analysts hold varied positions on how to cope with declining conventional oil supplies. Some fear that advocates of climate change action think that peak oil would help to solve climate change through higher prices and declining supplies. High oil prices, alternatively, could increase demand for coal. Other peak oil analysts just seem to doubt any energy scenario but those that lead to economic collapse.
14. Regarding vote suppression that already exists, see www.brennancenter.org, the website of the New York University School of Law group that studies the problem and has produced numerous excellent publications in recent years that are available through the website.
15. Regarding ugly forces in America see, for example, David Neiwert, *The Eliminationists: How Hate Talk Radicalized the American Right* (Boulder: Paradigm Publishers, 2009) or recall the attempts to require people of Hispanic descent in parts of Arizona to continuously document their citizenship for police or the virulent hostility to the construction of mosques in New York, Tennessee, and California.
16. Private capital is available, but someone must convince oil companies to not spend the money searching for the last drop of oil and using the money for executive compensation and currying political favor.
17. Most postcarbon alternatives are capital intensive. A postcarbon world also likely requires a "smarter" electrical grid, reconfiguration of urban areas, and a transportation system that includes more high-speed rail and urban transit. As well, most existing buildings of all kinds need an energy efficiency upgrade.
18. Oil companies tout their investments in alternative energy, but the amounts are a small share of their income compared to the cost of searching for more oil or extracting bitumen from the oil sands.
19. It is instructive here to recall the environmental disasters and foregone public expenditures during World War II or the Cold War. The health impacts of uranium mining, for example, were catastrophic.
20. Another way of making the same point is to say, as Joseph Nye has, that: "The world of traditional power politics was typically about whose military or economy would win. In today's information age, politics is also about whose 'story' wins." Joseph S. Nye "The New Public Diplomacy," www.project-syndicate.org (February 10, 2010). Accessed December 22, 2013.
21. Again, American reaction was muted by a docile press, as documented by Michael Isikoff and David Corn in *Hubris* (New York: Crown, 2006).
22. See even the usually sympathetic (moderate to conservative) British and Canadian press (*The Times* or the Toronto-based *Globe and Mail*) during the period 2003 to 2006.

23. See, for example, Pew Global Attitudes Project, "Global Unease with Major World Powers" (June 27, 2007). Available at www.pewglobal.org. For contrasting more recent figures in the Obama era by nation, see, same source: "Opinion of the United States," for 2013. Accessed January 18, 2014.
24. For a discussion of this latter option, see, Robert Paehlke, *Democracy's Dilemma: Environment, Social Equity and the Global Economy* (Cambridge: MIT Press, 2004).
25. Of particular concern is the Supreme Court's *Citizen's United* decision, as well as attempts at vote suppression in several states. These issues are discussed further in chapter 4.
26. Tony Blair's autobiography argues, in effect, that "we could not have known" that Saddam did not have WMDs. See, *A Journey: My Political Life* (New York: Knopf, 2010).
27. Lawrence Martin, "No Defense for the Staggering Pentagon Budget," *Globe and Mail* (February 10, 2007), p. A25.
28. See, Dalia Sussman, "Polls: Much Skepticism about Iraq," www.nytimes.com (August 31, 2010).
29. However, some military assets such as radar installations and antimissile defenses, for example, must be forward positioned to be effective for territorial defense.
30. Measures of success in this regard may include the war in Iraq and excesses in electronic eavesdropping.
31. See Gary Hart, "The Lessons of Iraq," www.huffingtonpost.com (March 19, 2007).
32. See, for example, Niall Ferguson, "A World without Power," www.foreignpolicy.com (July/August, 2004).
33. Kagan sometimes seemed to fit better with the group identified as hyper-realists. His specialty within that realm was insulting the motives of Europeans.
34. Conservative, rather than neoconservative, in that realists are typically more willing to allow that American power has limits and that working within those limits is in part what statesmanship is about.
35. Paul Krugman observes that Bush (in Washington-based media circles) was "treated as a highly effective leader who knew what he was doing right up to Katrina." Many other Americans had begun to doubt this earlier. See, Paul Krugman, "Shorting Out the Wiring," www.krugman.blogs.nytimes.com (October 5, 2013).
36. See, for example, Peter Beinart, *The Good Fight: Why Liberals—and Only Liberals—Can Win the War on Terror and Make America Great Again* (New York: Harper Collins, 2006).
37. Some might reply that America looks elsewhere *because* Latin America is now democratic. This view misreads the history of US-Latin American relations. See, for example, Peter H. Smith, *Talons of the Eagle: Dynamics of US- Latin-American Relations* (New York: Oxford University Press, 1996).
38. Romney's campaign assertions regarding Russia and China exemplify this pattern of thoughtlessness.

39. In a recession this glaringly begs the question of cost effectiveness, especially when one considers that advocates claim that these weapons are needed to counter North Korea and Iran. The cost of this system would vastly exceed the military budgets of those nations combined.
40. See www.socialprogressimperative.com and Nicholas Kristoff, "We're Not No. 1!" www.nytimes.com (April 2, 2014).
41. Declines in conventional oil reserves also contribute to oil price increases, but gradually rising energy prices are far less disruptive and *if anticipated* reduce the demand more efficiently and smoothly than abrupt price spikes.
42. Björn Hagelin, Mark Bromley, and Siemon T. Wezeman, "The Volume of Transfers of Major Conventional Weapons: By Recipients and Suppliers, 1999–2003." See Stockholm International Peace Research Institute (www.sipri.org).
43. Jonathan Rauch, "All Over but the Pullback," www.washingtonpost.com (December 4, 2005).
44. John Rawls, *The Law of Peoples* (Cambridge, MA: Harvard University Press, 1999), p. 91.
45. Social policies will not be broadly harmonized in the short term, but minimum standards can be established within purchase contracts (as they were following the 2013 Bangladesh clothing factory catastrophe). Some matters like the legalization of unions could be included in trade treaties were there the political will.

2 A Tale of Three Cities: Kyoto, Baghdad, and New Orleans

1. Many nations, individuals, and corporations are making an effort, but the results to date are insufficient. See American Meteorological Society (AMS), *State of the Climate in 2012*. Published in the *Bulletin of the AMS*, 94 (August, 2013).
2. See Robert Paehlke, *Some Like It Cold: The Politics of Climate Change in Canada* (Toronto: Between the Lines, 2008) regarding the politics of Kyoto in Canada. Evidence that the earth is warming is not diminished by the off-putting language of some climate scientists in the famous-in-conservative-circles stolen emails.
3. See the photos and graphics in Al Gore, *An Inconvenient Truth* (New York: Rodale, 2006).
4. Naomi Klein, "Climate Change is the Fight of Our Lives—Yet We Can Hardly Bear to Look at It," www.theguardian.com (April 23, 2014).
5. See Mike Berners-Lee and Duncan Clark, *The Burning Question* (Vancouver: Greystone Books, 2013).
6. Solar energy capacity in America doubled during Obama's first term.
7. See Ian Bailey and Hugh Compston (eds), *Feeling the Heat: The Politics of Climate Policy in the Rapidly Industrializing Countries* (Basingstoke, Hampshire: Palgrave Macmillan, 2012). China, for example, suffers from

horrendous air pollution and wants to become a leading producer of solar panels.
8. David Orr, "Governing in the Long Emergency," www.resilience.org/2013-05-14/governance-in-the-long-emergency. Accessed May 16, 2013.
9. See the *Stern Review on the Economics of Climate Change* available at: www.webarchive.nationalarchives.uk.gov dated July 7, 2010 and the American Geophysical Union August 2013, statement update at www.agu.org.
10. See the Stern Report as well as George Monbiot, *Heat: How to Stop the Planet from Burning* (Toronto: Doubleday Canada, 2006); David Goodstein, *Out of Gas: The End of the Age of Oil* (New York: Norton, 2004); and Michael T. Klare, *Resource Wars: The New Landscape of Global Conflict* (New York: Owl Books, 2002).
11. However, biomass, with plausible technological breakthroughs, could supply a good proportion of liquid fuel needs if those needs were reduced through automobile efficiency improvements and increased transit use. It is an uncertain option, though, given concerns regarding food prices, land use, and net carbon.
12. Biomass from grain has serious net energy problems. See David Pimentel, "Energy Balance, Economics and Environmental Impacts are Negative," *Natural Resources Research* 12 (June, 2003), pp. 127–134. Many also argue that clean coal is simply impossible. See also Tom Philpott, "Biofuel Skeptic Extraordinaire," www.grist.org (December 8, 2006). For an argument that clean coal is an oxymoron see www.thisisreality.org.
13. Regarding the energy content in the US stimulus bill, see Michael Grunwald, "How the Stimulus is Changing America," www.time.com (August 26, 2010).
14. See Gwynne Dyer, *Climate Wars* (Toronto: Vintage Canada, 2008).
15. Rapid growth in North American oil use began after World War II so this depletion has been more rapid than is usually assumed. For the early history of oil use, see Sam H. Schurr, *Energy and Economic Growth in the United States* (Washington: Resources for the Future, 1962) and for historic data on world oil consumption, see www.eia.doe.gov.
16. For the view that oil reserves are very limited, see www.peakoil.net or www.theoildrum.com. For relative optimism about reserves and doubts about peak oil see Cambridge Energy Research Associates "Why the 'Peak Oil' Theory Falls Down—Myths, Legends and the Future of Oil Resources," www.cera.com (November 10, 2006).
17. Regarding settlement and energy demand see, for example, Peter Newman and Jeffrey Kenworthy, *Cities and Sustainability: Overcoming Automobile Dependence* (Washington: Island Press, 1999).
18. James Howard Kunstler, *The Long Emergency: Surviving the Converging Catastrophes of the Twenty-First Century* (New York: Grove/Atlantic Books, 2006).
19. See Paehlke, *Some Like It Cold*.
20. For a quick summary of a key study on this point see Hilary Osborne, "Stern Report: the Key Points," www.theguardian.com (October 30, 2006).

21. In this lobbying effort the auto industry was of course joined by the oil industry.
22. Only a few years after oil prices declined in 1985, gas guzzlers again became Detroit's staple, and heavily advertised, offering. The decline in oil prices resulted from energy efficiency gains as a result of both high prices and public initiatives. Repeating this pattern for a third time (pre-1973, post-1985, and post-2008) goes beyond market failure into pig-headedness.
23. Most developing countries have signed Kyoto but have, under that treaty, been exempted from reductions since their per capita emissions and their historic emissions are still far, far below those of North America and Europe.
24. Ontario, after delays, plans to soon lose all coal-fired power plants.
25. Brad Plumer, "China May Soon Get a Carbon Tax," www.washingtopost.com (February 21, 2013).
26. One notable exception to this generalization are carbon emissions from slash and burn agriculture in poorer nations in Southeast Asia, China, and Latin America.
27. See Paul Krugman, "An Affordable Truth," www.nytimes.com (December 7, 2009).
28. Editorial, "Climate Signals," www.nytimes.com (November 7, 2005).
29. See www.apolloalliance.org.
30. I first saw the assertion as a "sig line" on the liberal weblog www.dailykos.com. Both books noted here are cited above.
31. See, for example, Barry G. Rabe, "Power to the States: The Promise and Pitfalls of Decentralization," in Norman J. Vig and Michael E Kraft (eds), *Environmental Policy* (Washington: Congressional Quarterly Press, 2006), pp. 34–56.
32. See www.toatmosphericfund.ca. Entry dated April 24, 2013. Accessed April 29, 2013.
33. December 11, 1997, is the date the Kyoto Agreement was opened for signatures.
34. For a discussion, see Molly Ivins, "Outrage of the Week," www.alternet.com (October 13, 2005). The normalization of torture was also apparent in the passage of the Military Commissions Act just prior to the 2006 midterm election (when many Democratic members were unwilling to appear soft on terrorism).
35. I like to think that by the time this book is published, however, the Obama administration will have rejected the Keystone pipeline project.
36. Naomi Oreskes, "The Scientific Consensus on Climate Change," *Science* 306, p. 1686.
37. Paul Krugman, "Enemy of the Planet," www.nytimes.com (April 17, 2006).
38. See "Inside Washington: Congressional Insiders Poll," *National Journal* 38, pp. 5–6.
39. A close examination of how conservative media viewing undermined public understanding of climate science was published in 2013: see Jay D. Hmielowski, et al., "An Attack on Science? Media Use, Trust in Scientists, and Perceptions of Global Warming," *Public Understanding of Science* (2013), pp. 1–18. Available at www.pus.sagepub.com.

40. Al Gore, "I Don't Plan to Run for President," www.yahoo.com (October 13, 2005).
41. In 2012, Romney's campaign advisors regarding foreign policy were primarily neoconservatives from the Bush–Cheney era. Romney frequently spoke of an "apology tour" regarding Obama's attempts to restore normal relations with long-standing allies. There are, however, also some signs of an emerging quasi-isolationism within the Republican Party led by Senator Rand Paul of Kentucky and others.
42. See Paul Rutherford, *Weapons of Mass Persuasion: the War against Iraq* (Toronto: University of Toronto Press, 2004).
43. This sense of things emerged from a reading of a December 28, 2006, diary in the political blog www.dailykos.com. The diary was by "Major Danby" and was entitled "Dick Cheney has a point."
44. This particular myth was put to rest on September 24, 2014, when President Obama, speaking to the United Nations said: "Iraq shows us that democracy cannot simply be imposed by force." See www.washingtonpost.com/politics/transcript-president-obamas-speech-at-the-un-general-assembly.
45. The list of blogs that emerged and grew during the early years of the war is very long and includes high-traffic sites such as Daily Kos, Balloon Juice, Eschaton, Hullabaloo, and Talking Points Memo.
46. It is plausible, for example, that Paul Wolfowitz thought that military action could launch a democratic transformation of much of the Middle East. It is also difficult to say how much of what was said was believed by George W. Bush. He might not know himself to this day. Generally, both the level of cynicism and the deep appreciation of what Americans might accept as a reason for war was impressive.
47. As well, in Florida a church was blocked from a public-burning of the Koran by a local fire department's refusal to grant a burning permit within the city limits.
48. Needless to say, September 11 had already made al Qaeda a genuine global threat, but the response did not focus on al Qaeda and the ways in which it could be weakened, contained, and dealt with directly.
49. Edmund Burke, the quintessential conservative political philosopher, made this point eloquently in the eighteenth century in his response to the French Revolution.
50. See, for example, Russell Kirk, *The Conservative Mind: From Burke to Eliot,* 7th edition (Washington, DC: Regerny Publishing, 2001).
51. This conclusion is captured in Israeli military historian Martin van Crevald's observation that the Iraq war was the greatest strategic blunder of the past 2000 years because it was initiated following on 60 years of history in which no such war had been successful. See Brian Whitaker, "Nowhere to Run," www.guardian.co.uk (November 29, 2005).
52. A third possibility is that enduring extensive casualties was seen as a test of the restoration of American mettle that the administration's new post-Vietnam media strategy would assure.
53. See, for example, George Packer, *Assassins' Gate: America in Iraq* (New York: Farrar, Straus and Giroux, 2005).

54. In 2013, for the first time a majority (52 %) of Americans agreed that "the US should mind its own business internationally" (up from 30 % in 2002). See www.pewresearch.org/fact-tank/2013/12.23/13-data-milestones-for-2013.
55. Reported at www.boomantribune.com (December 3, 2005) based on a discussion in *The Economist*.
56. See several polls available at: www.pewglobal.org.
57. Long after it had been thoroughly disproved, Dick Cheney was still implying that Saddam Hussein had had links to 9/11 and a depressing number of Americans accepted this as truth. One technique used to perpetuate this mythology was to mention Iraq or Saddam Hussein and al Qaeda in the same paragraph without explicitly saying that there was a connection.
58. See Ewan MacAskill, "Romney Election Triumph Would Sink US Reputation in Europe, Poll Finds," www.theguardian.com (September 11, 2012).
59. See Dinesh D'Souza, *The Roots of Obama's Rage* (Washington, DC: Regerny Publishing, 2010). Some, even some conservatives, have commented that this book reads like a bad conspiracy theory.
60. See Nick Wing, "Dana Rohrabacher, GOP House Science Committee Member: "Global Warming is a Total Fraud," www.huffingtonpost.com (August 12, 2013).
61. Romney spoke of fewer ships than in 1917; Obama replied that America had fewer horses and bayonets as well. See www.theguardian.com/world/2012/oct23/third-presidential-debate-obama-wins/. Accessed October 24, 2013.
62. Only in 2013 has extensive discussion of the minimum wage and low wages in the retail sector been widely engaged.
63. The so-called coalition of the willing quickly fell away to primarily troops from Britain, Australia, and Italy. Most had acted in the absence of enthusiasm from their own citizenry and by 2008 virtually all non-American troops had left Iraq.
64. The near certainty of the absence of such weapons was plainly stated by both Hans Blix, Chief UN Weapons Inspector and Mohamed ElBaradei, Head of the International Atomic Energy Agency, prior to the invasion. See Hans Blix, *Disarming Iraq: The Search for Weapons of Mass Destruction* (London: Bloomsbury Publishing PLC, 2005).
65. See Eric Boehlert, *Lapdogs: How the Press Rolled Over for Bush* (New York: Free Press, 2006).
66. To this end, the Bush administration scrapped treaties regarding antimissile missiles and announced the possibility of restarting nuclear testing.
67. For many it only exposed incompetence, but the real lesson runs deeper than that. American military strength has been achieved in part through a failure to attend to social justice needs. As well, during the Reagan and George W. Bush administrations, it was achieved on borrowed money (and during the latter was aided as well by a financial and housing bubble that was undermining the economy as a whole).
68. The phrase "getting government down to a size that it can be drowned in a bathtub" is from Grover Norquist, a leading conservative political strategist.

69. Kate Pickett and Richard Wilkinson showed some of the many ways this is true in their book, *The Spirit Level: Why Greater Equality Makes Societies Stronger* (New York: Bloomsbury Press, 2011). Many social ills (poor health, happiness, crime, mental illness), it turns out, are higher in more unequal wealthy societies, even among the middle class and the rich. This makes the contemporary trend of rising inequality all the more ominous. See also Joseph E. Stiglitz, *The Price of Inequality* (New York: Norton, 2012).
70. Eric Le Boucher, "Arrêtez la salade verde!" www.lemonde.fr (November 11, 2006). Translation and original citation from author Jerome á Paris on www.dkos.com same date.
71. George F. Will, "Leviathan in Louisiana," www.msnbc.com (September 12, 2005).
72. Maureen Dowd, "Lost in the Desert," www.nytimes.com (November 22, 2006).
73. This is not to say that some rooftop rescues were not accomplished rapidly, especially by fellow citizens, but there seemed to be no ability to deliver even drinking water to elderly people and children, many of whom had slogged for hours through filthy flood waters in sweltering heat and humidity.
74. Recall that many who "looted" had previously waited for days with no help whatsoever. Some had clawed their way through their own roofs with small tools or their bare hands in the dark and then trudged through chest deep filth for miles. Many had family members or neighbors who were dead or missing. It is incomprehensible that some were at risk of being charged with a crime in these circumstances. The *police* should have commandeered the contents of stores and distributed food and water to those in need. Payment could have been arranged later but should have been unnecessary since the content of stores was already destined for landfills and insurance claims.
75. See Trymaine Lee, "Rumor to Fact in Tales of Post-Katrina Violence," www.nytimes.com (August 26, 2010).
76. In fairness, armies must be ordered to act by civilian authorities that were busy choosing shirts for TV appearances and playing guitars in photo ops with popular country singers.
77. Local government could have done more in the years before Katrina struck, but following the disaster local governments often performed better than those at the state and national levels.
78. Arguably, the failure to achieve security in Iraq in the three years prior to Katrina had laid the groundwork for the dramatic shift in opinion triggered by that single riveting event.
79. Rush Limbaugh, ever the diplomat, in yet another attempt to stir racism among the benighted called Obama and Christie's connection a master-servant relationship.
80. Quoted in www.mediamatters.org September 9, 2005, from a radio broadcast on that same date.
81. Freedom is overused in American political discourse, but the word has great meaning to many around the world. It explains America's continuing appeal even among those repelled by some of its actions.

82. How normal is made clear by Rank who notes that 40 percent of Americans between 25 and 60 will spend at least one year below the official poverty line and more than that will experience unemployment or near poverty. See Mark R. Rank, "Poverty in America is Mainstream," www.nytimes.com (November 2, 2013). Accessed November 4, 2013.
83. Michael Harrington, *The Other America: Poverty in the United States* (New York: Scribner, 1997), originally published in 1962.
84. A trajectory wherein poverty can again be publically discussed began here and led toward Occupy Wall Street, and later to raise the minimum wage campaigns and President Obama's widely noted inequality speech of December 4, 2013.
85. Many in neighboring communities were welcoming, but many were decidedly not. Many refugees from the floods walking on abandoned highways were turned back by armed police and/or white vigilantes "protecting their neighborhoods."
86. It would be exceeding difficult to determine by how much climate change altered those odds, but average water temperatures in the Gulf had been higher for several years. This change will not necessarily increase the number of hurricanes, but it can increase the intensity of those that do occur.
87. See Mark Pelling, *Adaptation to Climate Change* (Abingdon, UK: Routledge, 2011).
88. See Ariella Cohen, "No-Go Zone," www.newsweek.com (August 25, 2010).
89. Eugene Robinson, "Where's Bush? Not in New Orleans" www.washingtonpost.com (December 16, 2005).

3 The Evolution of Citizenship: From Athens to Earth

1. Doug Miller, "Citizens of the World Want UN Reform," www.globeandmail.com (April 8, 2005), web-exclusive comment reporting a Globescan poll conducted in 2005.
2. Regarding "endless yesterdays"—I owe a footnote to Max Weber who spoke of the eternal yesterday of traditional rule. See Robert Paehlke, *Environmentalism and the Future of Progressive Politics* (New Haven: Yale University Press, 1989), p. 178.
3. Several points in this section, and this chapter, were previously discussed (and debated) online. See Robert Paehlke, "Global Citizenship: Plausible Fears and Necessary Dreams," www.greattransition.org (June, 2014).
4. See Kate Parlett, *The Individual in the International Legal System* (New York: Cambridge University Press, 2013).
5. One group that often needs international help is refugees. Indeed, 11 to 15 million persons, mostly in camps, are stateless—unable to prove who they are or where they belong. See Victoria Redclift, *Statelessness and Citizenship* (Abingdon, Oxford: Routledge, 2013).

6. There are UN associations in many nations. United States: www.unausa.org. Canada: www.unac.org.
7. For information on the 2009 World Social Forum, see: www.fsm2009amazonia.org.br.
8. The COP for the Kyoto climate change treaty held in Copenhagen and Durban, for example, had broad public participation. Information on these meetings is available at www.unfccc.int and such participation will continue at future meetings. Another example is the Joint Public Advisory Committee (JPAC) of the Commission for Environmental Cooperation (CEC), an organization focused on the environmental and social effects of the North American Free Trade Agreement (NAFTA). For this, see www.cec.org/jpac.
9. The Massachusetts Institute of Technology (MIT) has made its course syllabi available worldwide. Google is putting massive libraries online. Al Jazeera has English language broadcasts available in much of the West adding to media diversity. UNESCO produced an online environmental encyclopedia compendium available at www.eolss.net that made valuable environmental information available to citizens and governments in poorer nations.
10. Miller, "Citizens of the World Want UN Reform," www.globeandmail.com (April 8, 2005), web-exclusive comment reporting a Globescan poll conducted in 2005.
11. For example, even if only one chamber of any global "legislature" (a general assembly analog) were directly elected within some or all nations and its powers were highly limited relative to a second chamber (a security council analog) comprised of delegates named by states and favoring powerful states, the elected assembly delegates could emerge in time as politically significant on the global stage.
12. It is not clear precisely how and what the American government monitors within global communications, but there is little doubt that it monitors extensively. American "signals intelligence" includes keeping track of who communicates with whom and some sort of computer key word monitoring of phone and electronic messaging.
13. Television is singled out here because it is ubiquitous yet controlled almost exclusively, in the United States, by a small number of large media corporations.
14. Alexander Keyssar, *The Right to Vote: The Contested History of Democracy in the United States* (New York: Basic Books, 2009).
15. In 2013 the Supreme Court overturned sections of the Voting Rights Act opening the way to selective (though not formally race-based) limitations on the opportunity to vote in several states.
16. Water from the tap is almost free compared to bottled water, which is more expensive per liter than gasoline. Health care in Canada is provided universally as a public service and costs significantly less per capita than health care in America, a predominantly private system—even with a significant proportion of Americans excluded from other than emergency access.
17. See David Boyd, *The Environmental Rights Revolution: A Global Study of Constitutions, Human Rights and the Environment* (Vancouver: University of British Columbia Press, 2012).

18. L. T. Hobhouse, *Liberalism* (Oxford: Oxford University Press, 1964).
19. T. H. Marshall and T. B. Bottomore, *Citizenship and Social Class* (London: Pluto Press, 1992). Page references in the text refer to this edition.
20. This point was brought home to me in the 2013 Morrison Lecture at Trent University given by Manfred Bienefeld (September 25, 2013).
21. Robert D. Putnam, *Bowling Alone: The Collapse and Revival of American Community* (New York: Simon & Schuster, 2001).
22. Robert Paehlke, *Democracy's Dilemma: Environment, Social Equity and the Global Economy* (Cambridge: MIT Press, 2003).
23. Most dramatic in this regard has been the decline of defined benefit pensions. During and following the financial meltdown of 2008, risk was transferred to individuals. The great mercy is that the attempt to make social security assets market-based in 2005 failed. Had that effort succeeded, today's economic situation might have been far worse.
24. Canadians and Europeans see security more in terms of societal functioning and the effectiveness of social programs than in terms of military might.
25. Quoted from *The Federalist* by Rocco J. Tresolini in his *American Constitutional Law* (New York: MacMillan, 1959), p. 83.
26. In recent years some American religious conservatives have argued that the founding fathers actually wished the United States to be a Christian nation. There is no historical basis for this view.
27. For a thorough discussion, see Will Kymlicka, *Multicultural Citizenship* (New York: Oxford University Press, 1995).
28. A transcript of the speech given on September 6, 2012, is available at www.npr.org.
29. Boutros Boutros Ghali was called out by American conservatives on the campaign trail during the Bush years. The notion of democratizing international relations is anathema to them, no small irony for a nation that was at the time trumpeting a goal of democratizing other nations through military might.
30. The late Senator Everett Dirksen (R-IL), the noted American conservative, once said of civil and voting rights legislation that there was no stopping an idea whose time had come. The same might be said today of global governance though it is unlikely that today's conservatives will be half as wise as Dirksen.
31. Perhaps the only multilateral options the Bush administration ever accepted were an abstention on a UN resolution regarding Darfur and generous funding for combating AIDS in Africa.
32. See John Perkins, *Confessions of an Economic Hit Man* (New York: Plume, 2005) and the website of the Berlin-based global civil society economic transparency movement Transparency International at: www.transparency.org.
33. See Robert Paehlke, *Democracy's Dilemma: Environment, Social Equity and the Global Economy* (Cambridge, MA: MIT Press, 2004).
34. Regarding many of these issues see, for example, Glenn Greenwald, *A Tragic Legacy* (New York: Three Rivers Press, 2008).

35. To begin thinking about such questions see: Benjamin Barber, *Jihad vs. McWorld: How Globalism and Tribalism are Reshaping the World* (New York: Ballantine Books, 1996).
36. One wonders if the bin Laden video helped to reelect President Bush by directing timely attention to the very issue (terrorism) where Bush had his strongest political advantage. Whether this possible effect might have been intentional will likely never be known.
37. I take the term blowback from Chalmers Johnson, *Blowback: The Costs and Consequences of American Empire* (New York: Holt Paperbacks, 2004).
38. See Brad Plumer, "The End of Fish in One Chart," www.washingtonpost.com. Published and accessed May 19, 2012, and Daniel Pauly, "Aquapalypse Now," www.tnr.com. Published September 28, 2009; accessed May 21, 2012.
39. Among the iconic species at risk are whales, tigers, and pandas.
40. Changes in government can sometimes diminish opportunities for sanctuary. This might apply to Afghanistan, but clearly not to Iraq where there were few terrorists prior to the American invasion.
41. Regarding the latter, see David Vogel, *The Market for Virtue: the Potential and the Limits of Corporate Social Responsibility* (Washington: Brookings Institution Press, 2006).
42. At the time there was a minority government in Canada and some visible doubts about the need for such a system among Canadians.
43. See, for example, Clyde Pestowitz, *Rogue Nation* (New York: Basic Books, 2003), and the remarks of Brent Scowcroft quoted in Maureen Dowd, "Defining Victory Down," www.nytimes.com (January 9, 2005).
44. Editorial: "The World According to Bolton," www.nytimes.com (March 9, 2005). Ambassador Bolton, ever the new-style diplomat, explicitly identified the one permanent member, and sole global power, as the United States.
45. See, for example, Eric Margolis, "US Buries the Truth," (Toronto: *Toronto Sun*, December 31, 2006), accessed on www.commondreams.org on January 3, 2007. Margolis contends that America did not want Saddam to reveal that it had supported Saddam during the invasion of Iran. More than that though, the administration did not want to establish a precedent of trials for deposed dictators in an international court lest it open the door to trials of those dictators that it might prefer.
46. See www.fsm2009amazonia.org.br and www.slowfood.org.
47. As well, increased travel is incompatible with climate action.
48. *Sorry Everybody: An Apology to the World for the Re-Election of George W. Bush* was published in book form in 2005 by Hylas Publishing.
49. Frank Rich, "How Dirty Harry Turned Commie," www.nytimes.com (February 13, 2005).
50. I doubt that the American electorate, given the media bias of the day, fully understood the international significance of the 2004 election. Many were voting against legalizing gay marriage more than for torture. Or they voted for Bush as a well-meaning leader, lacking elite "airs," rather than rejecting participation in climate initiatives. Many in the rest of the world, however, saw the choice in different terms.

4 From New American Century to Global Age America?

1. See survey data at www.pewglobal.org.
2. See, for example, Greg Grandin and Naomi Klein, *The Last Colonial Massacre: Latin America in the Cold War* (Chicago: University of Chicago Press, 2011).
3. See, for example, Clyde Prestowitz, *Rogue Nation: American Unilateralism and the Failure of Good Intentions* (New York: Basic Books, 2003).
4. Paul Wolfowitz, Robert Kagan, Lewis Libby, Stephen Cambone, and John R. Bolton among others signed (or wrote) the *Rebuilding America's Defenses* document published in 2000 and were also involved in the planning of or rationale for the occupation of Iraq. The planning began well before September 11, 2001.
5. William Kristol and Liz Cheney offered a widely noted assertion that called Obama Department of Justice officials "the Al Qaeda Seven" for providing defense counsel to those on trial (as required by the US Constitution and military regulations).
6. These and other actions repositioning from Europe and Asia to the Middle East presumably gave pause to every nation with oil, and set many wondering whether they too might eventually be on the list.
7. Chief among those factors were McCain's obvious discomfort with economic policy and his selection of an inexperienced extremist as a running mate (an important matter considering McCain's age).
8. Gerrymanders, a long-standing American tradition, are also complex. One reasonable objective would be the creation of more relatively more competitive seats. See Ed Kilgore, "The Fix Is In," www.dlc.org May 31, 2005).
9. Some conservative libertarians have an isolationist streak and prefer reduced military spending as part of small government.
10. George W. Bush indeed went out of his way to cool anti-Muslim attitudes, but rarely hesitated to stir up fear of "Islamic terrorism."
11. Quoted in "Lee Atwater," www.wikipedia.org.
12. Those attacks included endless claims that Obama had not been born in the United States or was secretly a Muslim.
13. Racism plays out in local politics as well. For example, a Republican leader in Atlanta recently (in 2013) made clear that he did not want to see public transit moving Atlanta city residents to a possible new suburban baseball stadium of the Atlanta Braves. See Ed Kilgore, "Take MARTA to Cobb and Rob," www.washingtonmonthly.com/political-animal (November 12, 2013). Urban governance failure in Detroit also has roots in racism. See George Galster, *Driving Detroit: The Quest for Respect in Motor City* (Philadelphia, University of Pennsylvania Press, 2012).
14. Following Dean's narrow loss in Iowa, all television networks repeated in an almost continuous loop, Dean shouting over the noise of a large crowd of young supporters. In this coverage of "the scream" that effectively ended his candidacy, the background noise was electronically faded so that his speech sounded hyperbolic and slightly demented.

15. See www.mediamatters.org/research/2014/01/16/study-how-broadcast-news-covered-climate-change-in-the-last-five-years for details.
16. For example, between June 2011 and February 2012, the proportion of guests on the Sunday news shows on the four main television networks were 70 percent Republicans and 86 percent men. This sort of pattern rarely changes. See www.fair.org (Fairness and Accuracy in Reporting). The pattern did not change in 2013; see www.mediamatters.org "REPORT: Once Again, Sunday Morning Talk Shows Are White, Male and Conservative" (October 11, 2013). Accessed October 14, 2013.
17. Robert W. McChesney, John Nichols, and Ben Scott, "Congress Tunes In" (May 5, 2005 at www.thenation.com). Needless to say, this assessment is provided by a media source in a magazine that has been published for a century. The point is not that information and progressive framing are kept from Americans, only that one must work hard to find it where neoconservative frames and trivia are literally in everyone's face.
18. Figures are from the Center for Responsive Politics via www.opensecrets.org. Accessed January 16, 2007.
19. Representative Buchanan was certified the victor, but through poor ballot design or machine malfunction, there was a very large undervote in this highly contested Congressional race. Several studies have indicated that had the expected number of voters cast ballots, Buchanan would have lost by a sizeable margin.
20. Figures available on www.opensecrets.org.
21. Indeed the poor are rarely even mentioned in American political life. See Charles P. Pierce, www.esquire.com/blogs/politics/cuts-to-food-stamps-110813.
22. 558 U.S. *Citizens United v. Federal Election Commission* (2010).
23. www.publicintegrity.org/print/13712.
24. Martin Gilens and Benjamin I. Page, "Testing Theories of American Politics: Elites, Interest Groups, and Average Citizens," mimeo. Forthcoming in *Perspectives on Politics* (Fall 2014).
25. See Gary May, *Bending Towards Justice: The Voting Rights Act and the Transformation of American Democracy* (New York: Basic Books, 2013). For a conservative voice in support of voting rights, see Norm Ornstein, "The Right to Vote," www.nationaljournal.com/washington-inside-out/the-right-to-vote-20131030.
26. See, for example, www.climatechange.ca.gov.
27. See: www.usmayors.org/climate protection and www.cityofseattle.net/mayor/climate.
28. Alex Haley, *Roots* (New York: Vanguard, reissued 2007).
29. A good summary of what has been done is offered in Ian Reifowitz, "Obama Has Done Nothing to Address Income Inequality. Right?" www.dailykos.com/story/2013/11/03/1251386/-Obama-has-done-nothing-to-address-income-inequality-Right? Accessed November 3, 2013.
30. Roger Cohen, "A Court for a New America," www.nytimes.com (December 4, 2008).
31. See Joseph E. Stiglitz, *The Price of Inequality* (New York: Norton, 2012).

218 Notes

32. Paul Krugman, "Graduates versus Oligarchs," www.nytimes.com (February 27, 2007).
33. See Emmanuel Saez, "Striking it Richer: The Evolution of Top Incomes in the United States," www.elsa.berkeley.edu (September 3, 2013).
34. For example, clothing workers in poor nations receive from 0.5 to 4.0 percent of the cost of clothing sold in wealthy nations. Doubling their wages would therefore add less than 10 percent to the retail cost of clothing. See www.ethicalfashionforum.com. See also Worker Rights Consortium "Global Wage Trends for Apparel Workers, 2001–2011," www.americanprogress.org (July 11, 2013). Accessed December 2, 2013.
35. The electoral implications of the demographic shift are intelligently discussed by Ronald Brownstein in "Bad Bet: Why Republicans Can't Win with Whites Alone," www.nationaljournal.com (September 5, 2013).
36. See, for example, Pew Research Center for the People & the Press, "Public Sees U.S. Power Declining as Support for Global Engagement Slips," www.people-press.org (December 3, 2013).
37. The importance of these speeches in this context came home to me reading a column by Leonard Pitts, Jr., "The Speech that Defined and Challenged Us," www.miamiherald.com (November 16, 2013).

5 Global Citizenship without Global Government

1. The United States may remain the greatest single military power, but it cannot indefinitely outspend most other nations combined. Recently, a noted moderate American foreign policy analyst advocated 'a breather' on foreign interventions to concentrate on domestic needs including restoring economic growth. See Richard N. Haass, *Foreign Policy Begins at Home: The Case for Putting America's House in Order* (New York: Basic Books, 2013). The conflicting needs here are not, in my view, temporary.
2. David Miller, *National Responsibility and Global Justice* (Oxford: Oxford University Press, 2007). See also Bruce Cronin, *Institutions for the Common Good: International Protection Regimes in International Society* (Cambridge: Cambridge University Press, 2003).
3. John S. Dryzek, *Deliberative Global Politics* (Cambridge UK: Polity Press, 2006).
4. National origin labels are often highly deceptive since ingredients and components are sourced from many nations and labeling rules may be vague or not immune to evasion.
5. In some locations they have been transformative as in the case of fair trade bananas from the Piura region of Peru. See www.cftn.ca/resources/blog/education-and-voice-how-peruvians-improved-their-lives-selling-fair-trade-bananas.
6. Among the earliest to make this case were Frances Moore Lappé and Joseph Collins in *Food First: Beyond the Myth of Scarcity* (New York: Ballantine

Books, 1977). More recently see Wayne Roberts, *The No-Nonsense Guide to World Food* (Toronto: Between the Lines, 2013).
7. See Robert Paehlke, *Democracy's Dilemma: Environment, Social Equity and the Global Economy* (Cambridge: MIT Press, 2004).
8. Unlike most nations, Chile, Mexico, Turkey, Hungary and, until recently, Greece have *reduced* income inequality. Clearly policy choices are relevant. See Joseph Stiglitz, "Inequality Is a Choice," www.nytimes.com (October 13, 2006).
9. See Michael A. Fletcher, "Income Inequality Hurts Economic Growth, Researchers Say," www.washingtonpost.com (January 26, 2014) and studies cited therein.
10. S. M. Lipset, *Political Man* (Garden City, NY: Doubleday, 1960).
11. William Ophuls, *Ecology and the Politics of Scarcity* (San Francisco: W.H. Freeman, 1977), p. 151 discussing how Rousseau distinguished his central concept, the "general will," from the "will of all."
12. See www.whc.unesco.org/en/about/.
13. Amory Lovins, *Reinventing Fire* (White River Junction, VT: Chelsea Green, 2011).
14. See www.simpol.org. The approach is called the Simultaneous Policy campaign.
15. Quoted in Chrystia Freeland, "The Advent of a Global Intelligence," *International Herald Tribune* (September 23, 2011), p. 2.
16. Peter Bachrach and Morton S. Baratz, "Decisions and Nondecisions: An Analytic Framework," *American Political Science Review* 57 (September 1963), pp. 632–642.
17. Joseph Stiglitz, "Developing Countries are Right to Resist Restrictive Trade Agreements," www.theguardian.com (November 8, 2013).
18. See Scott Carlson, "Defense Insider: Sustainable Communities are Key to the Future," www.grist.org (November 11, 2011).
19. See www.army-energy.hqda.pentagon.mil/netzero/. See also the recent report of the CNA (Corporation) Military Advisory Board, *National Security and the Accelerating Risks of Climate Change* (May 2014) Available at: www.cna.org/sites/default/files/MAB_2014.pdf. The CNA Military Advisory Board includes more than a dozen retired generals and admirals.
20. Jim Dwyer, "A National Security Strategy That Doesn't Focus on Threats," www.nytimes.com (May 4, 2011).
21. Mr. Y, *A National Strategic Narrative*, available from www.wilsoncenter.org, published 2011, p. 5.
22. Ibid., p. 6.
23. Paul Collier, *The Plundered Planet: How to Reconcile Prosperity with Nature* (New York: Penguin Books, 2011), p. x.
24. Tariq Banuri and Niclas Hällström, "A Global Programme to Tackle Energy Access and Climate Change," *Development Dialogue: What Next Volume III* (September, 2012), pp. 265–279. See also Felipe Calderon, "The New Climate Economics," www.project-syndicate.org (September 22, 2013).
25. For a partial explanation see, for example, Harold Meyerson, "The Lansing-Beijing Connection," www.washingtonpost.com. Published December 12,

2012; accessed December 13, 2012. One possible response to restrictions on unionization in China is citizen pressure on retailers to adopt responsible contractor policies. Another, as noted, is to include the right to unionization in trade agreements.

26. The Chinese government has recently become more open about air quality problems. See Simon Denver, "In China's War on Bad Air, Government Decision to Release Data gives Fresh Hope," www.washingtonpost.com (February 3, 2014).
27. Considerable credit in this regard should go to many American foundations, most notably perhaps the post-Presidential work of Bill Clinton regarding global development, health, women's rights and the effects of climate change. See www.clintonfoundation.org.
28. See www.gtinitiative.org.
29. These would include www.nokero.com and www.kiva.org and hundreds of others.
30. Susan Clark and Woden Teachout, *Slow Democracy* (White River Junction, VT: Chelsea Green, 2012).
31. See Steve Killelea, "The Peace-Prosperity Cycle," www.project-syndicate.org (October 22, 2013).
32. Jake Richardson, "94% Renewable Electricity by 2017 is Goal for Nicaragua," www.cleantechnica.com. Published January 6, 2013; accessed July 27, 2013.
33. Sami Grover, "Kenya to get 50% of Electricity from Solar by 2016" www.treehugger.com (January 21, 2014), citing The Guardian.
34. Robert J. Allen, Steven C. Sherwood, Joel R. Norris, and Charles S. Zender, "Recent Northern Hemisphere Tropical Expansion Primarily Driven by Black Carbon and Tropospheric Ozone," *Nature* 485 (May 16, 2012), pp. 350–354.
35. Regarding women's rights two important recent steps are the creation of the UN Entity for Gender Equality and the Empowerment of Women – www.unwomen.org – in 2010 and global reaction to the powerful example of Malala Yousafzai in 2012 and since.
36. See, for example, Andrew Wong, "Is Bitumen Good for Canada?" www.alternativesjournal.ca/science-and-solutions/bitumen-good-canada. Accessed May 15, 2013.
37. The Brundtland Commission, named for the former Norwegian Prime Minister that chaired it, popularized the term sustainable development.
38. Thomas Piketty, *Capital in the 21st Century* (Cambridge, MA: Harvard University Press, 2014).
39. See, for example, Jeff Faux, "Thomas Piketty Undermines the Hallowed Tenets of the Capitalist Catechism," www.thenation.com (April 21, 2014).
40. The importance of wicked problems in relation to development was brought home to me in two October 2011 lectures at Trent University by Lucie Edwards, a noted, recently retired Canadian diplomat.
41. The text of Lovins's talk is available in *Alternatives: Perspectives on Society and Environment*, volume 8 (Summer/Fall, 1979), pp. 4–9.

42. One of the many communicators of such possibilities is Solutions Journal, a widely accessible online publication available at: www.thesolutionsjournal.com.
43. See the discussion by Harold Meyerson, "Democracy Is on the Retreat in Europe," www.washingtonpost.com (December 6, 2011).

6 Conclusion: Building Global Citizenship

1. Michael Lind, "Against Cosmopolitanism," in *Breakthrough Journal*, No. 1 (Summer 2011), p. 30.
2. Lind, p. 33.
3. Ibid.
4. Terry Glavin, "About China: Canadians Need to Talk about What's Happening Under our Noses," www.transmontanus.blogspot.ca (December 10, 2011). Accessed December 2, 2013. Glavin is a conservative whose work appears in the *Ottawa Citizen* and the *National Post*.
5. Anka Lee, *How Standing Up for Chinese Workers Helps Our Economy: A Policy Brief* (Washington D.C.: Progressive Policy Institute, 2012).
6. For an explicitly low carbon development strategy (for Guyana) see: www.lcds.gov/gy.
7. Martha Nussbaum, *Cultivating Humanity* (Cambridge: Harvard University Press, 1998). For Nussbaum's eloquent case for global citizenship see *Not for Profit* (Princeton: Princeton University Press, 2010).
8. This phrase from the Great Transition Institute (www.gtinstitute.org) discussed below.
9. See www.un.org/millenniumgoals.
10. See Mary Landers, "Solar Has a Bright Future in Georgia," www.savannahnow.com (September 2, 2013). Accessed September 3, 2013. See also Grace Wyler, "A War over Solar Power Is Raging within the GOP," www.newrepublic.com (November 21, 2013).
11. One exception to this was environmental policy. In the 1970s heyday of environmentalism American legislation added provisions for public involvement in environmental regulatory decisions. See Robert Paehlke, "Democracy and Environmentalism: Opening a Door to the Administrative State," in Robert Paehlke and Douglas Torgerson, eds., *Managing Leviathan: Environmental Politics and the Administrative State* (Peterborough, ON: Broadview Press, 2005), pp. 25–43.
12. See www.simpol.org. A case is made here that *simultaneous* action is more easily accomplished.
13. It is not the *medium* of television *per se* that enabled Bush, but the pattern of ownership and regulation.
14. See, for example, Peter M. Shane, ed., *Democracy Online: The Prospects for Political Renewal through the Internet* (London: Routledge, 2004) and Elaine Ciulla Kamarck and Joseph S. Nye, eds., *Governance.Com: Democracy in the Information Age* (Washington: Brookings Institution Press, 2002).

15. Regarding the rising influence of the political blogs see Lowell Feld and Nate Wilcox, *Netroots Rising: How a Citizen Army of Bloggers and Online Activists is Changing American Politics* (New York: Praeger, 2009) and Jerome Armstrong and Markos Moulitsas Zuniga, *Crashing the Gate: Netroots, Grassroots, and the Rise of People-Powered Politics* (White River Junction, VT: Chelsea Green, 2006).
16. All quotes here from Bill McKibben, "A Movement for a New Planet," www.thenation.com (August 19, 2013). Accessed August 20, 2013.
17. See, for example, www.ewb-usa.org. There are equivalent organizations in Canada, Britain, Australia, and elsewhere.
18. See www.sdinet.org.
19. Newspapers were in libraries on microfiche or one could clip stories, but the whole process is now vastly easier, making it more open to citizens, those not doing full-time research.
20. Ordinary citizens, lacking experienced editors, it might be argued, may be prone to errors. Intellectual snobbery notwithstanding, they are called to task by thousands of amateur editors. Moreover, they do not need to answer to wealthy publishers or to avoid offending advertisers.
21. Yearly Kos, the second annual gathering of participants in the website Daily Kos, in Chicago in 2007, drew thousands and featured all Democratic candidates for president, and dozens of Congressional candidates.
22. Newspapers accept letters to the editor, but those are selectively printed and are a small proportion of a paper's content. In the early days of radio someone not wealthy might start a radio station, but that era is long past other than perhaps through campus and community stations. The internet takes citizen communication opportunities ahead by orders of magnitude.
23. See Mary Kaldor, *Global Civil Society: An Answer to War* (Cambridge, UK: Polity Press, 2003).
24. See www.earthcharterinaction.org.
25. See www.humanwave.com, www.onthecommons.org, and www.facebook.com/ElectoralRebellion.
26. Importing nations inspect imported food, but many agencies have been cut back severely. Inspections are infrequent and pesticide residues, for example, are very rarely assessed.
27. The most horrific example of this came in 2013 in Bangladesh when more than 1000 clothing workers perished in a fire reminiscent of events in America's garment industry more than a century earlier. See Sarah Butler, "Three Factory Safety Deals in Bangladesh Aim to Improve Conditions," www.theguardian.com (October 23, 2013) and Worker Rights Consortium, "Global Wage Trends for Apparel Workers, 2001–2011," www.americanprogress.org (July 11, 2013).
28. See www.transfairusa.org, www.fairtradefederation.com, and www.ifad.org. The last provides a broader view of rural development needs.
29. See Gavin Fridell, *Fair Trade Coffee: The Prospects and Pitfalls of Market-Oriented Social Justice* (Toronto: University of Toronto Press, 2007).
30. There is extensive discussion of environmental ethical investing at www.greenmoneyjournal.com.

31. See Mark Lifsher, www.latimes.com (January 4, 2012) and Jamie Raskin, "The Rise of Benefit Corporations," www.thenation.com (June 8, 2011).
32. Micro-loans were made famous when Muhammad Yunus and the Grameen Bank of Bangladesh won a Nobel Prize. See www.grameen-info.org. See also Muhammad Yunus's autobiography *Banker to the Poor* (New York: Oxford University Press, 2001).
33. See, for example, www.kiva.org.
34. Dan Roberts, "Is the World Falling Out of Love with US Brands?" *The Financial Times* (January 5, 2005), downloaded from www.yaleglobe.yale.edu.
35. www.avaaz.org.
36. Ben Garside, "Norway Pledges $300 million/year to Green World's Power," www.reuters.com (January 18, 2012).
37. See Kwame Anthony Appiah, *Cosmopolitanism: Ethics in a World of Strangers* (New York: Norton, 2007).
38. www.wideningcircle.org.
39. www.wideningcircle.org.
40. www.gtinitiative.org.
41. The conference emphasized the post-2015 development goals and was held November 10–15, 2013. See www.civicus.org.
42. See www.world-governance.org.
43. World Economic Forum, *Insight Report: Global Risks 2012*. Available from: www.weforum.org.
44. Frances Moore Lappé, *Eco-Mind* (New York: Nation Books, 2011).
45. www.pachamama.org.
46. Kofi Annan, "A United Call for Action on Climate Change," www.washingtonpost.com (January 22, 2014).
47. See Arlie Hochschild, "How to Foster Compassion in Children," www.latimes.com (September 2, 2013). Accessed September 3, 2013. See also Tracy Kidder, *Mountains Beyond Mountains* (New York: Random House, 2003) – a biography of Paul Farmer and www.pih.org.
48. See Sarah Dougherty, "This Is What Politicians Debating Global Warming Will Look Like Soon," www.globalpost.com (March 26, 2014).
49. Yotam Ottolenghi and Sami Tamimi, *Jerusalem: A Cookbook* (New York: Random House Appetite, 2012).
50. Americans tend to misjudge how much they presently contribute, at least in terms of the proportion of the federal budget going to foreign aid. See: Ezra Klein, "The Budget Myth,..." www.washingtonpost.com (November 7, 2013). Accessed December 2, 2013.
51. Global Peace Index 2012 data suggests that domestic and international violence and avoiding it cost the world cost the world $9 trillion or more than 10% of GDP. See Steve Killelea, "The Peace-Prosperity Cycle," www.project-syndicate.org (October 22, 2013). Accessed October 25, 2013.
52. The links among believing that one can influence political outcomes, citizen political participation and political efficacy is treated extensively in political science dating back to the 1960s. See, for example, the classic Gabriel Almond and Sidney Verba, *The Civic Culture* (Boston: Little Brown, 1963).

53. Francis Fukuyama, "The Future of History," in *Foreign Affairs* 91 (January, 2012), p. 53.
54. See: Task Force on Inequality and American Democracy, *American Democracy in an Age of Rising Inequality* (Washington, D.C.: American Political Science Association, 2004) available at www.apsanet.org. See also Piketty, op cit.
55. Guy Standing, "The Precariat: Why It Needs Deliberative Democracy," www.opendemocracy.net/print/63869, p. 3.
56. Ibid., p. 6.
57. Regarding some positive effects of global economic integration on global equity see Francis Stewart and Albert Berry, "Globalization, Liberalization, and Inequality: Expectations and Experience," in Andrew Hurrell and Ngaire Woods, eds., *Inequality, Globalization, and World Politics* (New York: Oxford University Press, 1999), pp. 150–186.
58. Branko Milanovic, *The Haves and the Have-Nots* (New York: Basic Books, 2012).
59. Thomas Schutz, "Has America Become an Oligarchy?" www.spiegel.de/international (October 28, 2011).
60. It is also notable that America stands out as having markedly lower life expectancy than comparably wealthy nations. See www.dx.doi.org/10.1787.888932916040.
61. Many politicians pretend that these forces are more beyond their control than they actually are. See Robert Paehlke, *Democracy's Dilemma: Environment, Social Equity, and the Global Economy* (Cambridge, MA: MIT Press, 2004).
62. See, for example, Ian Reifowitz, *Obama's America: A Transformative Vision of Our National Identity* (Washington, DC: Potomac Books, 2012). See also Maureen A. Craig and Jennifer A. Richeson, "On the Precipice of a 'Majority-Minority' America: Perceived Status Threat from the Racial Demographic Shift Affects White Americans' Political Ideology," *Psychological Science*, published online April 3, 2014.
63. See Rich McEachran, "African Social Enterprises Pave the Way for Solar Power while Stimulating the Local Economy," www.the guardian.com (December 3, 2013). See also www.nokero.com, www.solar-aid.org and www.solarsister.org.
64. See Julia Pyper, "EPA Bans Sooty Ship Fuel off U.S. Coasts," www.scientificamerican.com (August 2, 2012). Accessed: December 2, 2013.
65. See "Global Civil Society Celebrates Failure of Talks at World Trade Organization," www.foodfirst.org (November 27, 2013).
66. Anna Lappe, *Diet for a Hot Planet* (New York: Bloomsbury USA, 2010).
67. See Robert Paehlke, *Democracy's Dilemma*.
68. Kemal Derviş, "The Inequality Trap," www.projectsyndicate.org (March 8, 2012).

Index

350.org, 112, 179
2008 recession/economic crisis
   American economy and, 10, 76
   borrowing for war and, 34
   electoral politics and, 74
   energy initiatives and, 46–7
   financial investments and, 140
   foreign investors and, 36
   fossil energy demand and, 47
   pensions and, 214n23

Abu Ghraib, 27
activism
   global citizenship and, 111–14, 159, 174–6
   importance of, 84, 89–90, 169
   the Internet and, 177–8
   venues for, 180–6
   voting as, 129
   work settings and, 145
   younger generation and, 137
   See also civil society organizations; global citizen's movement
adaptation
   to climate change, 44–5, 81, 82, 165
   of hegemonic dominance, 38–9, 131–2, 162, 188
Afghanistan, 5, 104, 107
African Americans, 79–80, 93, 122–4
agriculture, 11, 73, 81, 198. *See also* food

AK-47s, 9
America
   advice to, 31–2
   arms sales by, 34–5
   concentration of power in, 103
   contributions of to citizenship, 97–9
   defensibility of, 23
   democracy in, 16, 17
   domestic politics of, 119, 121–2
   electoral politics of, 120–1, 123–4, 129–31
   gap with rest of world, 58
   global economic integration and, 131–6
   global governance and, 156–9
   hegemony of, 14, 117–18, 171
   illusions about power of, 75, 83–4
   inequality in, 193–4, 212n82
   military bases of, 21–2
   national security of, 153–5
   political culture of, 122–8, 130–1
   political system of, 119–21, 129–30
   social citizenship in, 97
   strengths of, 158, 188
   transformation of, 136–7
   See also America, global view of; Bush administration; democracy; military expenditures; Obama administration

America, global view of
  Bush administration and, 1–2, 64–6, 69, 117–18
  global citizenship and, 115
  Hurricane Katrina and, 77–8, 83–4
  Iraq war and, 14, 35, 67
  Obama's election and, 3
American Recovery and Reinvestment Act (2009), 47
Americans for Prosperity, 127
Amnesty International, 88, 146, 180
Annan, Kofi, 189
Apollo Alliance, 53
Arab Spring, 32, 105, 107, 144, 145, 179
Architects without Borders, 179
arms races, 12–13, 22, 56, 69, 139, 163. See also nuclear capabilities
arms sales, 34–5
Army Corps of Engineers, 78
art, 122, 190–1
Athens, ancient, 92
Atwater, Lee, 123
Australia, 45, 55, 59, 109, 161, 210n63
automobile industry, 50–1, 208n22
Avaaz, 146, 185

Baghdad, Iraq. See Iraq war
Baker, James, 26
Banana Republic (clothing stores), 183
banks/financial institutions
  deregulation of, 10
  military spending and, 35–6
  need for regulation of, 141, 149, 158, 167, 200, 202
Banuri, Tariq, 155
Barenboim, Daniel, 190
Beck, Glenn, 77
biomass, 45, 207n11, 207n12
Biosphere Reserves, 149

Bipartisan Campaign Reform Act (McCain-Feingold law) (2002), 127
Blair, Tony, 17, 54, 109, 111, 205n26
blogs, 60–1, 145, 177–8, 179, 209n45
Bolton, John, 67, 109–10, 215n44, 216n4
Boutros-Ghali, Boutros, 100, 214n29
Brazil, 12, 53, 135, 160, 171
Bremer, Paul, 63
Britain, 10–11, 93, 109
Brittle Power: Energy Strategy for National Security (Lovins and Lovins), 154
Buchanan, Vernon, 125
Bunker C oil, 198
Burke, Edmund, 95, 209n49
Bush, George H. W., 123
Bush, George W.
  campaign funds raised by, 125–6
  foreign policy of, 55
  media treatment of, 124, 205n35
  on Muslims, 61
  on war, 31
  See also Bush administration
Bush administration
  conservative criticism of, 118
  deterrence and, 22–3
  economic crisis and, 36–7
  failure of, 1, 4
  global negative reaction to, 64–5, 105
  global support for multilateralism and, 109–11, 114–15
  homeland security needs and, 74
  lack of checks on power of, 100–1, 103, 117–18
  rejection of global governance by, 89–90, 97

rejection of global obligations by, 54–5, 56
rejection of Kyoto by, 45, 51, 56
rejection of multilateralism by, 17
rejection of United Nations by, 54, 67, 118
terrorism and, 24–5
use of military power by, 71
war in Iraq and, 26–7, 59–64, 70
Butler, The (film), 137

California, United States, 183–4
campaign funds, 125–7, 129
Campaign Reform Act (McCain-Feingold law) (2002), 127
Canada
 climate change and, 43, 45, 52, 54, 111, 208n24
 defensibility of, 23
 global governance and, 161, 191
 opinion of America in, 64
 rejection of ABM development by, 109
 social spending in, 72, 102, 213n16
Capital in the 21st Century (Piketty), 151, 163
carbon emissions
 economic effects of, 50
 global citizenship values and, 108, 154
 as global risk, 51–2, 56, 73, 106
 increase in, 156
 Kyoto compliance and, 51–2
 strategies for reduction of, 53, 160, 165, 187
carbon taxes, 10, 32, 52
cell phones, 27, 165, 183, 195, 197
Center for Public Integrity, 127
Chalabi, Ahmad, 62–3
Charles Leopold Mayer Foundation, 188

checks and balances, 9, 14–15, 97–8, 100–3
Cheney, Dick, 1, 18, 26–7, 60, 66, 100, 208n21, 210n57
Cheney, Liz, 216n5
China
 arms sales by, 35
 as candidate for great power status, 12, 26, 171–2
 climate change and, 43, 44, 45, 51–2, 53, 56, 134, 156
 defense and, 22
 economic crises and, 35, 37
 economic growth of, 156, 160, 172–3, 192–3
 global citizenship and, 135, 155–6
 income gap in, 143–4, 192–3
 military spending of, 4
Christians, 71, 77, 99, 214n26
Christie, Chris, 76, 211n79
Citizens United, 127
citizenship, 87–105
 America's contributions to, 97–9
 checks & balances and, 100–4
 duties of, 91, 93, 99
 evolution of concept of, 91–7
 global obligations of, 175–6
 global vs national, 87–8, 104–5, 153
 rights of, 91–3, 94, 99
 See also global citizenship
CIVICUS (World Alliance for Citizens), 188
civil society organizations
 American-based, 157
 campaigning by, 187
 Canadians and, 161
 global governance and, 108, 113–14, 146, 152, 200–1
 importance of, 102, 108, 163
 issues addressed by, 88–9, 113, 142–3, 146, 151–2, 180–2, 188–9
 new media and, 178–9, 185

Clark, Susan, 158
class
  changes in, 192–3
  Hurricane Katrina survivors and, 77
  income gaps, 120, 132, 135, 143, 192–3, 193
  middle class losing ground, 69, 132
  political discourse on, 68–9
  See also inequality; poverty
climate action
  American resistance to, 50–1, 56, 67, 68, 73, 134
  economic growth and, 50, 53, 135
  global approach to, 52, 53–4, 81–2, 134
  national attitudes toward, 161, 187
  responsibility for, 38, 72–3
  See also climate justice
climate change, 42–59
  adaptation to, 44–5, 81, 82, 165
  art depicting, 190–1
  changes needed to deal with, 10–11, 44–5, 48–50, 196–9
  denial of, 2, 44, 57, 66–7, 124
  economic development and, 173
  effects of, 42–3
  fossil energy demands and, 43, 47
  Hurricane Katrina and, 71–2, 72–3, 80–1
  military action and, 45
  new media and, 179
  Obama administration and, 46–7, 171
  poverty reduction and, 155–6, 197
  sociopolitical impacts of, 132, 143
  transnational networks regarding, 113
  as wicked problem, 164–5
climate justice, 52–3, 155, 173, 189, 196–7
Clinton, Bill, 56, 220n27
Clinton, Hillary, 64, 127

CNN, 74
coal, 43, 52, 156, 204n13, 207n12, 208n23
Cohen, Roger, 133
Cold War, end of, 5, 27, 118
collective strategic forces, 29–30
Collier, Paul, 155
colonialism, 61–2, 70
communication, transnational, 144–5
  global citizenship and, 113, 140, 147, 148, 166, 170, 174
  new media and, 180
communications initiatives, 185–6
communications technology, 140, 144–5, 165–6
  cell phones, 27, 165, 183, 195, 197
  See also Internet, the
CONCORD (European Confederation of Development NGOs), 188
conferences of the parties (COPs), 89, 213n8
conservatism/conservatives
  beliefs/views of, 122, 130–1, 136
  "genuine," 62, 63
  global goals and, 175
  Hurricane Katrina and, 71, 77
  Iraq war and, 62
  judicial activism and, 128
  media advantage of, 124–5
  reentrenchment of in America, 2
  restoration of New Orleans and, 82–3
  rights of citizenship and, 95, 99
  See also neoconservatism/neoconservatives; Republicans
Constitution, US, 66, 97–8, 121
cookbooks, 191
Copenhagen climate conference (2010), 66–7
Cordal, Isaac, 190–1

corporations
  benefit corporations, 183–4
  global integration of, 153
  opposition to Kyoto and, 50–1
  power of, 101–2
  trade agreements and, 152–3
cosmopolitanism, 170–1, 187, 194, 197–8
Crusades, 61
cultural heritage treasures, 148–9, 196

Daily Kos (blog), 178
debt, 10, 16, 34, 35–7
defense policy, defensive, 21–5, 30
deficits, public, 10, 35–6, 132
democracy
  checks & balances of, 97–8, 100–3
  deliberative, 158, 193
  duties of, 91, 93, 99
  global citizenship and, 174–5, 191–4
  hegemonic power and, 14–15, 16–17, 119
  inequality and, 135, 192–4
  the Internet and, 178–80
  liberal constitutionalism and, 98–9
  oil and, 32–3
  rights of, 91–3, 94, 99
  scale of, 146, 148, 158–9
Democracy Now (website), 179
Democrats, 67, 121, 125, 129
Denmark, 43, 53, 187
Department of Homeland Security, 74
Derviş, Kemal, 200
deterrence, 22–3
developing nations
  energy use by, 51–2
  exemption of from Kyoto, 208n23
  food politics and, 183
  fossil fuels and, 52–3, 173, 189, 197

development
  cell phones and, 195, 197
  climate change and, 155–6, 173
  food politics and, 143
  global citizen's movement and, 146
  global citizenship and, 157, 159, 180–1
  Hurricane Katrina and, 80
  vs military expenditures, 33–4
  oil revenues and, 32–3
  sustainability and, 195
  See also industrialization/industrial work
discrimination. *See* race/racism
Doctors without Borders, 88, 161, 180–1
dog whistle politics, 77, 123–4
domestic spending
  constraints on, 102
  education, 20, 72, 119, 158, 160, 165
  health care, 17, 20, 72, 97, 121, 165, 213n16
  importance of, 94
  military spending and, 33–4, 72, 120
Dowd, Maureen, 74
drones, 19, 23, 29, 104
Dryzek, John S., 141
due process, 91, 92
Dukakis, Michael, 123

Earth Charter initiative, 157, 181
economic stimulus plans, 46–7
economy, American
  climate change and, 10–12, 50–1, 53, 57–8
  foreign governments supporting, 35–7
  inequality and, 135
  Iraq war and, 34
  See also 2008 recession/economic crisis

economy, global
  citizen initiatives in, 182–4
  climate change and, 46–7, 48–9, 106–7, 173
  debt and, 36
  food politics and, 142–3
  global citizenship and, 139–41, 152–3
  global governance and, 192
  global taxation and, 200–1
  hegemony and, 3–4
  inequality and, 134–5, 143–4, 193
  military power and, 6
  national interests and, 30–1, 154–5
  policies regarding, 163
education, 20, 72, 119, 158, 160, 165
Elders, the, 189
elections
  international bodies and, 90
  in Iraq, 62–3
  midterm elections of 2006, 74
  Republicans and, 120–1
  See also presidential campaigns/elections
Electoral College, 120
Electoral Rebellion for Global Democracy, 181–2
elegant solutions, 164–6
emergency response, 29–30, 73–5, 80
endangered species, 143, 196, 200
energy initiatives, 46–7, 187
energy policy, 154–5. *See also* Kyoto Protocol (1997)
energy transition, 10–12, 13, 43, 46–50
Engineers without Borders, 179
Environics (polling firm), 64
environmental protection
  America's leadership on, 56, 157
  global citizenship and, 106–8, 143, 188
  poverty reduction and, 155–6, 195–6
  as solution, 165

epistemic communities, 113
Europe
  arms sales by, 34–5
  as candidate for great power status, 12
  climate action in, 53, 159
  economic crises in, 141
  electoral politics in, 90, 182
  financial transaction tax in, 200
  global governance and, 119–20
  global leadership and, 135, 159
  opposition to Bush administration in, 15, 19
  See also specific countries
exceptionalism, American, 3, 54, 66, 136, 157–8, 162
Exxon Mobil, 57

fair trade goods, 108, 112, 142, 182–3, 199
Farmer, Paul, 190
Federal Emergency Measures Administration (FEMA), 74
federalism, 98, 121, 130
Federalist Papers, The (Madison), 98
feed in tariffs, 151, 155
financial institutions/banks
  deregulation of, 10
  military spending and, 35–6
  need for regulation of, 141, 149, 158, 167, 200, 202
Financial Transfer Tax, 200
fisheries, 106, 199
food
  locally produced, 49, 142, 143, 165, 185
  organic, 108, 182–3
  politics of, 142–3, 198–9
  sharing of, 191
forests, 165
Forum for a New World Governance, 188–9
fossil fuels
  China's use of, 156
  demand for, 43, 44, 47–8, 52–3

developing nations and, 52–3,
    173, 189, 197
  global citizenship and, 107
  prices of, 32–3, 206n41
  taxes on, 13, 52, 197–8
  transition from, 10–12, 13, 43,
    46–50
  US rejection of Kyoto and, 56–7
  See also carbon emissions;
    renewable energy
Fox News, 66, 73, 124
France, 35, 73, 93, 184
freedom of assembly, 91, 92
freedom of religion, 92, 98–9
freedom of speech, 91–2, 99
freedom of the press, 91, 92
Friedman, Thomas, 32–3
fuel efficiency standards, 46, 50–1
Fukuyama, Francis, 192, 193
fundamentalism, religious, 25, 92,
    107, 124

Gap (clothing stores), 183
gay marriage, 131, 215n50
GCAP (Global Call to Action
  against Poverty), 188
general will, Rousseau's concept of,
  147, 149, 151
geo-green strategy (Friedman's), 32
Georgia, United States, 175
Germany, 35, 43, 49, 53, 182, 184
Gilens, Martin, 127–8
Gini coefficients, 149
Ginsburg, Ruth Bader, 128
global brain, 150–1
Global Call to Action against
  Poverty (GCAP), 188
global citizen's movement
  communication and, 112–14,
    144–5, 174, 177–9
  emergence of, 2, 8, 104–9, 111
  impact of, 186–7
  inequality and, 162, 195–6
  issues addressed by, 198–9
  need for, 142–4

  organizations advocating, 187–91
  policy innovation and, 166–7
  possible structure of, 87, 146–7
  reduction of hegemonic power
    and, 174–5
  use of soft power by, 16, 184,
    186
  wicked problems and, 164–6
global citizenship, 100–16, 139–67,
  169–202
  actions taken as expressions of,
    111–14
  American involvement in, 157–8
  Bush administration and, 109–11,
    114–15
  civil society organizations and,
    88–9, 180–2
  communication in, 173–4
  core challenge to, 155–6
  duties of, 107–8
  economic expressions of, 182–4
  emergence of, 87, 104–6, 111–14,
    169–70
  environment and, 106–8
  food politics and, 142–3
  global decision-making and,
    88–9, 140
  global economy and, 139–42
  the Internet and, 177–80
  issues needing attention of,
    149–50
  leadership on, 157–62
  necessity of, 84–5
  new perspectives through,
    151–5
  North Americans and, 191–5
  organizations working for,
    187–91
  policy innovation and, 166–7
  possibilities of, 88–91, 195–202
  power of, 54, 187
  rights of, 107–8
  Rousseau and, 146–51
  trade processes and, 90–1, 101–2
  venues for, 180–6

global economic integration
  America and, 119, 131–6
  citizenship and, 96
  concentration of wealth and, 96
  of corporations, 153
  democratic checks & balances and, 102
  democratic global governance and, 192
  inequality and, 141, 143–4, 150
  moderation of neoliberal approach to, 15
  national interests and, 30–1
  need for reduction of injustice and, 107
  production of goods and, 142, 182–3
  redistribution of wealth and, 199–201
  rules of conduct and, 38
  state-to-state attacks and, 6, 21
  trade practices and, 101, 152–3, 182–5
  See also under economy
global governance
  American involvement in, 157
  Bush administration's rejection of, 54, 89–90
  checks & balances and, 14–15, 97–8
  components to, 14–17, 148–9
  fear of loss of influence and, 90, 119, 150, 156–9, 171
  vs global citizenship, 88, 140–1, 146–7
  ideal forms of, 89
  Kyoto Accord as attempt at, 39, 42
  national attitudes toward, 156–61, 186–7
  national initiatives and, 187, 200
  need for, 110
  North Americans' resistance to, 191
  objections to, 170–1, 197–8
  possibility of, 69
  through civil society organizations, 152, 200–1
  through nongovernmental initiatives, 108, 113–14, 146, 181–2
global issues, 150
  as wicked problems, 164–6
global leadership, 37–8, 58–9, 156–62
Global Poverty Project, 190
globalization
  civic rights and, 99
  national security and, 154
  political efficacy and, 191–3
globally shared events, 170
Gore, Al, 54, 56, 58, 120, 124
great powers, 5, 12, 132, 139, 162–3, 172
Great Transition Initiative (GTI), 157, 187–8
Green Tea Coalition, 175
greenhouse gas (GHG) emissions
  Canada's, 191
  China's, 52, 56
  economic development and, 155
  as global risk, 189
  increase in, 73
  reduction of, 50, 81, 160, 185, 187, 199
Greenpeace, 161, 179, 180

Hällström, Niclas, 155
Harper, Stephen, 111, 161
Harrington, Michael, 79
Hart, Gary, 25
health care, 17, 20, 72, 97, 121, 165, 213n16
hegemonic power
  basis of, 14
  checks on, 9, 14–15, 100–3
  climate change and, 55
  collapse-of scenario, 10–12, 69
  cost of, 4–5, 9, 17–18, 85, 132
  decline-of scenario, 12–13, 38, 69
  defined, 4

designation of, 14
evolution-of scenario, 14–17, 69
global citizenship and, 108–11, 139, 157
hubris of, 30–1
inequality and, 69
internal interests and, 70–1
last temptation of, 37–9
limiting of, 5–10
opportunity costs of, 39, 71–2, 74–6, 78–9, 82–3
preference for status quo by, 7, 37–8
routes out of, 10–17, 69–70
vulnerability of, 5–6, 31
Hochschild, Arlie, 190
hockshop hegemony, 35–6
Horton, Willie, 123
House of Representatives, 121, 125, 134
human rights
citizen organizations for, 180
as global rights, 108
importance of, 99, 114
national leadership on, 16, 159
violations of, 101, 118, 160, 164
Human Rights Watch, 180
Humanwave, 181
Huntsman, Jon, 67
Hurricane Katrina, 71–83
climate change and, 71–2, 72–3, 80–1
effect of on America's image, 77–8, 83–4
emergency response during, 73–5, 80
inequality and, 75, 78–9, 211n74
Iraq war and, 71, 76–7
Hurricane Sandy, 73, 76, 204n11
Hussein, Saddam, 60, 110, 210n57
hyper-realism, conservative, 26–7, 205n33

ICC (International Criminal Court), 15, 54, 101, 120, 133, 159

idealism, neoconservative, 26
IMF (International Monetary Fund), 102
improvised explosive devices (IEDs), 9
income gaps, 120, 132, 135, 143, 192–3
Inconvenient Truth, An (Gore), 54
Independent World Television, 185
India
as candidate for great power status, 12, 171
climate change and, 43, 44, 51, 53
economic growth in, 160
income gap in, 193
as leading arms importer, 35
industrialization/industrial work
America and, 75
citizenship and, 88, 95–6, 160
climate action and, 51–2, 53
inequality and, 134–5, 193
jazz and, 79–80
oil prices and, 32
transfer of to other nations, 43, 52
inequality
in American campaign discourse, 68–9
changes needed to deal with, 199–201
cost of, 132, 134–5
the environment and, 155–6
in Europe, 120
global attention to, 151, 163
global citizenship and, 195
global economy and, 143–4
Hurricane Katrina and, 78–9
price of indifference to, 72
voices regarding, 163
as wicked problem, 164–5
See also poverty
insecurity, 19–20
intelligence, 29, 213n12
Inter Press Service, 185
International Criminal Court (ICC), 15, 54, 101, 120, 133, 159

234   Index

International Monetary Fund
   (IMF), 102
International Panel on Climate
   Change (IPCC), 113
Internet, the
   access to information through,
      213n9
   elegant solutions through, 165
   fair trade processes and, 183
   as global brain/general will,
      150–1
   global citizenship and, 113,
      144–5, 177–80
   Iraq war and, 60–1, 177–8
investments, financial
   2008 recession and, 140
   energy transition and, 13
   ethical/green, 108, 142, 183–4,
      222n30
   possibility of global tax on,
      200–1
   in renewable energy, 160–1,
      204n18
   Russian economy and, 36
   social programs and, 102
IPCC (International Panel on
   Climate Change), 113
ipsnews.net, 185
Iran
   as candidate for great power
      status, 12
   democracy in, 93
   deterrence by, 22, 24
   diplomatic engagement with, 158
   Iraqi war with, 110
   military expenditures of, 4, 206n39
   occupations of, 107
   view of daily life in, 186
Iraq
   government of, 62–3
   hegemonic dysfunction in, 39
   occupation of, 5, 60, 62–3, 83
   view of daily life in, 179
   weapons in, 34–5
   withdrawal from, 104, 109

Iraq war, 59–71
   as cause of decline in America's
      image, 35, 64–5
   Hurricane Katrina and, 71, 76–7
   Kyoto protocol and, 45–6
   media and, 7, 27, 60–1, 177–8,
      179, 209n45
   planning of, 9, 26, 61–4
   political support for, 19, 27–8
   problems of unilateralism in, 69–70
   public support for, 20
   purposes of, 6–7
   terrorism and, 23–4
   trade and, 184
Israel, 22, 26, 181–2, 190

Japan, 35, 37, 44, 45, 160
jazz, 79–80, 190
Jerusalem: A Cookbook (Ottolenghi
   and Tamimi), 191
job security, 20

Kagan, Robert, 26, 205n33, 216n4
Kenya, 160
Kerry, John, 67, 126
Kids for Peace, 190
King, Martin Luther, Jr., 137
King Baudouin Foundation, 87, 89, 90
Kissinger, Henry, 4–5, 26
Klare, Michael, 54
Klein, Naomi, 42–3
Koch brothers, 57, 127
Korb, Lawrence, 5
Kristol, William, 26, 216n5
Krugman, Paul, 53, 57, 135,
   205n35
Kunstler, James Howard, 49
Kyoto Protocol (1997), 42–59
   American nonparticipation in, 1,
      50–1, 54–5, 56–8, 171
   as attempt at cooperative global
      governance, 42
   Blair administration's support
      for, 109
   developing countries and, 208n23

failure of, 58–9
failure to live up to agreements of, 43–4, 50
importance of, 46–50
Iraq war and, 45–6

labor rights/conditions, 91, 153, 173, 182–3, 206n45, 220n25
land use, 108
Lappé, Frances Moore, 189
Latin America, 30, 159, 185
Lee, Anka, 172
levees, 78, 80–1
al Libi, Abu Anas, 133
Libya, 64, 133, 179
Limbaugh, Rush, 77, 211n79
Lincoln, Abraham, 137
Lind, Michael, 170–2, 197–8
Lipset, Seymour Martin, 145
loans, 33, 140–1, 165, 184
lobbying, 126
local goods, 49, 142, 143, 165, 185, 199
local scale
  action through, 112, 185
  initiatives at, 158–9
Lovins, Amory, 150, 154, 165
Lovins, Hunter, 154
loyal opposition, 15

Madison, James, 98
Mandela, Nelson, 189
Marlboro, 184
Marshall, T. H., 95–6
Martin, Lawrence, 18
mass production, 79
McCain, John, 66, 129, 130, 216n7
McCain-Feingold law (Bipartisan Campaign Reform Act) (2002), 127
McChesney, Robert W., 125
McKibben, Bill, 179
media
  climate change denial in, 57, 73, 124

  conservative dominance of, 124–5
  democratic rights and, 91, 92, 99
  global citizenship and, 144–5, 177–80
  Iraq war and, 7, 24, 27, 60, 71
  response to Hurricane Katrina in, 73–5, 77
  See also Internet, the; television
Mexico, 193, 203n10, 219n8
micro-loans, 33, 184, 223n32
Middle East
  America's approach to crises in, 64
  arms imports to, 34–5
  attempt to remake through occupation of, 61–2
  oil and, 32–3
  renewable energy and, 160–1
  See also specific countries
military expenditures
  campaign money and, 127
  climate change and, 12–13
  domestic politics and, 70
  economic crises and, 10, 12–13
  elegant solutions to, 165
  European, 120
  global citizenship and, 110, 141, 148, 158, 163, 171
  of loyal opposition, 15
  opportunity costs of, 21, 33–5, 72, 82, 132
  security through, 17–21, 31
  size of America's, 4
  support for, 19, 119
military power
  counter-attacks to, 70
  global citizenship and, 174
  need for on-call emergency military force, 29–30
  not as consequential as it was, 4–7, 8–9
  psychology of desire to use, 18–21
  restraint in hegemonic use of, 16–17, 68
  unilateralism based on, 69–70

Miller, David, 140
Milner, Yuri, 150
minorities
　constitutionalism and, 98–9
　dog whistle attacks against, 123–4
　increase in numbers of, 131, 194
　in New Orleans, 77
　Obama campaign and, 123–4, 129
　political power of, 129, 135
　voting restrictions and, 93, 128
missiles, 22–3, 109
Mitochondrial Eve, 169
Monbiot, George, 10–11, 13
Monde, Le (Paris), 73
morality
　conservative emphasis on, 130–1
　of global citizenship, 176
mortgages, 36, 140–1
mosques, campaign against construction of, 18, 46, 61
multilateralism
　in antiterrorist actions, 24, 25, 29–30
　Bush administration's resistance to, 89–90, 109, 118, 214n31
　Canada's traditions of, 161
　challenges to, 55–6, 170
　establishment of, 100–1
　European support for, 119–20
　global citizenship and, 109–11, 172
　hegemonic mindset and, 28
　of historic American goverments, 118
　of Obama administration, 18, 104–5, 133
　See also unilateralism
music, 79–80, 122, 190
Muslims, 18, 25, 61
Mykleby, Mark, 154–5

national interests, 30–1, 150, 151, 153–5, 159, 162–3
national security, 152, 153–5, 214n24. *See also* military expenditures; military power
nation-state, the
　as basis of law, 88, 102, 171
　global citizenship and, 170–1
　vs individuals, 108
natural disasters. *See* Hurricane Katrina
neoconservatism/neoconservatives
　Iraq war and, 59–60, 62–3
　mindset/views of, 63–4, 118, 130–1
　view of resistance to power by, 18–19
　See also conservatism/ conservatives
Net Zero energy program, 154
Netroots Nation, 180
New American Century, 9, 118, 203n7
new media. *See* Internet, the
New Orleans
　community response to Hurricane Katrina in, 75
　cultural gifts of, 79–80
　memories of, 76
　poverty in, 79
　restoration of, 82–3
　as sinful, 71
NGOs (nongovernmental organizations), 88–9, 112, 188. *See also* civil society organizations
Nicaragua, 160
Nichols, John, 125
nondecisions, 152
nongovernmental organizations (NGOs), 88–9, 112, 188. *See also* civil society organizations
North Korea, 4, 24, 206n39

Norway, 187
nuclear capabilities
  Bush-Cheney years and, 118
  deterrence and, 22
  Iran and, 158
  military strength of, 6
  terrorism and, 23–4, 29, 71
  weapons of mass destruction (WMDs), 6, 21, 22–3, 23–4, 60, 70

Obama, Barack
  American leadership and, 78
  American political culture and, 129–31
  on Assad, 203n2
  campaign funds raised by, 126, 129
  on citizenship, 99
  conservative attacks on, 28, 66, 68, 118, 158
  election of, 2, 3, 7, 46, 58, 64–6, 83, 129, 133
  new media and, 178–9
  racist attacks on, 123–4
  terrorism and, 18
  See also Obama administration
Obama administration
  climate change and, 46–7, 171
  domestic politics and, 121–2
  foreign policy of, 68
  international affairs and, 55, 104–5, 119, 133
  neoconservative criticisms of, 118
  public opposition to, 64–5
occupations
  capacity for resistance to, 8–9
  failure of, 5–6
  of Middle East, 61–2
Occupy movement, 151, 162
oil
  Bunker C oil, 198
  Iraq war and, 46, 61
  Middle Eastern conflict and, 32–3

  reserves of, 48
  transition away from, 10–12, 13, 43, 46–50
  See also fossil fuels
oil prices, 32–3, 206n41
On the Commons, 181
on-call emergency military force, 29–30
Ontario, Canada, 54, 208n24
opendemocracy.net, 185
opportunity costs
  Hurricane Katrina and, 39, 71–2, 74–6, 78–9, 82–3
  of military expenditures, 21, 33–5, 72, 132
Orr, David, 44, 153–4
Other America, The (Harrington), 79
Ottolenghi, Yotam, 191
Oxfam, 88, 146, 180

Pachamama Alliance, 189
Page, Benjamin, 127–8
Pakistan, 24
Palestine, 34, 182
Palin, Sarah, 67
paranoia, 21, 31, 65, 66–7, 85, 201
Partners in Health, 190
Patagonia, 184
peak oil, 11, 204n13
Perle, Richard, 26
Piketty, Thomas, 151, 163
policy innovation, 166–7
political advertising, 123, 126–7
political efficacy, 96, 176, 191–2, 194
polls
  regarding America's image, 35, 64
  regarding global citizenship, 87, 89, 90
  regarding Iraq war, 20, 35
Porter, Michael, 33
Porter, Wayne, 154–5

poverty
  in America, 83–4, 212n82
  the environment and, 155–6
  growth of, 79
  military spending and, 172
  new media and, 179
  in New Orleans, 79
  organizations working to end, 190
  policy decisions on, 135–6
  sustainability and, 195–6
  See also income gaps; inequality
Powell, Colin, 60
power, asymmetrical, 24
power, separation of, 97–8, 121
precariat, 193
presidential campaigns/elections
  of 2000, 120
  of 2004, 67, 104, 114–15, 125–6
  of 2008, 2, 93, 118–19, 129, 178–9
  of 2012, 2, 35, 55, 67, 68, 93, 99, 129, 136
  racism in, 123
Project for the New American Century (PNAC), 9, 118, 203n7
psychology of desire to use military power, 18–21
public services. *See* domestic spending
publiceye.ch, 183
Putin, Vladimir, 24

al Qaeda, 60, 61–2, 209n48, 210n57

race/racism
  American politics and, 122–4, 128, 136–7, 216n13
  democratic rights and, 91, 93
  Hurricane Katrina and, 75, 77
Rauch, Jonathan, 35
Rawls, John, 37
Reagan, Ronald, 123, 130
realism, conservative, 26–8, 82, 109, 110, 205n34

Red Cross, 74
religion, freedom of, 92, 98–9
religious conservatives, 71, 77, 214n26
religious fundamentalism, 25, 92, 107, 124
renewable energy, 44, 45
  communications technology and, 166
  conservatives working on, 175
  Europe as leader on, 159
  global South and, 160–1
  national security and, 154
Republicans
  American exceptionalism and, 136, 157–8
  American political culture and, 130–1
  campaign against mosque construction by, 18, 46, 61
  campaign money and, 125–6, 127
  climate change denial by, 57, 66–7
  criticism of Bush by, 118
  criticism of Obama by, 66, 118
  environmental legislation and, 157
  Iraq war and, 35
  media advantage of, 124, 217n16
  memories of New Orleans and, 76
  movement of to the right, 65
  national elections and, 120–1
  on oil reserves, 48
  race and, 122–3, 194, 216n13
  See also conservatism
Resource Wars (Klare), 54
retaliation, 22
Rich, Frank, 115
rights, civic, 92, 94, 95–6
rights, collective, 99
rights, economic, 91, 94, 95–6, 108
rights, environmental, 94, 108

rights, global, 108
rights, political, 91–3, 94, 95–6
rights, social, 94, 95–6
rivalries, military
　costs of, 139
　dangers of, 12–13
　economic limits to, 26, 132
　global citizenship and, 162–3, 171–3
Riverbend (pseudonym), 179
Roberts, John, 128
Robinson, Eugene, 83
rogue hegemons, 7, 16, 17, 36, 117, 171
Rohrabacher, Dana, 66–7
Romney, Mitt, 2, 12, 35, 67, 68, 209n41
Roots of Empathy, 190
Rousseau, Jean-Jacques, 146, 148, 149–50, 150–1
Rove, Karl, 60
Rumsfeld, Donald, 26–7, 60
Russia
　agricultural crisis of, 73, 81
　arms sales by, 34–5
　as candidate for great power status, 12
　climate action of, 53
　economic crisis and, 36
　economic growth and, 160
　military spending of, 4
　objection of to American anti-ballistic missiles, 22
　occupation of Afghanistan by, 5

Saez, Emmanuel, 135
Santorum, Rick, 126
Saudi Arabia, 32, 35, 37, 43, 48, 160–1
savings rates, 10, 36
Scowcroft, Brent, 1, 26, 118
Senate
　allocation of seats in, 121
　blocking of federal action by, 134

　campaigning for, 125, 126, 127
　rejection of Kyoto by, 56, 58
September 11, 2001, 1, 54, 60, 61, 117
Shack/Slum Dwellers International, 179
Shelby County v. Holder (2013), 128
shopyourvalues.org, 183
Sierra Club, 175
al-Sistani, Ali, Ayatollah, 62
Slow Democracy (Clark and Teachout), 158
social citizenship, 95–7
social media, 129, 150–1, 178–9. *See also* Internet, the
Social Progress Index, 33
social services. *See* domestic spending
socialism
　citizenship and, 95, 174
　Obama accused of, 66, 68, 158
soft power, 15, 16, 37, 182
solar energy, 45, 156, 160–1, 175, 197, 206n6
solar panels, 53, 160, 197
sorryeverybody.com, 114–15
Soviet Union, 4, 5, 107, 117–18
species loss, 73, 81, 106, 143, 196
Standing, Guy, 193
state-to-state attacks, 21
Stiglitz, Joseph, 152, 153
subsidiarity, 146, 157, 188, 194
Supreme Court, 127, 128, 134
sustainability, 44–5, 108
　national security and, 153–5
　poverty and, 195–6
swing states, 120
Syria, 4, 64

talkingpointsmemo.com (TPM), 178
Tamimi, Sami, 191
tar sands, 52, 161, 204n18

taxes
  on carbon, 10, 32, 52
  on financial transactions, 200–1
  on fossil energy, 13
  on fossil fuels, 13, 197–8
  global citizenship and, 170–1, 197, 200–1
  political discourse on, 93–4
  on the wealthy, 68, 97
taxpayers, 93–4
Tea Party, 175
Teachout, Woden, 158
Telecommunications Act (1996), 125
television
  conservative dominance of, 124–5, 217n16
  decline of dominance of, 61, 145
  free speech rights and, 99
  Hurricane Katrina images on, 73–5
  Iraq war images on, 7, 27
  political advertising on, 123, 126
  racism and, 123
terrorism
  appeal of as strategy, 24
  defensive defense against, 24–5
  as limit on hegemonic power, 5, 6–7
  military strength as no defense against, 6–7, 29–30
  oil and, 32–3
  opposition of by moderate Muslims, 18
  resistance to, 107, 133
  as territorial threat, 21
  war on terror, 19, 24–5, 71
Texas, United States, 81, 128, 130
therealnews.com, 185
Tobin tax, 200
too big to fail principle, 35–6
Toronto, Ontario, Canada, 54
Toyota, 51
trade agreements
  global citizenship and, 90–1, 152–3, 176–7, 206n45

  international, 15
  lack of checks on, 101–2
transportation, 13, 49, 185, 198, 204n17
treaties
  citizen involvement in, 89
  negotiations of, 101, 176
  regarding climate, 161
  regarding nuclear weapons, 118, 210n66

UNESCO, 149, 190, 213n9
unilateralism
  of Bush administration, 118–19
  costs of, 25–6, 69–70, 184
  Iraq war and, 27–8, 69–70, 109–10
  restraint of, 12, 15–16
  See also multilateralism
unions, 91, 153, 173, 183, 206n45, 220n25
United Nations
  global citizenship and, 89, 146, 148–9
  importance of, 90
  need for, 7
  US relations with, 54, 67, 109–10, 118, 157
  World Heritage sites of, 148–9
United States. *See* America

Vietnam, war in, 5, 7, 27, 31, 60, 117
violence, political, 107
voter turnout, 120–1, 129, 131, 135
voting
  American system of, 120–1, 128, 129
  right to, 91, 93, 182
Voting Rights Act (1965), 128, 213n15

wages
  fair trade concerns regarding, 108
  global impacts of, 134–5, 172–3

median, 36
minimum wage, 15, 132, 152, 183, 200
war on terror, 19, 24–5, 71
Washington Post, 9
weapons
  psychological need for use of, 18–21
  sales of, 34–5
  See also military expenditures
weapons of mass destruction (WMDs), 6, 21, 22–3, 23–4, 60, 70
wheat crops, 73
wicked problems, 164–6
Widening Circle, the, 187–8
Will, George, 74
will.i.am (William Adams), 178

wind energy, 11, 44, 45, 53, 130, 160–1
Wolfowitz, Paul, 26, 209n46, 216n4
women, 92, 93, 123, 179
women's rights, 160, 220n35
World Alliance for Citizens (CIVICUS), 188
World Economic Forum, 189
World Heritage sites, 148–9
World Jazz Day, 190
World Social Forum (WSF), 89, 113, 176, 181
World War II, 5, 118, 122
World Wildlife Fund, 88

Yes We Can (song), 178–9
YouTube, 178, 190

The manufacturer's authorised representative in the EU is Springer Nature Customer Service Centre GmbH, Europaplatz 3, 69115 Heidelberg, Germany. If you have any concerns regarding our products, please contact ProductSafety@springernature.com

Printed and bound by CPI Group (UK) Ltd, Croydon, CR0 4YY

23/03/2026

02076682-0015